Electronic Aids to Navigation:
Radar and ARPA

Electronic Aids to Navigation: Radar and ARPA

Roger Lownsborough I. Eng., F.I.E.I.E.
Senior Lecturer in Communications Engineering
Southampton Institute of Higher Education

David Calcutt M.Sc., C.Eng., M.I.E.E.
Senior Lecturer in the School of Systems Engineering
University of Portsmouth

Edward Arnold
A member of the Hodder Headline Group
LONDON MELBOURNE AUCKLAND

© 1993 Roger Lownsborough and David Calcutt

First published in Great Britain 1993

British Library Cataloguing in Publication Data

Lownsborough, Roger
  Electronic Aids to Navigation: Radar and ARPA
  I. Title II. Calcutt, D.
  623.8933

  ISBN 0–340–59258–3

Typeset in 10/11 pt Times Roman by Wearset, Boldon, Tyne and Wear
Printed in Great Britain for Edward Arnold, a division of Hodder Headline PLC, Mill Road, Dunton Green, Sevenoaks, Kent TN13 2YA by St. Edmundsbury Press, Bury St. Edmunds, Suffolk. Bound by Hartnoll's Ltd, Bodmin, Cornwall.

Preface

During the past few decades pulse radar systems have become one of the most important aids to navigation, acting as the eyes of the ship during periods of reduced visibility. In more recent years, the information obtained from radar has been processed by a computer to extend the basic function into one of an automatic anti-collision device (Automatic Radar Plotting Aid—ARPA), to give advance warning of potential navigation risk, and to enable the appropriate avoiding action to be taken.

This book, the second in the series 'Electronic Aids to Navigation', sets out to explain both pulse radar and ARPA systems as used in a marine environment. A systems approach has been used rather than a mathematical or analytical treatment in order to simplify the explanation, and, with the exception of the section dedicated to ARPA, detailed circuit descriptions have been avoided in order to present the reader with an overview of radar systems without bias to any one manufacturer or their specific equipment. It is our considered opinion that, provided the user knows what each part of the system does, and how it interfaces with the other parts, then the way is clear to work on any radar equipment regardless of its pedigree.

The text of this book is aimed towards students, to contribute to part of an HNC or HND course, which in turn would lead towards a formal radar maintenance certificate. Additionally, deck officers wishing to study for the on-board radar maintainer qualification would also find it useful. With this type of reader in mind, the depth and content of each chapter allows for study, either in a sequential format, or by reference to several chapters dedicated to the same aspect of the system but handled at progressively greater depth.

The content is arranged in the form of a series of building blocks, with each chapter building on to a preceding chapter; starting with the basic concept of range and bearing determination, and developing, in a sequential manner, towards a complete radar system. The sequence chosen for the chapters has been based on personal experience of teaching radar systems for ten years, and from tried and tested recipes which have proven to be digestible to students.

R. Lownsborough
D. Calcutt
1993

Acknowledgements

As with any technical publication much is owed to various individuals, manufacturers and organisations who gave freely of their time and expertise. The authors are grateful for all the assistance given, often at short notice, and the courteous and efficient responses. To mention names would perhaps be invidious but certainly credit should be given to the following:

Kelvin Hughes, for permission to use details from their *Concept* Radar range. Thanks also to Andy Norris, Technical Director, David Hannah, Chief Engineer and especially to Peter Stevens who must have dreaded receiving yet another letter or telephone call requesting assistance but never failed to give prompt and courteous assistance. John Beattie of Racal Marine Group Limited for his advice on ARPA symbols. The International Maritime Organisation for permission to reproduce an extract from their publication *Performance Standards for Navigational Equipment*. This appears as Appendix 1. The International Electrotechnical Commission for permission to reproduce Amendment 1 to IEC 872 which appears as Appendix 2.

Finally, Roger would like to thank his wife Dilys, for without her support and extended tolerance he would still be facing a blank sheet of paper; and David is equally grateful for the patience and forebearance shown by his wife Daphne when he announced that he was going to assist in the writing of yet another book. Both authors also offer thanks to Roger's very good friend Peter Harrison for supplying much of the artwork which supports this text; and to Roger's colleagues Bob Pritchard and Roger Forster for playing Devil's Advocate when proof reading.

R. Lownsborough
D. Calcutt
1993

Contents

Part One

PRIMARY AND SECONDARY RADAR

1
Primary pulse radar

1.1 Introduction

During the Second World War the United States Navy adopted the acronym RADAR for what had previously been called 'Radio Echo Detection' equipment. The initial letters of RAdio Detection And Ranging form the word RADAR, and describe the function of the equipment when used as a navigation aid.

Today, there are many types of radar, each with a dedicated role and designed for a specific purpose. This book deals only with the pulse radar systems used in marine navigation and collision avoidance.

The inception of radar as a concept can be traced back to the beginning of radio transmission and reception; to the works of Hertz in 1886, Hülsmeyer in 1903 and Marconi in 1922. The suggestion put forward by Marconi was for the design of apparatus whereby a ship could radiate a divergent beam of radio rays in any desired direction; the rays, if coming across a metallic object such as a ship would be reflected back to a receiver thus revealing the presence of the ship. Marconi's idea was not adopted at the time as no practical application could be envisaged. It was many years after before a true radar system was developed.

In marine navigation, radar is employed to detect the presence of ships, coastlines and other objects, and to provide a navigator with information as to the bearing of a 'target' and its relative distance. Radar is especially useful when negotiating congested waters, during darkness, or in periods of reduced visibility.

'Marine radar' encompasses two systems: Primary pulse radar, which is the system used on board a vessel for the detection of targets; and Secondary radar—where an object can reveal its presence under conditions when it would not normally provide a good target, or to differentiate it from many other targets in the same area.

The book sets out to explain radar using a systems rather than a mathematical approach. The initial concepts are developed to cover both analogue and digital radar systems, and lead the reader to modern day Automatic Radar Plotting Aid (ARPA) collision avoidance radar. They also broach the latest developments of portable displays and Search and Rescue Radar Transponder (SART) beacons intended to form part of the Global Maritime Distress and Safety System (GMDSS).

1.2 Primary pulse radar

If we disregard the complexities of modern radar equipment and initially just consider the underpinning concepts which form the foundations of radar, a complete system can be developed. The primary pulse radar system is that used on vessels for the detection of targets for navigational purposes, and is generally referred to in the marine context as 'radar'. In consideration of the basic concepts an analogue system will be considered, with digital radar signal processing covered in later chapters.

The measurement of range

One of the prime considerations must be the determination of the range, or distance between the observer and the distant object (target).

The formula:

$$\text{Distance travelled} = \text{Velocity} \times \text{Time of travel}$$

is the starting point.

If we said: 'A vehicle travelled at 10 miles per hour, continuously for a total of 5 hours, how far has it travelled?', we could expect the answer to be: 50 miles. However, in giving this answer we are making the assumption that the speed of the vehicle remained constant at 10 miles per hour throughout the journey, and was not affected by the terrain or other factors. If we are to measure distance accurately, constant velocity must be maintained throughout the period of time measurement.

By using radio waves we have satisfied that requirement, as it is well known that electromagnetic energy travels at the speed of light with a constant velocity. Hence we have the original of the first word in the acronym, Radio.

$$\text{The velocity of light is } 300\,000\,000 \text{ m/sec.}$$

By using radio waves we see straight away the need to carry out the time measurement electronically rather than mechanically. A simple experiment using a torch, a mirror and a stop-watch would prove the impracticality of any other suggestion.

The electromagnetic energy is radiated in the form of a train of rectangular pulses, each of very short time duration. The reason why rectangular pulses are chosen is that the leading edge of the transmitted pulse being vertical will ensure that the leading edge of the returned (echo) pulse is vertical. If this was not so it would be impossible to measure the time interval between the transmission and reception of a pulse with sufficient accuracy.

Consider the transmission of one single pulse, and refer to Fig. 1.1. At the instant the pulse is transmitted an electronic timing device is started. The pulse travels with constant velocity until it strikes a distant object. The object will reradiate some of the

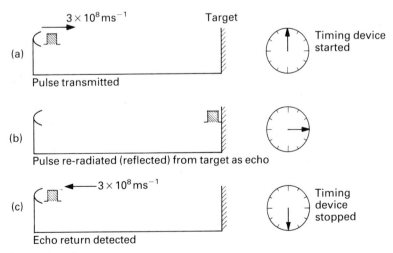

Fig. 1.1 Measurement of target range

energy back towards the origin; the reradiated energy will travel with constant velocity until it is detected by a receiver and the timing device stopped.

The distance travelled by the pulse can now be determined from the original equation.

Suppose the time interval between the transmission of the pulse and its subsequent detection had been 1 second, then we would know that the pulse had travelled a total distance of 300 000 000 metres. However, this is not the range of the target, but the round-trip distance from the transmitter, out to the object and back again to the receiver.

If then, a one-second time interval had been measured, the range of the distant object would be 300 000 000 metres divided by 2, ie 150 000 000 metres.

The units and figures dealt with so far in this chapter are not practical, and in reality are modified.

300 000 000 m/s is reduced to 300 m/μs.

The unit of marine navigation is the nautical mile, 6076 ft, 1852 metres or 2025.3 yards. The radar mile being defined as 2000 yards. This gives an acceptable difference between a nautical mile and a radar mile of approximately 1%. As yards are the units employed,

300 000 000 metres/second equates to
328 000 000 yards/second or,
328 yards/μ second.

In terms of radar range, therefore,

164 yards per micro second (12.2μ second per radar mile).

The description of range measurement has deliberately been over-simplified, and no mention has been made of the fact that the transmitted pulse has to be radiated from a directional antenna aimed directly at the target.

The measurement of direction

In addition to knowing the range of a target a navigator needs to know the bearing of the target in relation to a fixed reference point. Once the navigator knows both the range and the relative bearing of the target its position can be determined in relation to the navigator's own position.

Directional information relating to the target is obtained by radiating the pulse train from a highly directional antenna. The pulses of energy are radiated from the antenna in the form of a fan-shaped beam. Refer to Fig. 1.2.

The antenna radiation characteristics, when observed in the horizontal plane form a very narrow beam (less than 2 degrees), whereas when observed in the vertical plane, a very wide beam (20 or perhaps 30 degrees) is produced.

To construct an antenna with such directional properties requires the dimensions of the antenna to be large in relation to the wavelength of the signal.

Wavelength is given as $\lambda = c/f$,

where λ = wavelength (metres)
   c = Velocity of propagation (300 000 000 metres/second)
   f = Frequency (Hertz)
For this reason, and to keep the antenna dimensions within practical limitations, the

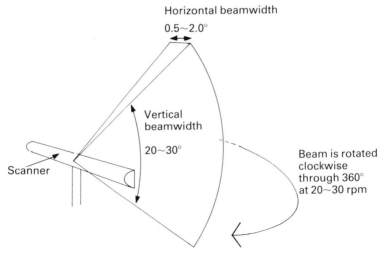

Fig. 1.2 Scanner radiated beam

transmission frequency of the radar is very high; typically 10 GHz for 3 cm wavelength radar and 3 GHz for 10 cm radar.

The pulse, or to be accurate, the train of rectangular pulses of energy are, therefore, directed over a very narrow arc. Only targets which lie within this arc will be able to return energy to the antenna as an echo of the transmitted pulse for subsequent reception and display. As long as the navigator knows the direction in which the antenna is pointing the relative bearing of the target can be determined.

To be of practical use, the radar has to display the range and the bearing of all targets lying within 360 degrees of azimuth. To effect this requirement the antenna is continually rotated throughout 360° at a constant rotational speed. Because the antenna's radiated beam continuously scans 360° it is referred to as a scanner, rather than an antenna.

The display of target range information

It was shown above how, by accurately measuring the time interval between the transmission of a pulse and its returned echo, it was possible to determine the range of a target. It was also noted that some electronic means of measuring the time interval was required.

Initially, this task was performed by an oscilloscope-type display, known as an 'A' scan display. As with an oscilloscope, the 'A' scan display had a single, horizontal trace, drawn by moving a spot of light across the screen of a cathode ray tube (crt), from left to right, at a constant rate. The source of the light spot is an electron gun assembly (located in the neck of an evacuated glass envelope or 'tube') in which a thermionic emitting cathode produces a stream of electrons. These are attracted along the length of the tube and focused (either through magnetic or electrostatic fields) into a narrow beam before impinging on a fluorescent coating on the inside of the tube screen.

The spot of light is caused to move by the force of a magnetic field produced by passing a current through a coil (or coils) situated around the neck of the crt. The current, whose value changes in a linear manner, is produced by a timebase circuit. The timebase causes the spot of light to be driven across the screen at a rate which corresponds to the displayed range. The current produced by the timebase circuit starts to rise, as a linear sawtooth, from zero at the instant the transmitted pulse is radiated from the antenna, up to a maximum value corresponding to the very edge of the crt. The crt screen is internally coated with material which continues to glow for a period of time after the spot of light has passed over it. The trace was made to deflect vertically at the instant of transmission, causing a 'blip' to appear on the trace. The returning echo from a target caused a similar vertical deflection of the trace, creating a second 'blip' which was off-set to the right of the transmission 'blip'.

Covering the screen was an etched sheet of glass with calibration marks in terms of range. Zero range was indicated as being coincident with the transmission blip, and the range of the target measured by the position of the echo blip in relation to the scale. With a highly directional antenna pointing in one, fixed direction, and with only a single target visible on the screen, an 'A' type display would appear as in Fig. 1.3.

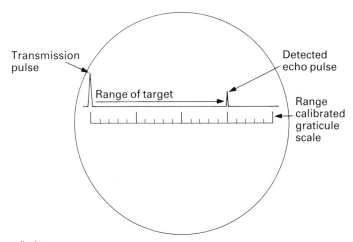

Fig. 1.3 'A' scan display

If the range of the target increased or decreased in relation to the observer, the echo blip would appear either further to the right, or further to the left on the display.

In the years which followed, technology evolved a more sophisticated display: the Plan Position Indicator (PPI).

A PPI display presents the navigator with a map-like representation of all targets within the range of the equipment. The display itself is a crt, having an almost flat, circular screen on which target information is presented as bright pin-pricks of light.

The target information is drawn on the screen by an electron beam focused into a very small spot. A chemical coating on the inside of the screen causes the screen to fluoresce at the point where the electron beam strikes it. The spot origin is the centre of the screen.

The electron beam can be deflected by an external magnetic field produced by passing a current through a coil, or set of coils located around the neck of the tube. By passing a sawtooth shaped current, rising linearly from zero up to some maximum value, through the coils the electron beam can be deflected to move the spot of light from the centre of the crt screen to the edge of the screen. As the spot moves across the screen, a second (phosphorescent) coating inside the tube screen glows, leaving a trail showing where the light has passed, thus producing a visible trace.

The spot of light starts to move across the screen in a linear manner at the instant the transmitted pulse leaves the scanner. The radius of the crt screen will represent the displayed range of the equipment, and so by providing a means of calibrating the screen in miles, the display of range can be achieved.

Suppose, for example, our radar equipment was set to display a maximum range of 6 miles, which corresponded with a target some 6 miles distant. At the instant the transmitted pulse leaves the scanner the spot of light commences to move from the centre of the crt screen towards the edge. At the time the pulse strikes the target at a range of 6 miles the spot of light will be exactly half-way across the screen. In the time that it takes for the returned echo pulse to return to the scanner, be detected by the receiver and displayed, the spot of light will have travelled the remaining distance and be at the edge of the screen. The detected echo picked up by the receiver will cause the spot of light to increase in brilliance, thus showing a bright spot at 6 miles which represents the target.

The current which causes the spot to be deflected across the screen is produced in a time-base generator. The time-base generator is triggered by a synchronising pulse produced in the transmitter at the instant the pulse is transmitted.

The display of target bearing information

We outlined above the principle behind scanning 360 degrees of azimuth with a rotating antenna radiating a narrow horizontal beam. Knowledge of the direction in which the scanner is pointing enables the navigator to determine the relative bearing of the target in relation to the scanners' location. To display this information on the PPI screen a bearing transmission system is employed. The bearing transmission system relays the angular position of the scanner to the display at all times, to effect a rotation of the trace on the crt screen.

A bearing transmitting device is located under the scanner, and mechanically linked through gearing to the scanner itself. As the scanner rotates, the bearing transmitter turns in the same direction as the scanner. Electrical signals are fed from the bearing transmitter, down cables to a bearing receiver located in the display. The bearing receiver acts to bring about the synchronous rotation of the trace, by either an electromechanical or an electronically operated system.

In an electromechanical system, the deflection coils are physically rotated around the neck of the crt. In an electronic system the coils remain stationary, with the trace deflection being direction resolved into sine and cosine components. Both systems produce the same end product: the rotation of the trace on the screen in the same direction and at the same speed as the scanner rotation.

When the beam is pointing 'dead-ahead', the ppi trace is aligned with the top of the screen at the 12-o'clock position. Rotation of the scanner and trace will then follow in a clockwise direction at a rotational speed of between 20–30 revolutions per minute. Should the pulse(s) radiated from the scanner impinge on a target when the beam is pointing 090 degrees relative to dead-ahead, the ppi screen will show the target echo as a bright spot of light at the three-o'clock position. The same will apply for any target within the 360 degrees of coverage.

A combination of the concepts outlined will present the navigator with a spot of light on the display which corresponds with a target in both range and bearing.

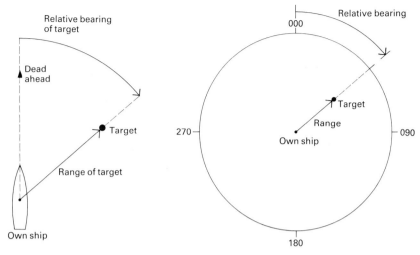

Fig. 1.4 Plan position indicator

Calibration of the ppi display in both range and bearing can be accomplished mechanically or electronically, the latter offering a higher degree of accuracy.

Calibration of range by mechanical means requires a transparent cursor being placed over the ppi screen, the cursor having lines etched into it, corresponding to predefined range increments, in accordance with the displayed range. By viewing the screen through the cursor it is possible to interpolate the approximate range of a target. An example is shown in Figure 1.5.

When this task is done by electronic means, a series of voltage spikes are superimposed on to the trace which, as it rotates, draw a series of concentric circles on the screen, each line representing range measurement intervals. The distance between the circles will represent range in relation to the selected display range on the equipment. The voltage spikes are referred to as calibration 'pips', and the resultant concentric circles as range rings. A range ring generator is used to produce the calibration pips. Figure 1.5 shows the production of range rings.

To enable the navigator to accurately measure the range of a target lying between two range rings a variable range marker (vrm) can be used. Whereas the range ring

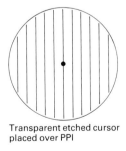

Transparent etched cursor
placed over PPI

Concentric range rings
equally spaced
own ship in centre

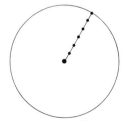

Calibration pips shown
brightening a stationary
timebase trace.
When trace is rotated the
tube afterglow produces
range rings.

Fig. 1.5 PPI range calibration techniques

generator produces a series of calibration pip voltage spikes, the variable range marker generator produces a single voltage spike, or strobe, which can be positioned anywhere across the screen by the navigator using a front panel control. The single voltage spike will prescribe a single circle of light on the screen, at any range depending on the setting of the variable range marker control. The control is connected to either a mechanical or an electronic display of range, to indicate to the navigator the range of the marker on the screen. Zero range is coincident with the scan origin.

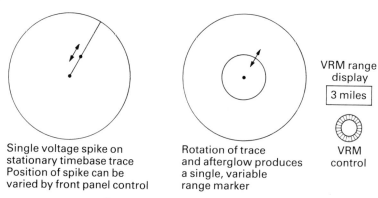

Single voltage spike on stationary timebase trace Position of spike can be varied by front panel control

Rotation of trace and afterglow produces a single, variable range marker

VRM range display

3 miles

VRM control

Fig. 1.6 Variable range marker on a PPI display

Calibration of bearing can also be accomplished either mechanically or electronically. The mechanical method requires an illuminated bearing scale to be located round the edge of the screen, showing calibration in 360, one-degree increments. The lines etched on the cursor, already mentioned, have the central line extended to over-lap the bearing scale physically. By rotating the cursor the navigator can place the central line of the cursor over the target and read off the relative bearing from the illuminated scale below it.

The electronic method involves the generation of a straight, dashed, radial line which appears on the ppi screen in a position determined by the navigator. The line starts at the trace origin, and extends the full width of the screen. On a correctly

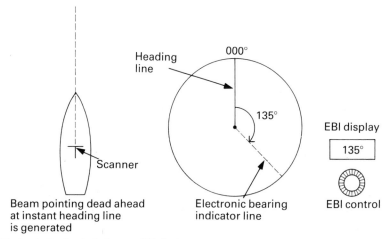

Heading line

000°

135°

EBI display

135°

Scanner

EBI control

Beam pointing dead ahead at instant heading line is generated

Electronic bearing indicator line

Fig. 1.7 Electronic Bearing Indicator on a PPI display

adjusted display, the electronic bearing indicator will be positioned at 000° when the bearing display read-out indicates 000°. As with the variable range marker, the electronic bearing indicator (ebi) control is connected to a display read-out which in this case is calibrated in degrees. By placing the dashed line over the target and reading-off the display read-out the navigator can measure the bearing of the target accurately. The electronic bearing indicator can be aligned anywhere over a 360° arc. Figures 1.7 and 1.8 show the use of an EBI.

To indicate to the navigator when the scanner is 'looking' dead-ahead, a heading line, or heading marker, is also superimposed on to the display. The heading marker circuit operation is triggered by closing a switch located in the beam assembly which does so at the instant the scanner points dead-ahead. The switch closure triggers a circuit which electronically generates a continuous, straight radial line, starting at the trace origin, and extending to the edge of the screen. The heading line will be coincident with 000° on the bearing scale of a correctly adjusted display.

A ppi display representing a target at a range of 3 miles, bearing 090° relative to own ships' head when the 6 mile range has been selected on the equipment is shown in Fig. 1.8.

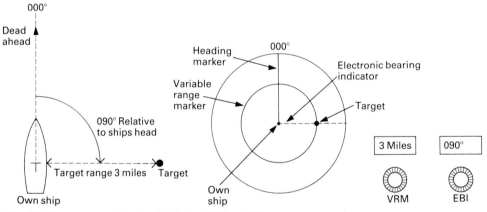

Fig. 1.8 Target range and bearing fixed using VRM and EBI

The main component parts of a basic primary pulse radar

PRF Generator The accurate timing of the interval between the transmission of a pulse of energy and the subsequent return of an echo from a target is one of the essential requirements of a radar. This is the function of the timebase generator. However, a circuit is required which will start the whole cycle of operation, namely the instant of time when a pulse is to be transmitted and the timebase circuit triggered. This will deflect the spot of light across the screen, from zero range at the instant the pulse is transmitted, at a rate of 1 mile every 12.2μ seconds.

As previously intimated, a continuous pulse train is radiated, the pulse repetition rate being determined by factors such as the displayed range, which will be discussed later. The timing initiator is essentially an oscillator which operates at a single frequency for each of the short, medium or long ranges, a separate frequency being employed for each of the three range bands. Because this circuit generates a frequency which determines the pulse transmission rate it is known as a pulse repetition frequency (prf) generator.

The Transmitter   The transmitter can be subdivided into two, linked units. The modulator, which is the unit which generates the rectangular pulse shape, and the magnetron—a device which produces high power pulses of rf energy at the transmission frequency.

The Modulator   The modulator can be regarded as a source of power which supplies the magnetron, and is, in effect, the magnetron eht power supply unit. Energy is supplied to the modulator from the equipment power supply at a relatively low level during the comparatively long periods in between transmitted pulses. The energy which is stored in the modulator is then released as a high-power, short duration discharge to the magnetron.

The concept is very similar to the charging of an electrolytic capacitor over a long period of time. Once the capacitor is fully charged it can be discharged by connecting a short circuit across its terminals. All the stored energy is then released in a very short period of time as a spectacular discharge.

The modulator, although having some similarities to the above description, is more sophisticated, but nevertheless, for the purposes of explaining a concept, it will suffice.

The commencement of the modulator charging cycle is initiated by a trigger pulse received from the prf generator, with a second, similar trigger pulse from the prf generator effecting the discharge cycle.

The modulator, in addition to supplying the magnetron with short-duration, high-power pulses of dc, eht, is the unit which sets the time duration of the transmitted pulse. Short pulse lengths being employed on short ranges, and long pulse lengths on long ranges, the reasons for which will be explained later in more detail.

A sample of the modulator pulse is extracted as a synchronising pulse to trigger the time-base generator unit which starts deflection of the centre spot at the instant the pulse is transmitted.

The Magnetron   The magnetron converts the dc pulses of energy from the modulator into radio frequency oscillations. The magnetron will produce the oscillations only for the duration of the modulator pulse as it is the modulator which provides the magnetron eht supply.

Duplexer   Commercial marine radar installations normally only use one scanner. To facilitate the use of a single scanner for both transmission and reception a change-over switch is required. It is not possible to leave the receiver and the transmitter connected simultaneously to the scanner, because the high-power pulse of energy from the transmitter would irreparably damage the receiver. An electronic switch has to be placed between the transmitter and receiver, therefore, which is capable of switching alternately between the two units. During the time that the transmitter is generating the pulse the switch connects the transmitter unit to the scanner, while during the subsequent period after the pulse, when target echoes are being received, the switch connects the scanner to the receiver unit.

Many modern marine radars have the transmitter and receiver unit (called a transceiver as it contains both units) mounted directly underneath the scanner. In such equipment the transmit/receive switch (TR) is mounted at the input point of the scanner.

In other radar equipments, the scanner and the transceiver may be a considerable distance apart. In such installations the transceiver and the scanner are linked by a hollow metal feeder known as waveguide, which carries the rf energy between the two. The duplexer will be located inside the transceiver unit at the entrance to the waveguide in such installations.

The device which performs the duplexing operation is known as a TR cell.

Bearing Transmission System   This system ensures that the scanner and the ppi trace remain locked in synchronisation in terms of direction and rotation, and thus enable directional information regarding the angular position of the scanner (and its highly directional beam) to be fed to the display. Target echo returns picked up by the scanner will, therefore, be displayed at the correct bearing relative to the ship's head.

Timebase Generator   On receipt of a synchronising pulse from the modulator (indicating the transmission of a pulse of energy) the timebase generator commences production of a linear, sawtooth-shaped current waveform which rises in amplitude, from zero up to a maximum value with time. The current, when passed through the deflection coils around the ppi tube neck causes the spot of light to be drawn from the centre of the screen towards the outer edge, due to the interaction between the magnetic field resulting from the current, and the electron beam which produces the spot of light.

Receiver   After the transmission of a pulse of energy the duplexer switch connects the scanner to the receiver to allow returned echoes of the pulse, which are picked up by the scanner, to be detected by a highly sensitive receiver. The detected signals are then processed in preparation for display. The signals appearing at the output of the receiver are known as 'raw video', and it is at this point in the system that analogue and digital radars differ, together with alternative display techniques which will be discussed later.

The basic component parts are shown in relation to one another in the simplified system diagram in Fig. 1.9.

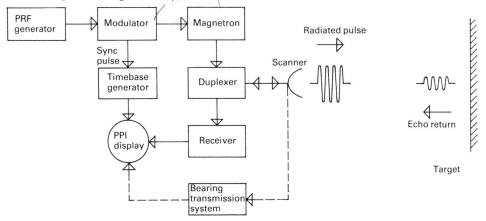

Fig. 1.9 Basic components of a primary pulse radar system

Operation of a basic primary pulse radar system

A trigger pulse from the prf generator initiates the charging cycle of the modulator. Some time later, the prf generator provides a second trigger pulse to discharge the energy stored in the modulator circuitry. A short duration, high voltage, rectangular pulse is fed from the modulator to the magnetron. A sample of the modulator pulse is fed, as a sync pulse, to the time-base generator to start the deflection of the spot from the centre of the crt to the tube edge. At the instant the modulator pulse is applied to the magnetron, oscillations build up inside the magnetron and radio frequency energy is produced. A powerful pulse of microwave energy passes through the duplexer which routes the rf pulse from the transceiver to the scanner from where it is radiated as a fan-shaped beam.

As the transmitted pulse propagates away from the scanner the sawtooth shaped current produced by the time-base generator continues to deflect the spot towards the outer edge of the screen, at a rate determined by the selected display range. Energy, reradiated from a reflecting target, is returned to the scanner and passed through the duplexer which, in the time immediately after the pulse was transmitted, will have reverted to connect the receiver to the scanner. A sensitive receiver detects the target's echo and processes the signal for subsequent display on the screen.

After a predefined period of time the cycle of operation comes to an end, with the time-base generator returning the spot back to the centre of the screen in readiness for the next trace.

During the reception period, the prf generator will have produced a trigger pulse to start the recharging of the modulator in readiness for the second pulse to be transmitted. The next trigger pulse from the prf generator discharges the modulator to produce the second pulse for the magnetron, and the second sync pulse for the time-base generator. For the whole of this time, the scanner has been turning, so the next transmission pulse will be directed a fraction of a degree to the right of the previous transmission.

Because of the relative timing cycles and rotational speed of the scanner, the scanner can be thought of as almost remaining in the same direction for reception as it was for transmission, although this cannot strictly ever be so. The bearing transmission system continuously supplies angular position information down to the display so, just as the next transmitted pulse is directed on a slightly different bearing, the next ppi trace will be painted on the screen at a slightly different bearing to the previous paint, in synchronism with the change in scanner direction.

The chemical materials coating the inside of the screen cause the previously painted trace to remain visible for a short period of time, and as a consequence this and the observer's persistence of vision, the end result appears as a continually rotating beam of light on the screen, with target information appearing as bright-ups in the same position (stationary targets only) every time the trace rotates.

The operating cycle described may, in practice, be repeated several thousand times per second.

Figure 1.10 shows the timing cycle over one period of operation using idealised waveforms.

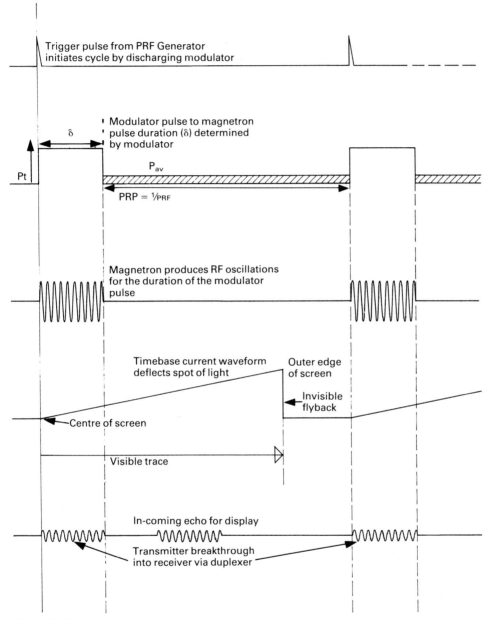

Trigger pulse from PRF Generator
initiates cycle by discharging modulator

Modulator pulse to magnetron
pulse duration (δ) determined
by modulator

δ

P_{av}

Pt

$PRP = 1/PRF$

Magnetron produces RF oscillations
for the duration of the modulator
pulse

Timebase current waveform
deflects spot of light

Outer edge
of screen

Invisible
flyback

Centre of screen

Visible trace

In-coming echo for display

Transmitter breakthrough
into receiver via duplexer

Fig. 1.10 Time related waveforms for a basic primary pulse system

2
Operating characteristics of a basic radar system

Chapter 1 described the basic operating cycle of a primary pulse radar system. In the description, mention was made of factors which are of great importance to the performance of a radar, and which are established at its design stage. Many of these factors are interrelated, and compromise often has to be made as an improvement of one could be detrimental to another. In this chapter each of the factors will be examined, and their interrelationship demonstrated.

2.1 Transmitted pulse duration (δ)

The transmitted pulse time duration, or 'pulse width' is determined by the design of the modulator circuit. A radar normally has more than one pulse duration, switched automatically as the displayed range is increased or decreased. When very short ranges are selected on the display the transmitted pulse width is made very short, typically 0.07μ seconds. Conversely, when long range is selected a long pulse duration is employed, typically 1μ second.

Some radars use three switched pulse durations, short, medium and long in accordance with the range selected on the display. The medium pulse duration would, most probably be between the two extremes noted.

2.2 Pulse repetition frequency (prf)

The pulse repetition frequency is determined by the prf generator, and describes the number of pulses of energy transmitted per second. As with the pulse duration, a radar will have more than one prf, the selected one being a function of the displayed range. On short ranges a high prf is employed, typically 2000 pulses/second. On long ranges a low prf is selected, typically 400 pulses/second.

2.3 Pulse repetition period (prp)

The pulse repetition period is the time duration of one complete cycle of operation. It is equal to the transmitted pulse width (δ) + resting period. The 'resting period' is the time interval after the transmission of a pulse when in-coming echoes can be received, and the modulator is being recharged in readiness for the next transmission pulse. The 'resting period' is equal to prp $-\delta$

2.4 Carrier frequency

The carrier frequency is the radio frequency on which the transmission is made.

Marine radar equipment is manufactured to operate in either one of two frequency bands.

'X' Band (λ 3 cm)   5200 – 11 900 MHz (λ 5.8 – 2.5 cm)
'S' Band (λ 10 cm) 1650 – 5200 MHz   (λ 18.2 – 5.8 cm)

Each band offers the navigator different advantages, the X Band producing a relatively high resolution picture which is excellent for precise navigation require-ments, but which suffers badly from the effects of sea and rain clutter. The S Band sacrifices high resolution of target information for the benefit of relative freedom from sea and rain clutter effects.

2.5   Peak power (P_t)

The useful power contained in the radiated pulse. The peak power is usually sufficient to ensure that the maximum range is limited only by the radar horizon and not by under-powered equipment. The peak power is often quoted as the nominal magnet-ron rating. Typical peak power values are 10 kW–30 kW for 3 cm and 10 cm systems respectively.

2.6   Average power (P_{av})

This is the peak power value (P_t) averaged out of the whole of the pulse repetition period. A comparatively small average power (typically 10 W) is supplied to the modulator from the equipment power supply unit for the comparatively long time of the resting period. The total energy stored in the modulator at the end of the resting period is then released in the short duration transmitted pulse.

2.7   Duty cycle (duty ratio)

The Duty cycle is used to denote the relationship between, prp in pulses/second; δ in seconds; P_{av} in watts; and P_t in watts.
   The Duty cycle or Duty ratio has no units, and serves only to show a relationship. The Duty cycle can be calculated in several ways:

Duty cycle = Pulse width (δ) divided by prp
            = Pulse width (δ) multiplied by prf
            = Average power (P_{av}) divided by Peak power (P_t)

Example:
A radar is known to have the following technical parameters:

P_t: 25 kW
δ: 0.6 μs on long range
       0.06 μs on short range
prf: 1000 pps on long range
       2000 pps on short range

from which it is possible to calculate (a) Duty cycle; and (b) P_{av}

$$\text{Duty cycle} = \delta/\text{prp}$$

prf is known, so prp can be calculated as 1/prf

prp on long range = 1 millisecond
    short range = 0.5 millisecond

therefore,
on long range duty cycle = 0.0006
on short range duty cycle = 0.00012

$$P_{av} = \text{Duty cycle} \times P_t$$

therefore,
on long range, $P_{av} = 0.0006 \times 25\,000 = 15$ W
on short range, $P_{av} = 0.00012 \times 25\,000 = 3$ W

2.8   Choice of values for the factors affecting the navigational characteristics of a marine radar

Transmitted pulse duration

The energy content of a transmitted pulse is given by

$$P_t \times \delta \text{ Joules,} \qquad (P_t \text{ in watts, } \delta \text{ in } \mu\text{s})$$

Using the reasoning: the stronger the pulse the stronger will be the returned echo, the weaker the pulse the weaker will be the returned echo. Therefore, if the energy content of a transmitted pulse is low, a small target may return an echo which is too weak to be detected by the receiver, and there is a real possibility that the target may not be detected. Therefore, for a given peak power (P_t), it could be argued that the pulse duration (δ) should be made as long as possible. Radiating a pulse which is sufficiently strong as to ensure that even the smallest of targets will return an echo of detectable strength is one of the arguments. However, if this is done it will increase the Duty cycle.

The Duty cycle is given by $\delta \times$ prf, and if the transmitted pulse duration is increased (and all other factors remain constant), the Duty cycle will increase, the Average power (P_{av}) will increase and the equipment power supply will have to deliver more energy to the modulator. This in turn will most probably increase the physical size and cost of the transceiver.

A broad transmitted pulse will also influence the receiver bandwidth. With a broad (long time duration) pulse the receiver bandwidth can be made narrow. By making the receiver bandwidth narrow the signal:noise ratio is improved. With a reduction in the noise level the receiver becomes more sensitive to weak echoes. This gives a second argument for the case to make δ as long as possible, disregarding the factors of cost and size.

There are, however, two reasons which argue the case for making the transmitted pulse duration as narrow as possible:

- range discrimination.
- minimum range.

Range discrimination

Range discrimination is defined as the ability of the radar to display as two separate targets the echoes from two objects which lie on the same line of bearing, but are separated by a short distance in range. Figure 2.1 shows this relationship. To achieve this requirement the receiver must detect two separate echoes, one from each target.

As stated in Chapter 1, the velocity of propagation of the transmitted pulse is 300 000 000 m/s. If a 1μ second pulse were radiated, the leading edge of the pulse

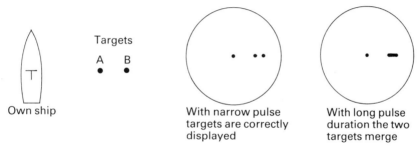

Fig. 2.1 Range discrimination

would be 300 metres from the scanner at the instant the trailing edge leaves the scanner.

If the two targets 'A' and 'B', shown in Fig. 2.2 were located 150 metres apart and subject to a 1μ second pulse, the following would happen, assuming that target 'A' does not cause shadowing of target 'B'.

At time, $t = 0$; the leading edge of the pulse is incident with target 'A' which will reradiate a portion of the pulse energy back towards the scanner as an echo.

At time, $t + 0.5μ$ seconds; the leading edge of the pulse has travelled 150 metres and is now incident with target 'B' which will also start to reradiate an echo. The leading edge of the echo from target 'A' will also have travelled 150 metres back towards the scanner. As target 'A' is still subject to the transmitted pulse it will continue to return an echo pulse for the remainder of the pulse.

At time, $t + 1μ$ second; The trailing edge of the transmitted pulse is now clearing target A and consequently the trailing edge of 'A''s echo return leaves the target, the leading edge now being 300 metres nearer to the scanner. The leading edge of 'B''s echo return has already travelled 150 metres, and consequently is coincident with the trailing edge of the echo from 'A'. Target 'B' will continue to return an echo pulse for a further 0.5μ second.

At time, $t + 1.5μ$ seconds, the trailing edge of the transmitted pulse now clears target 'B', and consequently the trailing edge of target 'B''s echo leaves the target. The leading edge of target 'B''s echo is now 300 metres nearer the scanner, and is coincident with the trailing edge of the echo from target 'A'. The two echoes return to the scanner as one continuous echo, and the radar cannot distinguish between the end of one echo and the beginning of the other as they are inseparable, being returned simultaneously from the two targets.

If, however, the two targets were to be separated slightly, to a distance of 180 metres, and still subject to a 1μ second pulse, the following would occur. (Refer to Fig. 2.3.)

At time, $t = 0$; The leading edge of the transmitted pulse is now incident with target 'A', which now starts to return an echo.

At time, $t + 0.6μ$ seconds, the leading edge of the transmitted pulse reaches target 'B' which starts to return an echo. The leading edge of the echo from target 'A' is already 180 metres nearer to the scanner on its return journey.

At time, $t + 1μ$ second, the trailing edge of the transmitted pulse clears target 'A', and the trailing edge of the echo from target 'A' clears the target. The leading edge of 'A''s echo is already 300 metres nearer to the scanner, whereas the leading edge of the echo from target 'B' is already 120 metres away from B on its return journey.

At time, $t + 1.6μ$ seconds; The trailing edge of the transmitted pulse clears target 'B', as does the trailing edge of its echo return. The leading edge of echo 'B''s is

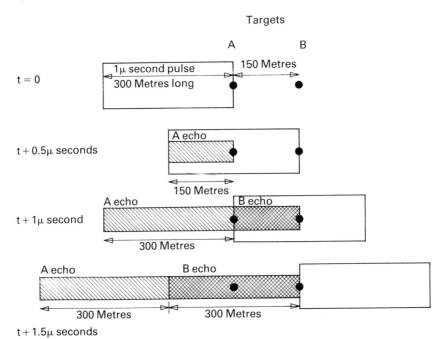

Fig. 2.2 Echo returns from targets inseparable

already 300 metres nearer to the scanner, but it is lagging target 'A''s trailing edge by some 60 metres. From this it can be seen that two separate echoes will be received from targets 'A' and 'B' which will be displayed as two separate echoes.

It can, therefore, be reasoned that if the two targets are separated by a distance

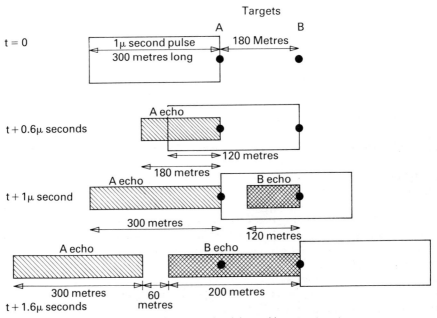

Fig. 2.3 Echo returns from targets A and B separated and detectable as two targets

which is greater than δ in metres (or yards) divided by 2 they will be displayed as two echoes. However, in saying that, the following should be borne in mind.

First, the reasoning and calculations supporting this argument have used a pulse duration which is not suited to short range operation. A 1μ second pulse would be used on long range working. This figure has only been used to provide the reader with simple figures for the purpose of calculation and illustration of the point. If a more plausible pulse duration is used, as in the case of short range operation, typically 0.07μ seconds, the theoretical distance which separates the targets would be 10.5 metres if they are to be displayed as two echoes.

Secondly, in the case of long range operation the dimension of the spot of light on the ppi will have a significant impact. Assuming that the minimum radius of the spot of light is 0.125 mm, then theoretically the minimum distance between adjacent spots would be twice the spot radius, i.e. 0.25 mm, assuming the operator's eye could resolve such a presentation. If a 16 inch (400 mm) ppi screen was used, and the equipment switched to the 48 mile range, then we can reason as follows:

The tube radius of 200 mm equates to 48 miles, then one mile would be represented by 4.16 mm. As a mile is taken as 2000 yards, then a spot size of 0.25 mm would equate to a separation of 120 yards (109.7 metres). From the above reasoning, a separation equivalent to half of the pulse duration is required. As 109.7 metres would be the dimension of a pulse of 0.365μ seconds, the transmitted pulse duration would have to be twice this figure: 0.73μ seconds. It would, therefore, be of no value to use a short pulse duration on long ranges as it would be unlikely that a human eye could discriminate between two adjacent pin-points of light.

To summarise, targets will be displayed as separate echoes if the distance they are apart is greater than:

$$\text{Transmitted pulse duration (μ seconds)} \times 164$$

The answer will be in yards.

Minimum range

The minimum range of a radar is the ability to detect and display echoes in close proximity to the radar. This is of importance when the vessel is negotiating narrow channels or berthing during darkness or in periods of reduced visibility.

To display targets in close proximity to ownship, it is necessary for the transmitted pulse to have terminated, and the duplexer to have reverted to the receive condition. When observing or tracking targets at very close range the navigator will have switched to the shortest display range, which in turn would have automatically selected the shortest pulse duration. If the shortest pulse duration was 0.07μ seconds, the leading edge of the pulse would be 21 metres away from the scanner at the instant the trailing edge of the pulse left the scanner. Ignoring the TR cell change-over time, it can already be seen that any target at a range under 10.5 metres (half the length of the pulse) would not be detected. When all other factors are included, the minimum range figure would be in the order of 15–20 metres. For a radar to comply with the current Department of Transport marine radar performance specification a target must remain visible down to a minimum range of 50 metres when the scanner is mounted 15 metres above the sea.

In addition to the transmitted pulse duration affecting the minimum range, the theoretical minimum range will also be affected by the time it takes for the duplexer transmit/receive switch to change-over from the transmit condition to receive.

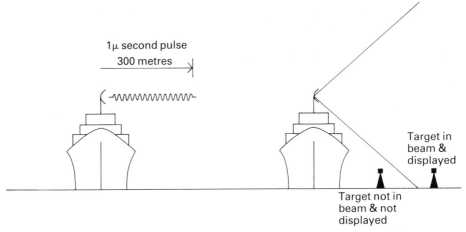

Fig. 2.4 Minimum range affected by transmitted pulse duration and scanner vertical beamwidth

Although this process is very quick it nevertheless does take a finite time to achieve, also the TR cell will become progressively sluggish with age, and, as no two TR cells are identical, no precise time can be quoted for this. Therefore, the theoretical minimum range cannot be less than:

(Pulse width $\{\delta\}$ + TR switch-over time [μ seconds]) $\times$ 164 yards.

Example:
A radar δ on long range is 0.6μ seconds,
          on short range is 0.06μ seconds

If the TR change-over time is 0.1μ seconds, the minimum range will be:
          on long range: 114.8 yards
          on short range: 26.24 yards

However, in practice the minimum range is affected by other factors:

- scanner height above sea level,
- vertical radiated beam-width of the scanner,
- sea clutter conditions,
- receiver paralysis.

Each of the above will be discussed separately, and their relationship with minimum range requirements will be demonstrated.

As can be shown, two conflicting criteria exist in relation to the duration of the transmitted pulse.

A long pulse, would satisfy the requirements for maximum energy in the pulse, returning strong echoes from even very small targets. It would also improve the detection of weak, long-range targets because the receiver bandwidth could be reduced, thus improving the signal:noise ratio.

On the other hand, there are two essential navigational requirements which must be satisfied, range discrimination and minimum range, both of which dictate the use of a short pulse.

In practice, the conflict can be satisfied by a combination of compromise and switching. On short display ranges when it is vital to maximise range discrimination and minimum range characteristics, a short pulse duration is automatically switched as a function of the range-change switch ($\delta \leqslant 0.07\mu$ seconds). On long ranges, where, as has been demonstrated, other factors produce limitations in relation to range discrimination the need for a short duration pulse becomes inconsequential.

Secondly, by switching to a long range the implication is that the navigator is not concerned with targets as close as 50 metres, for example, when navigating in mid-ocean. The requirement which must now be satisfied is the detection of relatively weak, distant targets. Therefore, when a long display range is selected an automatic switching process changes the transmitted pulse length to long ($\delta > 1\mu$ second) pulse.

Pulse Repetition Frequency (prf)

The pulse repetition frequency is determined by the prf generator circuitry, and defines the number of rf pulses of energy transmitted per second. The prf generator produces trigger pulses which,
(a) initiate the start of the modulator charging cycle, and
(b) produce the trigger pulse to discharge the stored modulator energy into the magnetron.

In the time period between two successive transmitted pulses, the 'resting period', the receiver is able to detect in-coming echoes as soon as the duplexer (TR cell) has changed from transmit to receive condition. This time period, which in turn dictates the pulse repetition frequency, is a function of the display range selected. When long pulse is selected on the display, sufficient time has to be allowed for long-range targets to return echo pulses before the next pulse in the train is transmitted. It was established in Chapter 1 that 12.2μ seconds must be allowed for each radar mile. Therefore, if a distant target at a range of 48 miles returned an echo, it would take $585.6\ \mu$ seconds from the time the pulse was transmitted to the return of the echo. As prf = 1/prp, $585.6\ \mu$ seconds corresponds to a frequency of approximately 1707 Hz. Theoretically, if the design maximum range of the radar was 48 miles, then the prf required for this range would be approximately 1707 Hz. In so doing, an echo returned from a target at 48 miles would be coincident with the next transmitted pulse.

In practice, the prf is lowered, thus extending the prp, and allowing all echo returns adequate time to return to the set and be displayed. If this was not done, and the original relatively high prf employed, the equipment would be prone to second trace (or even multiple trace) echoes. A second trace echo is one which returns to the equipment after a second pulse and trace has been initiated; the 'second trace echo' originates from the previous transmitted pulse but, because the prp is too short (the prf is too high) the second pulse was transmitted before the echo could return. As a consequence, the returning echo will be displayed on the next consecutive trace, but at an erroneous range.

Figure 2.5 shows graphically how a second trace echo can be displayed. The radar has a prf of 1000 pps, and is operating on the 48 mile range. A second trace echo is displayed at an apparent range of 11 miles on the second (subsequent) trace. A prf of 1000 pps corresponds to a prp of 1000μ seconds. The equivalent range from the transmission of the first pulse to the transmission of the second pulse will, therefore, be $1000/12.2\mu$ seconds = 81.96 nautical miles. As the second trace echo appears on the second trace at an apparent range of 11 miles, whereas the true range is $81.96 + 11 = 92.96$ miles.

Had the equipment been designed with a lower prf, for example 800 pps, this would have given a p.r.p of 1250μ seconds equating to slightly in excess of 102 miles. The

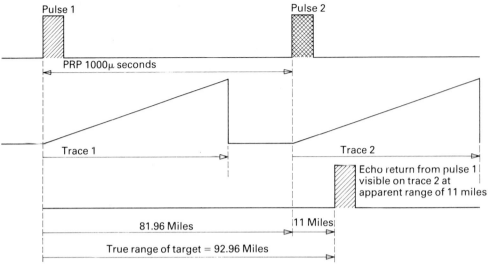

Fig. 2.5 Second trace echoes

timebase scan period for a 48 mile range is $48 \times 12.2 = 585.6\mu$ seconds. With a prf of 800 pps, the timebase scan would have run for the first 585.6μ seconds of the prp (ignoring δ which is sufficiently small as to be insignificant) after which the timebase would be blanked for the remaining 664.4μ seconds. The blanked period is known as the 'dead time'. An echo returning from a distance of 93 miles after 1134.6μ seconds would, therefore, arrive during the period when the timebase is not visible (well before the transmission of the next pulse) and would not be displayed at all.

It should be noted, however, that target echo returns which fall within the designed display range will be displayed on the screen at the correct range. It is only second (and sometimes multiple) trace echoes which would be displayed at an incorrect range. The 'dead-time' period plays a vital role for the technique of 'retimed video' in digital radar processing, as will be explained in a later chapter.

However, had the equipment design incorporated some means whereby the prf frequency could be swept over a relatively narrow frequency range, the effect would be to cause all second (and multiple) trace echoes to change their position on the screen with every paint, thus revealing themselves as erroneous targets to the operator. All normal 'true' echoes would remain unaffected by this technique and would continue to be displayed at their correct range.

Having seen the justification for employing a low pulse repetition frequency to allow long range echoes time to return and to obtain a degree of freedom from second trace echoes, a direct conflict of requirement is once more encountered.

Number of echo returns from a target

The case which can be argued for employing a high pulse repetition frequency is the necessity to 'hit' the target with at least five and preferably ten or more echo pulses to build up the brightness of the spot in an integrating fashion so that each echo shows as a bright spot of light. To achieve this we require a high prf in order to hit the target with as many pulses as possible while the target is in the scanner beam-width.

In estimating the number of times a target is hit by successive pulses of energy the following additional factors have to be taken into consideration:

- The horizontal aspect of the target and its physical length will determine how long the target remains in the scanner's beam. A 'supertanker' having an overall length of 1000 feet presenting a broadside aspect will obviously remain in the beam for a much longer period than, for example, a channel navigation buoy whose total reflective area is approximately $10\,m^2$ regardless of the aspect presented. For the reasons outlined above, when calculating the number of echoes received from a target, something known as a 'point target' is considered; one which does not have an excessive length or unusual aspect.
- The rotational speed of the scanner. For a given prf, pulses radiated from a scanner which turns slowly will hit the target many more times than one which turns rapidly. In close relation to this factor is the angular velocity of the scanner, the time the scanner takes to sweep over a finite number of degrees. In the case of marine radar the scanning requirement is for a complete 360 degrees.
- The horizontal beam-width of the scanner's radiation. Chapter 1 described the radiated beam as resembling a fan, having a narrow horizontal beam-width and a broad vertical beam-width. For as long as the target remains within the horizontal beam it will continue to provide echo returns from successive strikes. From this it can be reasoned that the wider the horizontal beam-width is made, the greater will be the number of hits and subsequent echo returns.

All of the factors combined in a formula give:

Number of echoes received from a point target =

$$\frac{(\text{Scanner horizontal beam-width}) \times (\text{Pulse repetition frequency})}{360 \text{ degrees} \times (\text{Scanner revolutions/60 seconds})}$$

$$= \frac{\text{HBW} \times \text{PRF}}{6 \times N}$$

where HBW = Horizontal beam-width in degrees, PRF = Pulse repetition frequency in pulses/second, and N = Revolutions per minute.

For example: if the horizontal beam-width of the scanner was 0.5 degrees, the prf was 2000 pps, and N, the number of scanner revolutions per minute, was 20 rpm, these figures would reveal

$$\frac{0.5 \times 2000}{6 \times 20} = 8 \text{ strikes of a point target (approximately)}.$$

It is assumed that all of these echoes are detected by the radar, and contribute to building up a bright spot of light on the screen as the phosphor coating on the inner tube face brings about an integrating action to produce a clearly identifiable echo return.

With the prf figure quoted in the example it would be assumed that the equipment is operating on short range from the reasoning of Section 2.8. When long ranges are selected the pulse repetition frequency is reduced as already explained, and the number of hits per target falls accordingly.

In addition to the reduction in prf, a second factor which will bring about a reduction in the number of hits of a target at long range is the apparent decrease in the aspect length due to the subtended angle. A target will present a physically longer projected area at short range when compared to long range, and will therefore be in the scanner's beam for a shorter period of time. As a consequence, long range targets provide a much weaker echo return, and may very often produce so few returns that the target brilliance is insufficient to be sustained by the afterglow between successive sweeps.

If the prf is increased to provide a greater number of echo returns from each target, and all other factors remain constant, it can be seen that the average power (P_{av}) will increase. This is because the Duty cycle = $\delta \times$ prf. Therefore, an increase in the prf will result in an increase in average power, and will also increase the possibility of second trace echoes.

As in the case of the pulse width, the conflict in requirements is partially solved by switching the prf in accordance with the display range switch; a high prf (typically up to 3200 pps) being used on the shortest range, and a low prf (possibly as low as 400 pps) for the longest ranges with even a third 'intermediate' prf used on ranges between the maximum and minimum.

Scanner horizontal beam-width

By definition, the horizontal beam-width of an antenna is the angle subtended by the half-power points in the polar diagram. See Fig 2.6.

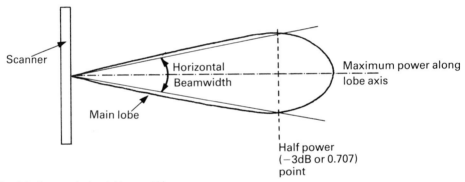

Fig. 2.6 Scanner horizontal beamwidth

The previous section argued for a wide horizontal beam-width in order to provide the largest number of echo returns from a target to produce a bright echo display. In direct contradiction to this argument is the necessity to reduce the horizontal beam-width to make it as narrow as possible.

A narrow horizontal beam-width is required for 'bearing discrimination'. Bearing discrimination is the ability of the radar to display as separate echoes targets which are at the same range, but closely spaced in bearing.

To be displayed as separate echoes, the targets must not be returning echoes at the same time; i.e. the trailing edge of the rotating horizontal beam must have cleared one object before the leading edge of the beam arrives at the second object. For targets to be displayed separately they must subtend an angle, when viewed from the scanner which is greater than the horizontal beam-width.

As shown in Fig. 2.7, objects at range (R) will show as separate echoes if the distance (d) between them is greater than:

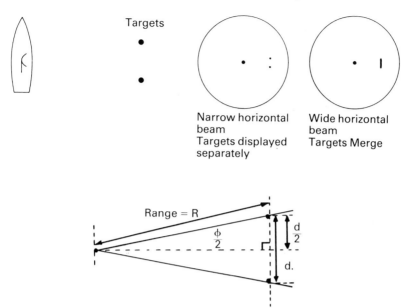

Fig. 2.7 Bearing discrimination

$$\sin \phi/2 = \frac{\text{Side opposite}}{\text{Hypoteneuse}} = \frac{d/2}{R} = \frac{d}{2R}$$

$$2R = \frac{d}{\sin \phi/2}$$

$$R = \frac{d}{2 \sin \phi/2}$$

$$d = 2 R \sin \phi/2$$

where d and R are in the same units.

A scanner offering a horizontal beam-width of 0.75° will have a bearing discrimination of 26.18 yards at a range of one mile, 261.8 yards at 10 miles, and 523.65 yards at 20 miles.

In addition to this, the horizontal beam-width will create a distortion in target length or width if it is excessively wide. Ref Fig. 2.8. The horizontal beam-width of a radar scanner has a relationship to the physical length of the scanner and also to the transmission frequency band.

At 'X' Band, scanner length 1.8 metres, hbw 1.3°
     scanner length 2.4 metres, hbw 1.0°

At 'S' Band, scanner length 3.9 metres, hbw 1.7°

In general, the greater the physical length of the scanner, the narrower will be the horizontal beam-width. Chapter 9 shows how these relationships are established. In addition, the larger the physical length of the scanner the higher will be the 'gain' of the scanner which in turn partially determines the ability to receive weak echoes.

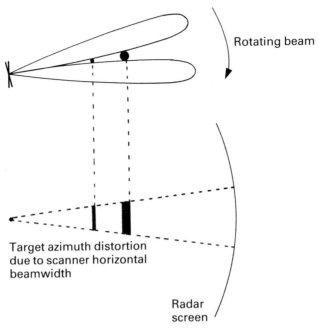

Fig. 2.8 Target azimuth distortion

Scanner rotation speed

In an analogue radar system using a ppi type display, the scanner should rotate fairly rapidly so as to up-date the display by repainting the picture. If this was not done the previous paint would have faded completely before the rotating trace could repaint the picture. The after-glow time, due to the persistency of the phosphor materials is covered below.

However, the scanning rate should be sufficiently slow so that all targets remain in the horizontal beam long enough to return several successive echo returns (see above). Also, to some extent, successive traces on the ppi overlap one another. If this did not occur it would, in extreme cases, be possible for targets to be 'lost in the gaps' between traces. In practice, rotational speeds are usually between 20 and 30 rpm for commercial marine radar.

Screen persistence

To present the navigator with a continual map-like presentation it is necessary that the crt screen phosphor material after-glow, in an analogue system, be at least as long as one revolution of the scanner. If it is made too short, the picture will have completely faded before the next paint; if it is made too long the picture will have a tendency to blur when the vessel alters course. In the latter case, blurring of the picture for any significant period of time will leave the navigator almost totally blind until the original picture information has faded to leave the new information clearly visible. In addition to this, when a ship's head-up display is selected—because it is highly unlikely that the vessel will ever steer a straight course but will be subject to continual yawing of only a half, or even one degree either side of the steered course—the picture information will also blur slightly. If the after-glow time is excessively long the fine detail of coastlines, essential for navigation position fixing, will become indistinct. This problem can be over come by the use of a North Stabilised display as discussed in Chapter 19.

Digital radar systems which employ raster-scan displays do not use the same display tubes as an analogue ppi system. The raster-scan display uses a short persistency picture tube, similar to those used for domestic television receivers, and relies on rapid up-date of information to maintain a picture as will subsequently be fully explained.

Scanner height

The height at which the scanner is mounted will have a bearing on both the minimum and the maximum displayed ranges. In Chapter 1 it was stated that the electromagnetic pulses of energy radiated from the scanner travel at the speed of light. As with light rays, the height of the scanner will play a significant role in the radar's performance. It is a fact that a tall person will be able to see a greater distance than a short person; the same reasoning can be applied to the height of the scanner. One which is mounted at a great height will be able to 'see' further than one mounted at a significantly lower height. As with optical rays, the radar beam will be subject to some degree of refraction or bending as it is propagated through the troposphere; however, the frequencies used for radar transmission do not suffer quite as badly as optical rays. The radar horizon is approximately some 6% greater than the optical horizon (which in turn is approximately 9% greater than the true, or geometric horizon) for 3 cm radar.

The distance to the radar horizon can be calculated from:

$$1.23\sqrt{ht}$$

where *ht* is the scanner height above sea level in feet; the answer being in miles, or,

$$4.06\sqrt{ht}$$

where *ht* is the scanner height above sea level in metres; the answer being in kilometres. (The distance to the geometric horizon being calculated by $1.06\sqrt{ht}$ and the optical horizon by $1.15\sqrt{ht}$; where *ht* is in feet and the answer in miles.)

Therefore, if a scanner is mounted 50 feet (15.24 metres) above sea level, the radar horizon will be approximately 8.69 miles (15.84 km).

An increase in the scanner height will obviously increase the distance to the radar horizon, and conversely, a decrease in height will reduce the distance to the radar horizon. Unfortunately, the price which has to be paid for increasing the distance to the radar horizon by raising the height of the scanner is the increased effects from sea (clutter) echo returns, and a reduction in minimum range capabilities.

Sea clutter echoes are caused by the reflection of energy from waves in a disturbed sea. When the sea is dead calm sea clutter echo returns are not observed. The height of the scanner in relation to the magnitude of sea clutter observed is a factor of the 'grazing angle' between the beam and the surface of the sea. This relationship is shown in Fig. 2.9 for both high and low scanner heights.

From Fig. 2.9 it can be seen that sea clutter echo returns extend further from the centre of the ppi when the scanner is high compared with those returned from a low scanner. The effects of sea clutter are more prevalent in the direction from which the weather prevails, where the waves present a concave (almost parabolic) surface capable of providing excellent reflections; and less prevalent in the leeward direction,

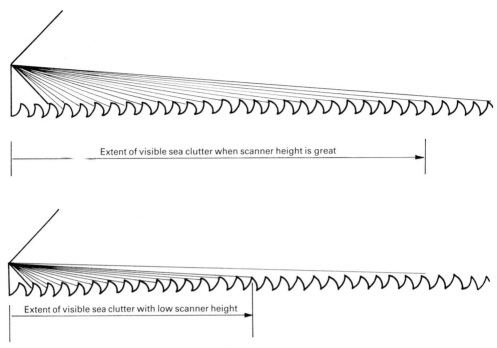

Fig. 2.9 The influence of scanner height on sea clutter

where the 'backs' of the waves present a convex surface which will reflect the energy away from the scanner, thereby not returning an echo.

To obviate the visible effects of sea clutter on the ppi, a sea clutter or 'swept gain' control circuit is incorporated in the equipment. The change in the minimum range feature brought about by increasing or decreasing the scanner height is related to the vertical radiated beam-width.

Vertical beam-width

The vertical beam-width radiated by the scanner is very much greater than the horizontal beam-width. The horizontal beam-width is deliberately made small in order to maximise the bearing discrimination capability and to minimise the apparent distortion of target length. The vertical beam-width is made intentionally wide in order to satisfy two additional requirements:

- minimum range
- the vessel rolling in a heavy sea.

Figure 2.10 illustrates how minimum range is affected by using two alternative vertical beam-widths. Close-range targets will not be displayed in the case of a narrow vertical beam-width (the factors outlined in the sections on Transmitted pulse duration and Minimum range, above, should also be taken into consideration in determining the minimum range), whereas the use of a very much wider vertical beam-width will increase the minimum range capability, and close-range targets will be displayed.

The vertical beam-width (typically 20°–30°) operates in conjunction with the factors

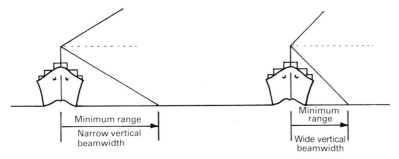

Fig. 2.10 Minimum range affected by vertical beamwidth

mentioned above, plus the scanner height above sea level in determining the minimum range. This is illustrated in Fig. 2.11.

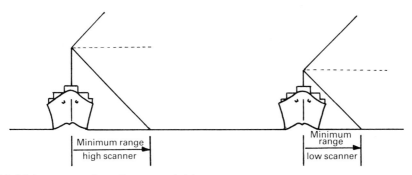

Fig. 2.11 Minimum range affected by scanner height

It is essential that close-range targets remain visible on the screen at all times despite the movement of the vessel caused by the elements, notably rolling. As a vessel rolls, there is a tendency for the radiated beam to be lifted above the surface of the sea. To counteract this, the vertical beam is made sufficiently wide so that under normal circumstances all close-range targets remain within the beam.

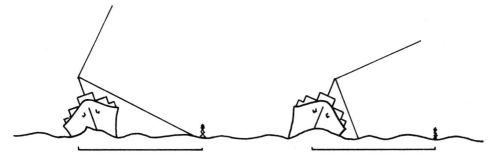

Fig. 2.12 Vertical beamwidth ensures target remains in beam as vessel rolls

Maximum range

The choice of prf was discussed above, and the inference of the significance of the prf and prp in relation to maximum range was noted.

The maximum range from which echoes can be returned sets a limit to the highest prf which can be used. The prf must be low enough (the prp long enough) to allow all echoes to have been returned to the radar before the next pulse is transmitted. Failure to do this would lead to the possibility of second trace echoes being displayed.

The relationship between the height of the scanner and the radar horizon has been noted. The maximum range scale on the equipment is not the maximum detectable range; this is determined by the distance to the radar horizon and not the range in use.

Working in conjunction with the height of the scanner in determining the maximum range is the height of the target.

Figure 2.13 shows the relationship between the height of the scanner, the (true)

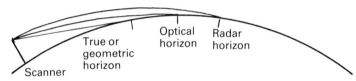

Fig. 2.13 Radar horizon

geometric horizon, the optical horizon and the radar horizon. If a target is situated beyond the radar horizon, providing it is of sufficient height, (and of significant reflecting properties) to protrude into the radar beam then the target will be detected and will return a displayable echo.

The simple formula previously quoted, $1.23\sqrt{ht}$ (or $4.06\sqrt{ht}$) is modified by this fact.

The maximum detectable range, assuming that the transmitted energy ($P_t \times \delta$), the reflecting properties of the target and other factors are adequate, can be determined from:

$$1.23 \left(\sqrt{H} + \sqrt{h}\right)$$

where H is the height of the scanner (feet)
        h is the height of the target (feet)
the answer being in miles.

(alternatively, $4.06 \left(\sqrt{H} + \sqrt{h}\right)$; H, h in metres, answer in kilometres).

Example:
Scanner height 120 feet above water-line, target height 300 feet above water-line. This target would return an echo from a maximum range of 34.7 miles, whereas the installation radar horizon is only 13.47 miles.

Similarly, a target 1685 feet high (a volcanic island for example) would return the same radar with an echo at a range of approximately 64 miles.

It should be noted that 'standard' atmospheric conditions are assumed to exist. Chapter 4 deals with propagation of radar waves.

Chapter summary

The factors outlined in this chapter serve to highlight some of the many compromises which have to be met in the design of a marine radar. The factors can be summarised as follows:

Scanner height:
increase: Gains   —better long-range capability.
            Losses —increased sea clutter echo returns.
                    poorer minimum range.
decrease: Gains   —Better minimum range.
                    Less sea clutter.
            Losses —Reduced maximum range.

Horizontal beam-width:
increase: Gains   —More echoes returns per target.
            Losses —Reduced bearing discrimination.
                    Less gain, therefore, reduced maximum range.
                    Distortion of target length.
decrease: Gains   —Improved bearing discrimination.
                    Narrower beam = higher gain, therefore improved maximum
                        detection range.
            Losses —Reduced number of echoes per target.
                    (This figure could be restored by rotating the scanner more
                        slowly, but would need a longer crt persistency, and would
                        not up-date the picture information quickly).
                    Scanner would be physically wider, and therefore would have
                        increased wind resistance which in turn requires a more
                        powerful turning mechanism.

Vertical beam-width:
increase: Gains   —Improved minimum range.
decrease: Loss   —Reduced minimum range.

Scanner Rotational speed:
increase: Gains   —Quicker 'up-date' of information on ppi.
            Losses —Need short persistency crt.
                    Reduced number of hits per target.
                    (This could be restored by increasing the prf, but this would
                        mean an increased risk of second trace echoes, and reduce
                        the useful range of the set due to the high pulse rate;
                        alternatively, could increase the scanner horizontal beam-
                        width but at the sacrifice of bearing discrimination.
decrease: Gains   —More hits per target.
            Losses —Need longer persistency crt
                    Slower 'up-date' of crt information.
                    Long persistency crt would cause blurring of picture when
                        course changes made.

Pulse width:

increase: Gains   —Reduction can be made in receiver band-width which improves *s/n* ratio, making receiver more sensitive to weak (long range) echoes.

More power in transmitted pulses, so stronger echo pulses.

           Losses   —Increase in Duty cycle, increase in P_{av}, 'bigger' transmitter and more cooling required etc.

Poorer range discrimination.

Poorer minimum range.

decrease: Gains   —Improved range discrimination.

Improved minimum range.

Decrease in P_{av} and Duty cycle, possibly smaller transmitter.

           Losses   —Less energy in transmitted pulse, therefore weaker echo returns.

Need wider receiver bandwidth which decreases *s/n* ratio, making receiver less sensitive to weak echoes.

Pulse repetition frequency:

increase: Gains   —Increased number of hits per target.

           Losses   —Increased chance of second trace echoes.

Increase in P_{av}, require bigger transmitter, more cooling etc.

decrease: Gains   —Less chance of second trace echoes.

Reduction in P_{av}.

Increased maximum range (theoretically).

           Losses   —Reduction in number of hits per target.

If taken to an extreme, the possibility of missing very small targets altogether.

P_t:

increase: Gains   —More energy in transmitted pulse, therefore stronger echo return from a given target. This will improve long range performance.

           Losses   —Higher P_{av} required if prf/prp remain the same. This necessitates a larger power supply unit.

decrease: Losses   —Correspondingly weaker echo returns necessitate higher antenna gain receiving aperture, and therefore longer scanner (for a given wavelength) plus a low noise, high gain receiver front end than previously.

3
Basic primary pulse radar system

In Chapter 1 a simple primary pulse radar system to illustrate the basic operating principles involved was outlined. In this Chapter a more complete system will be described.

An analogue radar system has been used for the description, as it is only after the detection of 'raw video' echo returns that the two systems differ significantly. As this difference only affects a very small portion of the whole system it has been excluded for ease of explanation but will be dealt with separately in Chapter 19.

Figure 3.1 shows a schematic diagram of a typical marine radar system. Figure 3.2 shows idealised waveforms which could be expected from the system.

3.1 PRF generator

This unit may be a free-running (not externally synchronised) oscillator, or one which is capable of being triggered from an external source, as in the case where more than one radar has to be synchronised to another to avoid mutual interference. Many alternatives have been offered by different manufacturers for this unit, ranging from deriving synchronising pulses from a high-frequency motor-alternator ac output; a bi-stable flip-flop using bipolar junction transistors relying on capacitor/resistor timing; logic gates with a series resonant circuit between input and output; down to a 555 timer circuit. It has been common practice in the past to produce at the oscillator output the highest frequency required by the equipment, and to divide the output down in frequency for progressively longer ranges. This is often seen as a numerical relationship in specifications: i.e. prf 3600: 900: 450 Hz; or 2000: 1000: 500 Hz.

The division of frequency can easily be achieved by logic divider circuitry. The prf generator will, as has been suggested, provide more than one output frequency in accordance with the range or ranges selected: high prf for the shortest ranges and the lowest prf for the longest. As the display range is changed so the prf generator output frequency is selected accordingly. The output from the unit is in the form of short duration, relatively low voltage spikes: 'trigger pulses'. Two such trigger pulses are required for one complete cycle of transmitter operation, the first initiates the charging cycle of the modulator circuit, the second providing the discharge trigger to the modulator circuit to fire the magnetron as the stored energy is released as a pulse.

Figure 3.3 shows typical, idealised waveforms to illustrate the timing cycle of the equipment.

3.2 Modulator

Almost without exception, the circuit principle used for the generation of a short-duration, high-voltage, dc pulse is an open-ended length of artificial transmission line.

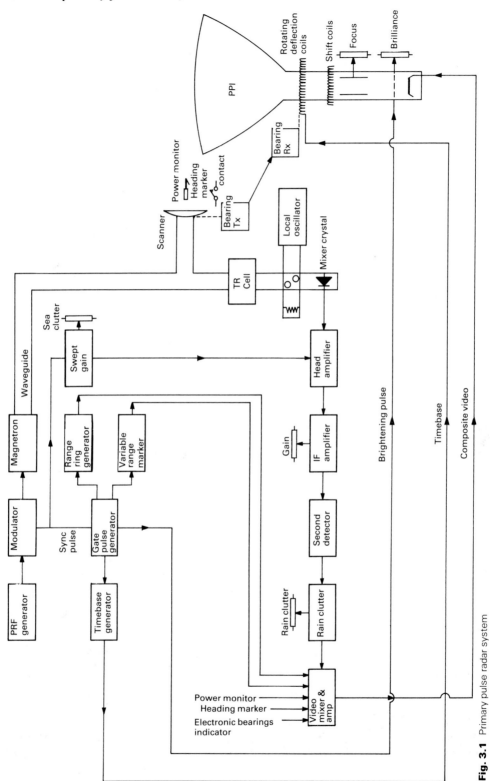

Fig. 3.1 Primary pulse radar system

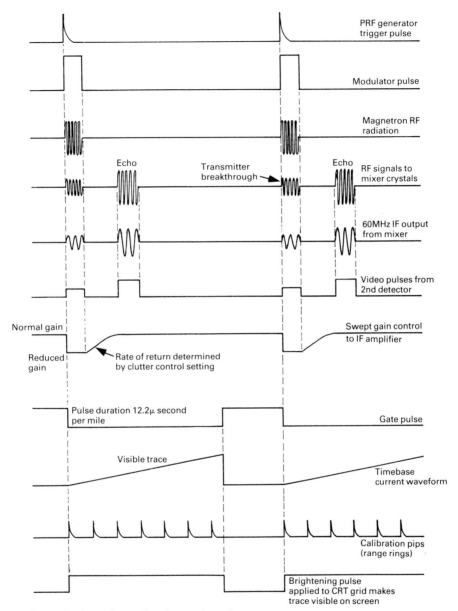

Fig. 3.2 Time related waveforms of a primary pulse radar system

The theory of transmission lines is covered in Chapter 5. The line can be adjusted to increase or decrease its electrical length to accommodate a longer or shorter pulse duration in accordance with the range selected. Trigger pulses from the prf generator switch a semiconductor device to allow the transmission line to charge-up from a modest dc voltage supply, typically 300–400 volts. With the artificial line fully charged a second trigger pulse from the prf generator brings about the discharge of the line. The discharge process requires a quick-acting switch action. Over the years, various devices have been employed, Trigatrons, Thyratrons and Thyristors. Most modern

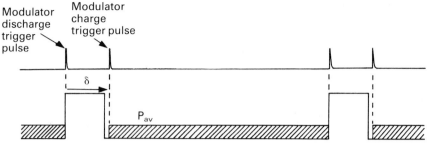

Fig. 3.3 PRF generator pulses controlling the charge and discharge of the modulator

radars employed silicon controlled rectifiers (thyristors) to initiate the discharge process, and a saturable core reactor to complete the switch action. This technique is explained in greater detail in Chapter 6.

The rectangular pulse of energy is delivered between the anode and cathode terminals of the magnetron causing it to operate. Trigger and synchronisation pulses are tapped off from the modulator pulse for the synchronisation of the gate pulse generator, the timebase generator and the sea-clutter circuits.

3.3   Magnetron

When subjected to the high-power modulator pulse, the magnetron bursts into oscillation for the duration of the pulse, converting the dc pulse into radio frequency oscillations. The frequency at which the magnetron oscillates is determined by the internal physical dimensions of the device and cannot normally be changed in marine radar applications. Chapter 7 describes how the magnetron operates and the factors which determine its frequency of operation. The microwave rf energy is coupled from the Magnetron into a wave-guide feeder.

3.4   Wave-guide

The wave-guide is the feeder, linking transmitter and receiver to the scanner. In 3 cm radar systems the wave-guide takes the form of a rectangular, hollow pipe through which the electromagnetic pulses zigzag their way to the scanner. Unlike most antenna feeder systems, the wave-guide is quite safe to touch when in operation. However, the open end of a wave-guide must never be looked into when the transmitter is in operation. Should there be any doubt as to the passage of rf energy along a wave-guide, a neon tube held near to the open end will ignite in the presence of rf energy. In 10 cm radar systems, where the dimensions of everything is correspondingly greater, according to the wavelength, a high-grade coaxial feeder is often substituted for the wave-guide due to financial constraints: wave-guides being quite expensive.

3.5   Duplexer (TR cell)

As has been established, a duplexer is necessary when the same scanner is used for both the transmission of pulses and the reception of their echoes. Because the transmitted rf pulse is very powerful and the receiver is extremely sensitive, the two cannot be connected directly on to a common feeder. Several techniques and devices can be employed to provide a duplexing facility, the most common being the TR

(Transmit/Receive) cell. This is a gas-filled device employing a spark-gap which, under normal conditions, allows the free passage of low power microwave rf energy (as for example received echoes). However, when subjected to high power rf energy, the spark gap ionises and presents itself as an electrical short-circuit. If such a device is placed across the receiver input, then every time the magnetron fires and produces a high-power rf pulse the TR cell will ionise, placing a short circuit across the entrance to the receiver. This prevents any appreciable amount of energy entering the receiver and damaging it. A small amount of the magnetron pulse does in fact leak past the TR Cell as 'transmitter break-through' but it is so relatively small as to be acceptable, and does not cause the receiver to become paralysed. When the transmitted pulse ends the cell de-ionises and behaves as an acceptor circuit, allowing echo returns to enter the receiver.

On occasion, a second gas-filled device may be employed. Known as a TB (Transmit Block) or ATR (Anti-Transmit/Receive) this device is intended to 'guide' all in-coming echoes into the receiver branch of the wave-guide, and to prevent them being dissipated in a useless manner by travelling down the transmitter branch of the wave-guide.

Ferrite circulators are now being employed with success in many modern radars. The application of these, and all duplexing techniques will be discussed in Chapter 12.

3.6 Scanner

The majority of commercial marine radars now use the 'slotted wave-guide' type of scanner as opposed to any other. Military radar systems continue to use these and other types of scanner as best fit the requirements. The scanner radiates the transmitted pulse as a fan-shaped beam, having a narrow horizontal and a broad vertical beam-width, the beam being continuously swept over 360° of azimuth at between 20–30 revolutions per minute. By convention, scanners rotate in a clockwise direction. There have, in the past, been radar systems employing a twin scanner system with one scanner mounted directly above the other and turned in synchronism by a single drive unit. In such systems the need for a duplexer could be dispensed with.

3.7 Bearing transmission system

The bearing transmission system serves to lock the rotation of the trace on the ppi screen with the rotation of the scanner, so that both rotate at exactly the same speed and in the same direction. Several alternative approaches to the design of a bearing transmission system are open to the designers, and have included: synchro systems, servo-mechanisms and digital pulse systems employing sine-cosine look-up tables. Regardless of the system used, the visible end result is always the same. Chapter 11 describes the various systems in greater depth.

3.8 Frequency changer

The returning echo will be at the same frequency as the transmitted pulse, e.g. approximately 10 GHz (10 000 MHz), a more accurate figure would be in the order of 9.4 GHz (9400 MHz) in the case of 3 cm radar systems. This is because the echo is a reradiation of part of the energy contained within the transmitted pulse. Radar systems have to employ such high frequencies in order to produce a scanner of practical dimensions which can radiate a very narrow horizontal beam. The use of a lower frequency would necessitate a scanner of such dimensions as to render the whole system impractical. In producing such a transmission frequency the development of the multicavity magnetron by Messrs Randell and Boot in 1940 removed many of the problems previously encountered.

However, processing the in-coming echoes at such high frequencies poses many problems which cannot easily be solved. Because of these problems a technique commonly used in communication receivers has been adopted, namely heterodyning—the beating together of two frequencies to produce a much lower one as the resultant. As the frequencies are above the audible range they are known as 'supersonic', and the whole process is known as 'supersonic heterodyning'. Receivers using such a technique are called 'superhets'; the radar receiver being one example.

The in-coming echoes at the original transmission frequency are mixed together with a locally produced oscillation, generated in the radar receiver by a 'local oscillator'. As the transmission frequency is so high the oscillation produced by the local oscillator must also be high; but it must differ slightly if the process is to be effective. If, for example, the original transmission frequency was exactly 10 000 MHz, and the local oscillator frequency was 9940 MHz, there would be a difference in frequency of 60 MHz.

Alternatively, with a 10 000 MHz echo return, the local oscillator frequency of 10 060 MHz would also produce a difference frequency of 60 MHz. By using the superhet principle the returning echo frequency can be reduced to one which can easily be processed. Thus, for every incoming echo at 10 000 MHz, the frequency changer will produce an output at 60 MHz, the same echo return but frequency translated to a lower part of the spectrum. The new echo is frequency known as an intermediate frequency, abbreviated to IF, with 60 MHz being a popular choice of designers. To effect the mixing process a non-linear device has to be employed. A crystal diode has such a characteristic and is used as the frequency changer. The local oscillator will be a special microwave device, either a klystron or, in modern equipment, a Gunn diode. Chapter 13 expands on this principle.

3.9   Pre-IF or head amplifier

As explained in the previous section, the incoming echoes are first reduced from the transmission frequency down to a more handleable intermediate frequency. Once at the IF frequency the echoes have to be amplified before they can be processed further. Echo returns are extremely weak despite the apparently high powered transmitted pulse (see Chapter 4, Radar Free-space range equation) and must therefore, be amplified before being taken any distance. The amplifier which performs this function is situated in the transceiver and forms part of the rf head assembly—hence its alternative name. The main IF amplifier is generally located in the display unit, which may be many feet away from the transceiver, and signals have to be amplified before being carried by coaxial cable between the two. The pre-IF amplifier does this job.

In the design of this amplifier, the main considerations are:

- Low noise. Any noise introduced at this stage will degrade the whole of the radar's performance as the noise will be further amplified and processed along with the signal. The level of the noise floor will restrict the receiver sensitivity as only signals which are above the noise level can be detected.

- High gain. A substantial amount of amplification is required to restore the echo returns to a level where they can be processed.
- Broad band-width. The system is dealing with rectangular pulse shapes. As a rectangular pulse is known to be composed of an infinite number of odd-harmonics a wide bandwidth must be a feature of the amplifier if the pulse shape is to be maintained. There is a trade-off here against noise, as increasing the band-width excessively will cause the noise floor to rise, thus making the radar insensitive to weak echo returns (which would be lost in the noise).
- Freedom from instability. In addition to providing a high degree of amplification, the amplifier must be stable. Instability could be detrimental to the display of echoes and could, in extreme cases, result in the total loss of an echo or echoes.

The amplifier is normally a series of cascaded stages, with a cascode configuration being frequently used within the first stages. The cascode configuration provides high voltage gain without the inherent inter-electrode (Miller) capacitance effects which normally act to reduce the gain at very high frequencies. Capacitive reactance, Xc being $1/2\pi fC$, is a very low value when the frequency 'f' is high, thus for a given inter-electrode capacitance 'C' a low impedance path will exist which could substantially reduce the stage gain of the amplifier due to feedback.

3.10   Anti-sea clutter

Sometimes called 'swept gain'. Sea clutter was introduced in Chapter 2. Due to the grazing angle of the radiated beam the effects of sea clutter are more noticeable near the centre of the screen, and gradually diminish as range increases. A circuit is therefore required which helps to minimise the severity of sea clutter echo returns which, because of their proximity to the scanner, are very strong at close range, but which decay as range increases.

The swept gain, or anti-sea clutter circuit operates on receipt of a synchronisation pulse derived from the modulator pulse as shown in Figs 3.1 and 3.2. At the instant the magnetron fires a pulse of rf energy, the swept gain control circuit cuts-off one or more of the first stages in the pre-IF (head) amplifier as shown in Fig. 3.4.

With the first stages of the amplifier cut off, the gain of the over-all amplifier is very much reduced. The first stages remain cut-off for the duration of the transmitter pulse (δ) in order to minimise the effects of ground wave leakage (break-through) of the transmitter pulse through the TR cell. If this was not done, the rf leakage through the TR cell entering the receiver would be of such amplitude as to cause saturation of the amplifier stages. With the head amplifier stages in saturation: (that is to say when the signal is so large that the amplifiers can not handle it and the devices either 'bottom' or 'saturate' in their attempts to provide amplification), the receiver would become temporarily paralysed, and unable to respond to near-by target echoes for a period of time—until the amplifier has recovered from the state of saturation. As this would take a finite period of time, close-range targets would be lost, and the minimum range of the radar could perhaps be extended to an unacceptable figure.

At the end of the transmitted pulse, the gain of the amplifier is gradually restored over a period of time, (The time period is in terms of μ seconds) from cut-off level back to normal at a rate determined by the setting of the display 'sea clutter' control. This in turn would be set by the navigator in response to the amount of sea clutter prevailing. In calm water, when the sea does not return clutter echoes, the sea clutter control setting would be at zero, and the gain of the amplifier would be restored quite quickly. If a very disturbed sea is running, however, returning a large amount of sea

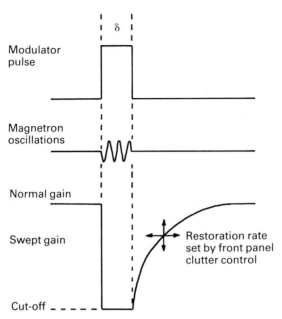

Fig. 3.4 Swept gain

clutter which extends across the screen centre, the control would be adjusted to a higher setting which in turn would slow-down the restoration time of the amplifier gain.

3.11   Main IF amplifier

The IF signal from the pre-IF (head) amplifier is fed to this unit which is situated in the display, often many feet away from the transceiver. Several (typically six) stages of amplification are provided in this unit. This unit serves to increase the amplitude of the echo return, and is also the unit where the main 'gain' control is situated.

3.12   Second detector

The first detection of the presence of an echo is at the crystal mixer (frequency changer) where the echo frequency is down-converted to an Intermediate frequency of, typically, 60 MHz. The second detector stage, which follows the main IF amplifier, acts in a manner identical to an amplitude modulated detector (envelope detector) in an a.m. radio receiver. A pn junction diode, together with a CR filter circuit, converts the 60 MHz IF echo pulses into rectangular dc pulses called 'video', by the elimination of the 60 MHz IF carrier.

3.13   Rain clutter

Rain (or to give it its) correct name, precipitation clutter and its effects are detailed above. The appearance on the screen of a distant rain cell is as a solid blob of illumination on the screen. It is possible for valid target returns from ships to be lost inside the clutter. Figure 3.5 illustrates this point.

The rain clutter circuit is normally offered as a parallel path to the video between

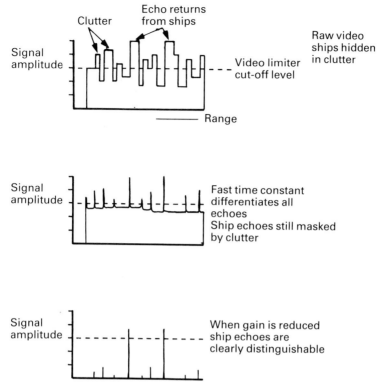

Fig. 3.5 Operation of rain clutter

second detector and video mixer stages. A fast time constant CR differentiator, when switched into circuit, breaks up the large blocks of echo return, leaving a voltage 'spike' coincident with the leading edge of the echo, and leaving almost nothing behind until the leading edge of a subsequent echo return (see Fig. 3.5). With the rain clutter circuit in operation, reducing the receiver gain, which reduces the clutter and target echo returns below the cut-off level of the video limiter, the ship targets become clearly visible once more.

3.14   Video mixer and video amplifier

The first stage of the video amplifier unit is the video mixer. The video amplifier receives inputs from:

- variable range marker circuit
- range ring generator
- heading marker circuit
- electronic bearing indicator circuit
- performance monitor
- video from the second detector.

These are mixed together so that they can all be displayed, simultaneously if necessary, without any interaction. The video amplifier is a broad-band, low gain amplifier incorporating a limiter stage to prevent excessively large amplitude video over-loading the crt. The output from the video amplifier is referred to as a 'composite' video signal, usually negative-going, to be applied to the cathode of the crt where it causes intensity modulation of the electron beam.

3.15   Gate pulse generator

This unit changes the very narrow trigger pulse from the modulator into a broad gate pulse. The width of the gate pulse is a function of the range in use, e.g. its duration being:

12.2 μ seconds on 1 mile range
36.6 μ seconds on 3 mile range etc.

The gate pulse generator performs 4 main functions:

- It is the brightening pulse generator.
- It triggers, and time controls, the time-base generator.
- It triggers, and time controls, the range-ring generator.
- It triggers, and time controls, the variable range marker generator.

All of the circuits listed have to operate in perfect synchronism otherwise the radar would cease to be a useful aid to navigation. By triggering this unit from a sample of the modulator pulse all operations can commence at the same instant the transmitter fires. The broad gate pulse produced by the unit defines the maximum time all the circuits have to complete their functions. When, for example, the 12 mile range is selected, the timebase generator has 12×12.2 μ seconds $= 146.4$ μ seconds in which to move the spot of light from the centre of the ppi screen to the outside edge; the range ring generator has 146.4 μ seconds in which to produce seven range rings (six visible rings, the seventh being coincident with the centre spot etc).

The role of brightening pulse generator is necessary because the time-base trace is intentionally kept cut off in order to protect the chemical coatings on the screen. The trace is lifted up to the threshold of visibility for the duration of the time-base scan, after which it is cut off once more during the fly-back period and following 'dead time'. When setting up a ppi brilliance control it should be adjusted, with the gain control turned off, until a visible trace is observed on the screen, and then backed-off until the trace is just no longer visible—a point known as the threshold of visibility.

3.16   Time-base generator

In essence, the time-base generator is an integrator CR circuit in which the capacitor is made to charge linearly from a constant current source, at a speed determined by the range in use. When very short ranges are selected the time-base trace has very little time in which to move the spot from the centre of the screen to the outer edge; ie $\frac{1}{4}$ mile range $= 3.05$ μ seconds. By contrast, on long range the time period is relatively long; ie 96 mile range $= 1171.2$ μ seconds for an identical 'journey'. Because of this increase in speed at which the spot of light has to move when short ranges are selected the precision 'drawing' of detail on the screen becomes rather ragged. Range rings, for instance, when viewed on the $\frac{1}{4}$ mile range appear thick and fuzzy, whereas on the long ranges, when the spot is moving relatively slowly they are drawn as fine pin-pricks of concentric light.

The linear sawtooth current waveform produced by the unit is then passed through power amplifiers to give the required several amps of scan coil current. To effect a linear rise of current through the coils, the accompanying time-base voltage waveform is a trapezoidal or pedestal waveform; the reasoning behind this will be given in Chapter 16.

3.17 Range ring generator

This unit is required to produce a series of voltage spikes or 'calibration pips' which brighten-up the timebase trace at precisely calibrated intervals which, when drawn out by the rotating trace, form a series of concentric rings of light, spaced a predetermined distance apart. The basis of this unit is an oscillator, the frequency of which is a function of the range in use and the corresponding distance apart the rings have to represent.

Example:
If rings are required at 1 mile intervals; then 1 cycle = 12.2 μ seconds, and as $f = 1/t$, = 81.96 kHz.
If rings are required at 2 mile intervals; then 1 cycle = 24.4 μ seconds, and $f = 40.98$ kHz etc.

As there is, once again, a clear numerical relationship between the respective frequencies, namely a factor of two, it is now common practice to have a single oscillator, running at the frequency required for the smallest distance between rings, and then to divide the output down using logic divider chains in conjunction with the selected range.

Thus, 655.73 kHz; 2 rings $\frac{1}{8}$ mile apart on $\frac{1}{4}$ mile range   divide by 2
      327.86 kHz; 2 rings $\frac{1}{4}$ mile apart on $\frac{1}{2}$ mile range   divide by 2
      163.93 kHz; 3 rings $\frac{1}{2}$ mile apart on $1\frac{1}{2}$ mile range
      or
      6 rings $\frac{1}{2}$ mile apart on 3 mile range   divide by 2
      81.96 kHz; 6 rings 1 mile apart on 6 mile range etc.

The accuracy of the range rings (and the variable range marker) must enable the range of a target to be measured with an error not exceeding 70 metres or 1.5% of the maximum range of the scale in use if type approval for the equipment to be used as an aid to navigation is to be sought. The brilliance of the range rings can be varied, and extinguished if required.

3.18 Variable range marker

Echoes appearing between fixed range rings can be ranged by interpolation. A more accurate method of determining the range of such targets is by employing a single, variable range ring position of which may be varied by the navigator and the corresponding range displayed on some form of read-out device. The accuracy of the variable range marker is the same as for fixed range rings, and the brilliance requirement is also the same.

3.19 Heading line

The requirement for the heading line (sometimes called a 'heading marker'), is that it shall be aligned with 000° when a ship's head-up presentation mode is used, with a maximum error not greater than $\pm 1°$, and a thickness on the screen not greater than 0.5°. A scanner turning at 24 rpm will, in one second, complete 0.4 of a revolution. As each revolution equals a 360° scan; then in one second 144° are scanned, in 250 m seconds 36°, in 7 m seconds 1°, and in 3.5 m seconds 0.5°.

To generate a heading line to meet type approval specification, a circuit must produce a pulse lasting no longer than 3.5 m seconds. The pulse brightens the timebase trace for this period to produce a brightly visible, straight line, which extends from the scan origin to the edge of the screen. If provision is included in the radar to reduce the brilliance of the heading line, it must not be possible to dim it to extinction. A biased switch is incorporated to enable the heading line to be temporarily removed from the display. Then a navigator can ascertain that no small target is being obscured by the heading line by holding the switch, but on its release the heading line returns to the display.

A micro switch or reed relay, located in the scanner assembly, is often used to initiate the production of the heading marker by the circuit. Provision has to be included for the adjustment of the heading line display position by a minimum of ±5° (usually by adjustment of a contact in the scanner assembly).

4
Propagation of radar waves

The propagation of radar waves has been introduced, together with other concepts in Chapter 1. In this chapter, propagation will be covered in more detail.

4.1 Introduction

Microwave energy radiated from the scanner propagates in the region known as the troposphere, the region of the atmosphere which extends upwards from the earth's surface in which the 'weather' occurs. As with optical rays, radar waves undergo refraction due to the conditions within the troposphere, and therefore, suffer a slight degree of bending towards the earth's surface, rather than travelling in direct, straight lines. Whereas the bending of optical rays depends on the effects of temperature and pressure which establish the index of refraction, radar waves are additionally subject to changes in the moisture content of the atmosphere. It is because the radar waves are subject to a different index of refraction that the distance to the optical horizon is less than to the radar horizon, together with the fact that their wavelength is much greater.

In establishing how radar waves propagate, a set of 'standard' atmospheric conditions are assumed to exist:

- a decrease in temperature with an increase in altitude,
- a decrease in moisture content with an increase in altitude.

These two factors which determine the index of refraction are shown in graphical form in Fig. 4.1.

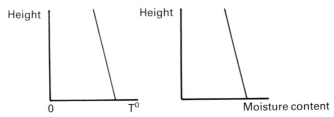

Fig. 4.1 Standard conditions

To enable the propagation path to be drawn as a straight, rather than a curved line, an 'effective earth radius factor' k is used, with $k = 4/3$ being taken as the conditions for standard propagation to occur. The effective earth radius factor acts to increase the physical radius of the earth by a factor of approximately one third.

Under standard propagation conditions it can be assumed that the maximum range of the radar will be determined by the height of the scanner and the height of the target as explained in Chapter 2

Any deviation away from the 'standard' atmospheric conditions will change the index of refraction and the degree of bending to which the waves are subjected. Such conditions are referred to as anomalous propagation conditions, and can either extend or reduce the maximum range experienced under standard conditions. Conditions which extend the maximum range are known as super-refraction, while those which reduce the maximum range are known as sub-refraction.

4.2 Super-refraction

One of the conditions which tends to bring about abnormal refraction is the passage of warm, dry air over a body of cool water. Evaporation of water from the surface produces an increased concentration of moisture near the surface of the sea. The initial increase in moisture content is known as a moisture lapse, with the moisture content decreasing more rapidly than usual with height. The moisture lapse is accompanied by an initial increase in temperature when plotted against height, see Fig. 4.2.

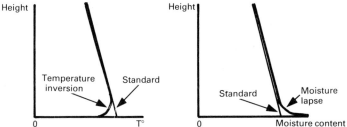

Fig. 4.2 Temperature and moisture conditions for super-refraction

Such conditions may exist on a relatively modest scale, where the relative humidity decreases more rapidly than usual from sea level up to scanner height, and where the temperature at the scanner height, or above, is greater than at sea level.

When such conditions occur the atmospheric refraction, and the subsequent bending of the waves, is increased. The radiated beam is bend downwards and consequently, elongated to follow the earth's surface for a much greater distance than usual. As a result, the maximum detection range is increased so that targets may be observed on the ppi screen at unexpectedly long ranges. Conditions which give rise to super-refraction have been observed more frequently than those which produce sub-refraction, particularly near coastlines in warm/tropical waters in the evening following a hot day.

Fig. 4.3 Effect of super-refraction

4.3 Ducting or trapping

A more severe form of super-refraction is known as ducting or trapping which produces extremely large maximum detection ranges, usually in the form of second or multiple trace echoes. The author has experience of fifth-trace echo returns in the Arabian Gulf area, where land masses produced firm, consistent echoes from over 300 miles range, on a vessel having a radar horizon of slightly under 16 miles.

The conditions which give rise to ducting or trapping are usually associated with a pronounced temperature inversion and a marked initial decrease in moisture content in the atmosphere when plotted against height. Such conditions cause the radar beam to follow the earth's surface more closely than normal, and even to strike the surface of the sea from where it is once more reflected upwards before being refracted back down to the surface. Such propagation is similar to the multiple-hop mode of high frequency (3–30 MHz) radio transmissions where reflection of a sky-wave component from the earth's surface is followed by refraction from the ionised layers back down to the earth for further reflection. However, unlike high frequency radio transmissions, the radar waves are confined within a relatively narrow duct which may have a height of only a few feet.

Rays which are radiated in an upward direction from the scanner are not affected by the ducting process, and consequently do not become trapped within a duct. It is only the relatively narrow beam which leaves the scanner at angles only a few degrees above the horizontal which are subjected to this process. The duct may be formed by a thin sandwich of warm air trapped between the cool surface of the sea below, and cool air above the layer. This effect is sometimes referred to as a 'waveguide' effect, a term which will be more easily understood after reading Chapter 8.

Fig. 4.4 Effect of ducting or trapping

4.4 Sub-refraction

The conditions which give rise to sub-refraction are more likely to be encountered in the polar regions, where the temperature of the sea is often markedly warmer than the air above. Such conditions are often clearly visible to the naked eye, with smoky-steam rising from the surface of the sea when a cold off-shore wind blows over the sea. The conditions for sub-refraction are shown in Fig. 4.5.

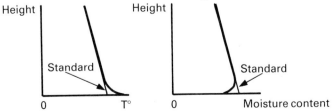

Fig. 4.5 Temperature and moisture conditions for sub-refraction

Sub-refraction may be due to the temperature decreasing more rapidly than normal from sea level to scanner, or the relative humidity initially increasing from sea level. The effect is to cause the beam to bend upwards, ie it bends down less than under standard conditions, rising clear of the earth's surface at a much reduced range than normal. As a result, target detection maximum range can be reduced by as much as 30% below normal.

Fig. 4.6 Effect of sub-refraction

Sub-refraction conditions may be ascertained as the cause of poor long-range performance by checking the operation of the equipment performance monitor. Chapter 10 refers to performance monitoring systems.

4.5   Summary of anomalous propagation conditions

As a rule-of-thumb, the radar beam will always bend away from the warmth. In super-refraction, where the air is warmer than the sea, the beam will bend further down and elongate. In sub-refraction the beam will lift up from the warm sea thus reducing detection range.

4.6   Effects of the earth's surface: Lobing

Up to this point, an 'idealised' beam of radiation has been considered, purely for the sake of clarity of explanation. The beam shape as discussed, would only exist under 'free-space' conditions, that is in the absence of any other objects which could modify or distort the pattern. Such conditions could only be found in deep space. In reality, the vertical beam does not exist as a single lobe of energy, but is in fact composed of many hundreds of individual lobes. The vertical beam lobe structure is modified by the presence of the surface of the sea (or land) over which the beam propagates.

During normal transmission, radar waves may propagate by either of two paths: directly, or by reflection from the surface of the sea. Figure 4.7 shows these two paths.

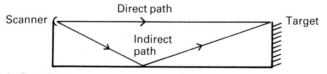

Fig. 4.7 Direct and reflected rays

The point at which the reflections occur may be anywhere from near the scanner up to the radar horizon. As a result of the two different path lengths the direct wave and the indirect wave may rejoin with a phase difference. If the two waves rejoin with zero phase difference they will reinforce one another, whereas if they are exactly out of phase they will cancel out. The phase difference is measured in terms of half wavelength multiples.

In addition to the two path lengths bringing about a phase difference, at the point of reflection the indirect wave undergoes an almost 180° phase shift at the sea surface. When the two features are taken into account, the waves will reinforce each other at multiples of odd half wavelengths, and will cancel at multiples of even half wavelengths.

In the region between the scanner and the radar horizon the direct and the indirect waves will progressively come into and pass out of phase, producing lobes of radiation separated by regions of almost zero radiation. At points where the two waves reinforce, the resultant lobe is much longer than would have been the case for the direct wave only. Ref Fig. 4.8.

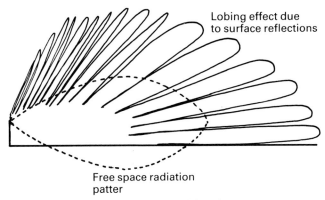

Lobing effect due
to surface reflections

Free space radiation
patter

Fig. 4.8 Main lobe modified due to the proximity of the earth's surface

4.7   The effect of rain, hail, sleet and snow

In microwave engineering these features of the weather are classified as 'Hydrometeors'. The effect of these everyday occurrences on a radar system can be quite dramatic, even to the extent of rendering the radar completely blind at times when it is needed most.

When operating under normal fair weather conditions the energy in a radar pulse is attenuated, mainly due to the presence of oxygen and water vapour in the atmosphere.* When precipitation, in the form of rain is present the attenuation factor increases considerably. Rain droplets cause attenuation by absorption of energy, and a reduction in returned echo strength due to scattering. Rain in the vicinity of targets can scatter unwanted echoes back to the radar as 'clutter' which may mask the wanted target.

The wavelength of the transmission and the diameter of the rain drops are significant factors in determining the amount of attenuation, and at S Band (10 cm) and longer wavelengths the amount of attenuation becomes so small as to be

---

* The attenuation of a radar signal, in the absence of precipitation clutter, is known as the 'free-space' loss (*dB*), and takes into account the attenuation experienced by the signal on both the outward and the return journey.
The Radar free space loss (L_{br}) is given by:

$L_{br} = 103.4 + 20 \log f + 40 \log d - 10 \log \sigma$
σ: target cross-section (m²)
d: distance to target (km)
f: frequency of the radar MHz

disregarded. However, at 3 cm wavelength the problem is quite acute, with targets normally visible at 25 miles in dry air being detected at only 22 miles in drizzle, 15 miles in light rain, 5 miles in moderate rain, and only 1 mile in heavy rain. The effects of fog and dry snow, although absorbing a finite amount of the energy, downgrade the display significantly, whereas sleet (wet snow) produces similar effects to rain.

The use of 10 cm radar as opposed to 3 cm will significantly reduce the effects experienced from both sea clutter and precipitation clutter, but at the sacrifice of target resolution. It is because of these relative benefits that many vessels have dual installations: 3 cm for high resolution navigation and 10 cm for inclement weather conditions.

The use of circular polarisation does, without doubt, obviate the problems due to precipitation clutter, but has not (as yet) found great popularity in the market. Circular polarisation requires a scanner which is capable of radiating circularly polarised electromagnetic radiation. A conventional scanner can not. One manufacturer who is progressing circular polarisation for the marine market offers a twin head scanner with a conventional horizontally polarised scanner mounted back-to-back with one which radiates circularly polarised energy. An electronic switch can bring either into use as circumstances dictate.

4.8   Spurious echoes and effects

Under certain circumstances echoes may appear on the ppi screen which do not correspond with any real target in the area being scanned. Such 'false echoes' may cause obscuring of real echoes, incorrect interpretation of the picture on the screen, or may simply be a nuisance to the navigator.

Spurious echoes may be caused by local sources (the ship's superstructure, or the radar installation itself), local sea conditions, weather conditions, other radar equipment operating in the vicinity, or the close proximity of very large targets.

Most of these echoes can be recognised as false or spurious echoes, and in many cases can be controlled by a skilled operator.

Sea Clutter

The appearance of echo returns from the sea is easily recognised. They usually cover an area (in the direction from which the wind is blowing) which contains a very large number of small echoes that change their position on the display with each paint, i.e. they are of a random nature. The extent of the area depends on the state of the sea. If the sea returns are of limiting amplitude, strong echoes from real targets in the area may be obscured by the clutter.

However, it is possible in most cases to detect targets in the clutter area by careful adjustment of the swept gain or sea clutter control. The amount of control used should be sufficient to ensure small target echoes are distinguishable, irrespective of whether the clutter is still visible or not.

Because, as explained in Section 3.10, the anti-clutter suppresses the sensitivity of the receiver for some period of time after each transmitted pulse, it should only be brought into operation when sea conditions make it necessary. Even so, the navigator should reduce or turn off the control at regular intervals to ensure that echoes from small targets in the non-clutter area near to the ship are not missed.

Careful manipulation of the anti-clutter control may also be employed to advantage in congested areas, such as rivers and harbours, where a mass of echoes from buildings and other ships give a confused picture. Careful use of the control will result in a clear and uncluttered picture of the boundaries of the river or harbour, and any outstanding landmarks. It can also minimise the 'side-lobe' effects referred to above.

Precipitation Clutter

Echo returns from rain, snow, hail and sleet are known as precipitation clutter, the echoes tending to have a more fuzzy, fleecy appearance than normal target echoes, although if the precipitation is particularly heavy—as in the case of a tropical down-pour—a solid echo with clearly defined boundaries may be returned.

The strength of precipitation clutter returns depends on the size of the moisture particles (particularly in relation to the wavelength of the transmission) and the spacing between them. If the ship is herself within the precipitation area, manipulation of the sea clutter control can assist in the detection of echoes from targets near to the ship which would otherwise by obscured by the clutter. However, when the precipitation clutter is at some distance from the ship, and consequently some distance from the centre of the display, it is necessary to use an alternative system. It is common practice to switch a differentiating circuit into operation in the video stages of the receiver.

In addition to the echo returns from precipitation clutter obscuring echo returns from wanted targets, the presence of precipitation clutter can have a detrimental effect on wanted targets due to other causes as outlined in Section 4.7.

Side lobe effects

In addition to radiating energy in the main beam (known as a lobe), a scanner will, by default, produce radiation at a much reduced intensity via other, subsidiary lobes located at either side of the main lobe, known as side lobes. Because these do not carry a significant amount of power they have no detrimental effect in the case of long range targets, as any echo returns would be well below the receiver noise threshold and consequently would not be detected. However, in the case of large targets at close range an echo will be returned from the side lobe radiation. For a given scanner, there may be several side lobes on either side of the main lobe as illustrated in Fig. 4.9

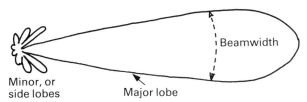

Minor, or
side lobes   Major lobe

                    Beamwidth

Fig. 4.9 Main lobe of horizontal beam and associated side lobes

Under the conditions where a large, nearby target is scanned, a visible echo will be returned from the side lobes and the main lobe as each lobe sweeps the target. However, because the side lobes radiate in directions other than the main beam, echo returns due to the side lobes will be displayed on the ppi screen when a particular lobe is pointing in the direction of the target, but at a bearing corresponding to the direction of the main beam. Echo returns due to side lobes will be displayed at the correct range, but it is only when the main lobe is pointing directly at the target that the echo will be displayed at the correct bearing. The usual effect is, therefore, for a single target to return a series of echoes, drawn as an extended arc on either side of the real echo.

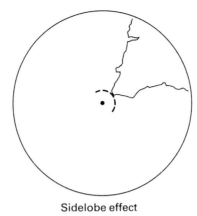

Sidelobe effect

Fig. 4.10 Visible effect of sidelobe echo returns

It is possible for a real echo lying under a spurious side lobe echo to go undetected, but judicious use of the gain and sea-clutter controls can eliminate or reduce side lobe echoes.

Radar interference

When a radar is operated in close proximity to other radar installations operating within the same frequency band it is possible to pickup and display a small portion of the transmitted pulses from the interfering radar. The interference usually takes the form of a series of curved or spiralling dashed lines which change in shape and position with each revolution of the trace.

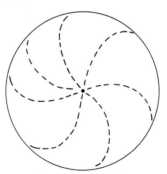

Fig. 4.11 Typical radar interference pattern (uncorrelated video)

The effects are most pronounced when the equipment is operating on long ranges, and can usually be recognised as an interference pattern rather than target echo returns. The visible effects of radar interference can be suppressed in modern radar equipment using processed video which will be discussed in Chapter 19.

Indirect echoes

Echo returns from a target at close range may be picked up either directly in the normal way, or indirectly by reflection from a nearby object. Reflections can come from masts, or the vessel's own funnel as shown in Fig. 4.12.

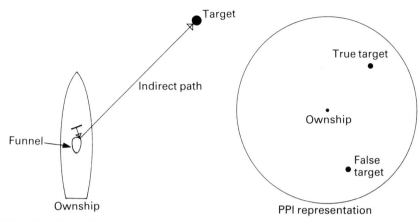

Fig. 4.12 Indirect false echo

The result of this is to produce two echoes on the screen, the true echo, at the correct range and bearing, and an indirect echo at almost the correct range but on the bearing of the object providing the reflection path. The difference in range of the indirect echo is due to the additional distance the reflected energy and echo return have to travel.

Careful siting of the scanner at installation can sometimes obviate this problem, or alternatively a metal sheet can be placed at scanner height on the reflecting object to deflect radiated energy upwards, thus blocking the reflection path. Indirect echoes very often appear in sectors of the display which are usually 'blind' due to the presence of the obstruction and can therefore be identified as false echoes and discounted. Indirect echoes may be due to reflections from other large objects and not necessarily from the ship's own structure. A large bridge spanning a river may return an echo of the navigator's own vessel, appearing to approach the bridge in the opposite direction and mimicking any change of course or speed.

Multiple echoes

Radiated energy from a ship's own radar may, under certain conditions be able to 'bounce' between two structures, with each bounce producing an echo return. If, for example, a vessel having a large reflecting surface (a supertanker in ballast presenting a high hull profile) running on a parallel course to own vessel will provide such a condition. A pulse radiated from own vessel will produce an echo return as normal, but a portion of the echo return could be reflected back towards the target from the hull of own vessel, and be re-reflected a second, third, or even more times. The result is the display of two, three, or more echoes appearing on the same bearing, at multiples of the true target's range.

Under such conditions, multiple echoes will continue to be returned for as long as the two vessels are parallel to one another. As soon as one vessel pulls ahead of the other the energy ceases to bounce between the two hulls and the multiple echo returns disappear, leaving only a single true echo. In docks, rivers and harbours, the presence of large buildings can produce multiple echo returns, resulting in a very confused picture.

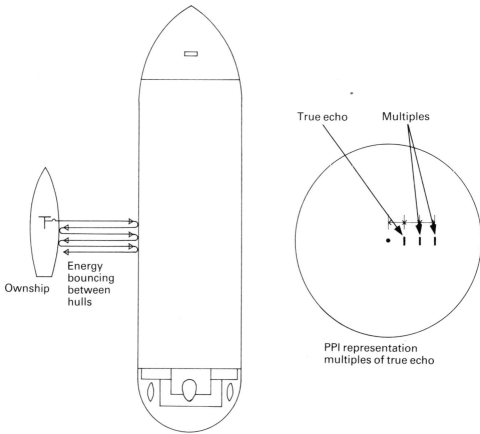

True echo   Multiples

PPI representation
multiples of true echo

Energy
bouncing
Ownship   between
hulls

Fig. 4.13 Multiple echo

Shadow sectors

Shadow sectors are areas of reduced radar visibility (sensitivity) produced by obstructions presenting a narrow profile when viewed from the scanner. Such objects could well be the vessel's own masts. The effect on the radar is similar to holding a finger a few inches in front of one's eyes and looking ahead. The finger obstructs the line of view, and it is not possible to see fully behind it. A mast will present a similar problem to a radar if it is of sufficient height and width. Targets which are in line with the scanner and the mast will be subjected to a weakened pulse due to absorption by the obstruction or reflection from it, and provide a weakened echo return over a very narrow sector. Because the mast will not completely block echo returns, but only reduce their intensity, the sector provided by the mast will give rise to a narrow arc of reduced sensitivity, known as a shadow sector.

Again, careful siting of the scanner at installation can often minimise of eliminate these effects. On vessels having a proliferation of masts the scanner is sometimes mounted on the foremost mast, thus giving a clear view ahead.

Blind sectors

When an obstruction of significant width is placed in the beam of the scanner it is
unable to 'see' through, or round the obstruction, and is therefore 'blind' over an arc
subtended by the obstruction. Such an obstruction could be caused by the funnel or
part of the ship's superstructure, and could also be a source of indirect echo pick-up.
Such blind sectors are very often visible as dark sectors appearing in the presence of
sea clutter. At the time of installation all blind and shadow sectors should be recorded
for future reference by the navigator.

In addition to obstructions due to funnels etc which generally render a vessel blind
in an astern direction, a vessel will be completely blind in a forward direction, and to
some extent along the sides as illustrated in Fig. 4.14.

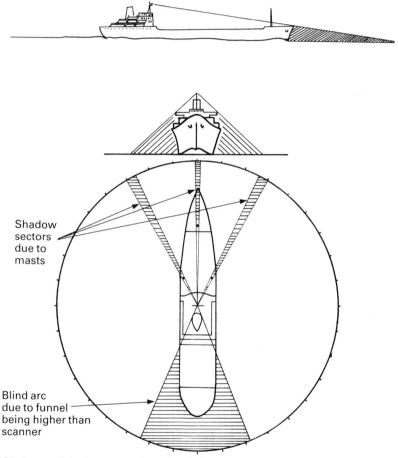

Fig. 4.14 Blind arcs and shadow sectors due to installation

Vessels which frequently have to navigate astern, such as ferries, which have
significant blind sectors astern very often have a second radar scanner installed on the
aft part of the vessel, thus giving a clear unrestricted view astern. Other vessels which
have an unduly restricted forward view, such as aircraft carriers equipped with
ski-ramp flight decks, may have a second scanner installed on the bow under the flight
deck to give a clear forward view.

Large land masses can produce blind or shadow areas in the regions beyond such masses. In ascertaining the extent of such effects, a good parallel is to imagine a land mass being illuminated by a powerful searchlight on a dark, moonless night. The beam would pick up rising high ground, casting a shadow on lower lying ground behind. The visible effect with a searchlight can be interpreted so that lit areas would be able to return a radar echo, and those which are in shadow being unable to return an echo. Such effects can drastically alter a coastline as displayed on a radar when compared to the chart (Fig 4.15).

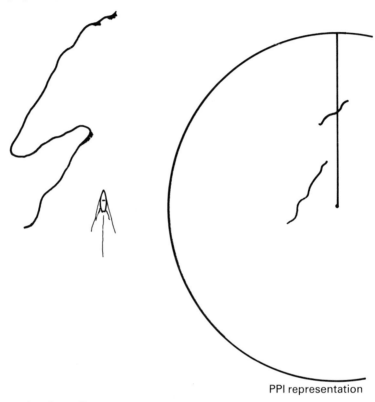

PPI representation

Fig. 4.15 Distortion of coast line

4.9 Free-space radar range equation

As has already been noted, the maximum range at which it is possible to detect a target is a function of:

- The curvature of the earth
- The height of the scanner
- The height of the target
- Atmospheric conditions.

Whether a particular radar set will then detect the target will depend on the attributes of that particular radar, e.g. its peak power, receiver sensitivity etc. It is possible that the same target might be detected at quite different maximum ranges by different radar sets. It is this feature of a radar's performance which will now be discussed.

As noted in Section 4.6, the lobing effects brought about by reflections from the earth's surface create a complex lobe structure. In this chapter, lobing effect will be excluded from the equation and a free-space condition will be assumed to exist.

A radar transmitter is assumed to develop a peak power (P_t) W for the duration of a pulse ($\delta\,\mu$ seconds) and to deliver this to an omnidirectional (isotropic) antenna.

The energy content of the transmitted pulse is, therefore, $P_t \times \delta$ Joules.

The antenna will radiate the energy in the form of a sphere, which is continually expanding at the speed of light.

If a target is located at a range of 'r' metres, then it follows that the radius of the sphere when the energy strikes the target will also be 'r' metres, and the total energy ($P_t \times \delta$ J) will be equally distributed over the surface of the sphere.

As the surface area of a sphere is given by: $4\pi r^2$, the energy density on the surface is, therefore,

$$\frac{P_t \times \delta}{4\pi r^2} \ \text{J/m}^2$$

If the area of the target facing on to the antenna is 'A_0' square metres, then the total energy striking the target is:

$$\frac{P_t \times \delta \times A_0}{4\pi r^2} \ \text{J}$$

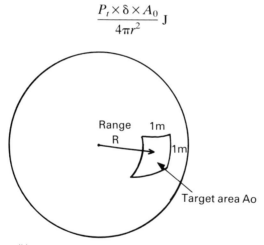

Fig. 4.16 Energy density striking target

As previously explained, marine radars use highly directional antennas (scanners), which have considerable 'gain' over an isotropic antenna, where:

$$\text{Antenna gain} = \frac{\text{Energy striking target using directional antenna}}{\text{Energy striking target using omni-directional}}$$

With an isotropic antenna, the energy is radiated equally well in all directions, and is consequently 'diluted', becoming even more so as time elapses and the sphere continues to expand at the speed of light. However, with a directional antenna, instead of the radiated energy being allowed to spill freely in all directions it is now focused into one single, narrow sector. The result is a considerable increase in the energy radiated in one direction only, with zero energy being radiated in all other directions.

A good parallel can be drawn using the principle of a theatre spotlight. Whereas a naked light bulb at the back of the theatre will provide some low-level of illumination on the stage as well as the rest of the auditorium, the addition of a reflector and lens assembly will produce a piercing spot of light on only a small portion of the stage, leaving the auditorium in almost complete darkness.

This focusing of energy in one direction when applied to antenna systems is known as 'gain', and is a passive value. It should not be confused with 'gain' produced from active devices such as semiconductors, thermionic valves etc. An antenna system cannot amplify, it can only focus radiated energy into a beam, giving an apparent gain to the system when compared to an isotropic antenna.

If the gain of the radar antenna is said to be 'G', and is now pointed at the previous target, then the energy striking the target is:

$$\frac{P_t \times \delta \times A_0 \times G}{4\pi r^2} \text{ J}$$

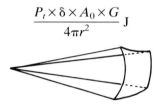

Fig. 4.17 Antenna focuses all energy on to target

Assuming that the target reradiates all the incident energy omnidirectionally, then a second sphere is established which will also have a radius of 'r' metres when it arrives back at the transmitter location.

The energy density on the surface of the second sphere will be:

$$\frac{P_t \times \delta \times A_0 \times G}{4\pi r^2 \times 4\pi r^2} \text{ J/m}^2$$

Because targets do not reradiate all of the incident energy, nor do they do so omnidirectionally, such factors as target shape, material and size make a substantial difference to the echo. The reflection coefficient (k) takes account of this deviation, and so the energy density, on arrival back at the transmitter is:

$$\frac{P_t \times \delta \times A_0 \times G \times k}{4\pi r^2 \times 4\pi r^2} \text{ J/m}^2$$

How much of the echo energy returned back to the transmitter is picked up by the antenna will depend on the receiving antenna aperture 'A_r'. This can be thought of as being similar to a butterfly net. When a large size net is used the butterfly can be caught quite easily, but if a small size net is used the catcher could swat around all day and still fail.

The receiving aperture of an antenna is related to the wavelength and, therefore, the frequency of the transmission. When very low frequencies are employed, the wavelength is very long and the physical dimension of the antenna is small in comparison. As a consequence, not very much of the potential whole of the signal is received. When the frequencies are very high (as in radar), the wavelength is very small and the antenna (scanner) is relatively large. As a result a substantial signal may be picked up.

When the antenna receiving aperture 'A_r' is taken into account, the amount of energy picked up as an echo is:

$$\frac{P_t \times \delta \times A_0 \times G \times k \times A_r}{4\pi r^2 \times 4\pi r^2} \text{ J}$$

The energy content of an echo can also be expressed as:

$$P_r \text{ (received power)} \times \delta \text{ (echo duration in } \mu \text{ seconds)}$$

Equating these two gives the energy content of a received echo as:

$$P_r \times \delta = \frac{P_t \times \delta \times A_0 \times G x k \times A_r}{16\pi^2 r^4} \text{ J}$$

This equation shows that the strength of an echo falls rapidly as the range increases. If the range is doubled the strength of an echo is decreased by a factor of one sixteenth. The strength of the echo is proportional to other factors, and doubling any one of them should double the strength of the echo.

If the returning echo ($P_r \times \delta$) is the minimum signal strength that the particular receiver can detect (P_{min}), then it must be returning from a target which is at the maximum detectable range (r_{max}) for that particular target.

The equation can now be written:

$$P_{min} \times \delta = \frac{P_t \times \delta \times A_0 \times G \times k \times A_r}{16\pi^2 r_{max}^4} \text{ J}$$

Transposing this, to make r_{max} the subject, will produce:

$$r_{max} = \sqrt[4]{1/16\pi^2 (P_t \times \delta)(1/P_{min} \times \delta)(A_r \times G)(A_0 \times k)} \text{ metres}$$

a simplified form of the free space maximum range equation.

From this equation, it will be seen that to double the maximum range of detection it would be necessary to increase the factors under the fourth root sign 16 times. Increasing the energy in the transmitted pulse is not an attractive proposition, in fact modern radars have, over the past three decades, reduced transmitter power from typically 75 kW down to 10 kW (or less in some cases, especially in the case of up-mast transceivers). There is, therefore, a tendency to make $P_t \times \delta$ smaller, but this is offset by the relatively large improvements that have been made in receiver sensitivity as the noise floor has been pushed increasingly further down. A -3 dB improvement in the receiver signal:noise ratio allows for the transmitter power to be reduced by a half and still achieve an identical performance. Figure 4.18 shows the effect of noise on performance.

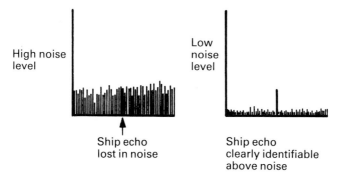

Fig. 4.18 Effect of receiver noise level on received echo

Increasing G and A_r, the scanner 'gain' and receiving aperture, are also very attractive to the designer because an increase in the size of the scanner will automatically increase its gain, and it is the product of these improvements that matter as far as r_{max} is concerned.

A_0 and k, the area presented by the target, its shape, material and reflecting properties are largely beyond the scope of the equipment designer, who cannot specify the targets to which the radar will be subjected during its working life. However, these parameters are of particular interest to the designers of military hardware, as a combination of special shapes and materials can render a target 'invisible' to radar detection. The 'Stealth' bomber is a prime example of modern technology pioneering in this field, where carbon fibres bonded by resin produce a very poor reflective surface to radar. In addition to the materials used, the absence of sharp corners and bends further reduces the potential to reflect radar transmissions.

5
Transmission Lines

A basic understanding of the characteristics of transmission lines is necessary as they are used extensively in radar systems for pulse forming networks, time delays, and lead to the development of waveguide and resonant cavities. In addition, the principles used in duplexing are derived from transmission line theory. This chapter is not intended to satisfy a purist, but is intended to provide a building block of ideas which will be shown later in application.

The open-wire feeder will form the basis of this chapter as it leads to several insights and important definitions, and also forms the basis of a solid state pulse modulator.

Waveguide, which is used as a transmission line (feeder) to link the transceiver and the scanner will be discussed separately in Chapter 8.

5.1 Open wire feeder

An open wire feeder consists of two parallel wires spaced a suitable constant distance apart, insulated from each other and from earth potential. When employed as a feeder a large amount of power is lost by radiation at the higher frequencies when the distance between the conductors in increased to approximately $\lambda/2$ and beyond. The factor which generally prohibits a reduction in the spacing below this figure is the power handling capability. Closely spaced wires would have a tendency to flash-over or arc across when carrying high frequency rf energy of any appreciable amount. However, when used for dc applications this aspect need not be a cause for concern.

Each wire of the open wire feeder may be considered to be made up of both resistance and inductance connected in series. Between the two wires there is capacitance (two conductors separated by an insulator form a capacitor) and because the insulation is not perfect, leakance can also be shown between the conductors as in Fig. 5.1.

The discrete components shown in Fig. 5.1 provide a model of an open wire transmission line. The line series resistance will produce a loss (I^2R), and similarly the leakance will also produce a loss (V^2G) on the line.

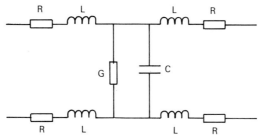

Fig. 5.1 Distributed resistance, inductance, capacitance and leakance on an open wire feeder

For the purpose of explanation only, the line will be considered to be loss-free—a situation which cannot be encountered in reality, and the resistance and leakance components will be discounted.

The 'Loss-free' transmission line

When the effects of resistance and leakance are removed, a chapter of open-wire transmission line can be represented as shown in Fig. 5.2

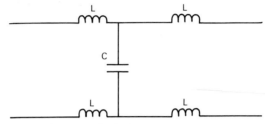

Fig. 5.2 Representation pf a loss-free open wire feeder

The distributed inductance and capacitance can be 'lumped' together as in Fig. 5.3. Each wire consists of a countless number of such sections, each possessing a small

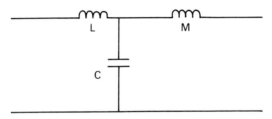

Fig. 5.3 Lumped values of capacitance and inductance

value of inductance and capacitance. Again for simplicity, the individual inductors and capacitors can be lumped together as shown, and connected to a dc supply.

It is assumed that the line is of infinite length, with only a small section being represented in Fig. 5.4.

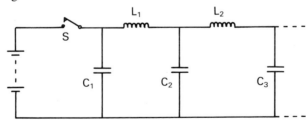

Fig. 5.4

When the switch (S) is closed, C 1 charges to *V* volts immediately, for there is nothing in the circuit to limit the current. C 2, however, will not be able to charge up so rapidly because its charging current must flow through inductor L 1. The voltage step appearing across C 1 is applied to L 1 and C 2 in series, and as C 2 is initially uncharged, the applied emf appears initially across L 1, through which current starts to increase at the rate of V/L amps per second. C 2 therefore, starts to charge towards V volts, but taking a finite time to do so. Sometime later, C 2 reached V volts, instigating a charge into C 3 and so on, rather like a series of buckets overflowing in a chain.

Because, in this hypothetical model, the line is assumed to be infinitely long, the supply will produce current to charge the line capacitors, one by one, *ad infinitum*, so that the voltage across the line rises to V volts as the charging current continues from capacitor to capacitor. From this, it can be seen that a wave (step) of voltage and current travels down the line, for an indefinite period of time, throughout which the battery provides energy which is stored in the line in the form of a magnetic field around the inductors and an electric field across the capacitors.

If 't' represents the time interval after the closing of the switch:

Energy supplied by the battery = Watts × Time
$$= V \times I \times t \text{ Joules}$$

Energy stored in the line $\quad = \frac{1}{2}CV^2 + \frac{1}{2}LI^2 \text{ Joules}$

As the line is loss-free:

$V \times I \times t = \frac{1}{2}CV^2 + \frac{1}{2}LI^2 \text{ Joules}$

But $I \times t = Q$, and $Q = CV$

$VQ = \frac{1}{2}CV^2 + \frac{1}{2}LI^2$

$CV^2 = \frac{1}{2}CV^2 + \frac{1}{2}LI^2$

$\frac{1}{2}CV^2 = \frac{1}{2}LI^2$

$CV^2 = LI^2$

$V^2/I^2 = L/C$

$V/I = \sqrt{L}/\sqrt{C} = Z_0$

Where V = voltage, I = current (amps), t = time, C = capacitance (farads), L = inductance (henrys), Q = coulombs, and Z_0 = characteristic impedance.

$Z_0 = \sqrt{L/C}$ ohms

Z_0 is known as the characteristic impedance of the line, and is independent of the length of the line. This is because the addition or subtraction of another length, or identical section of line merely increases or decreases the existing values of inductance L and capacitance C by the same amount.

The velocity with which the waves of V and I travel down the line can be used to show that a line may be used as a time delay or pulse-forming network.

The time taken to charge one section of a line can be obtained as follows:

When C is fully charged, the voltage V_c across it is equal to the supply voltage V

$V = Vc$

$V = Q/C \quad (Q = I \times t \text{ and } Q = C \times V)$

$V = It/C \quad$ (where 't' is the time required to charge one section)

$V/I = t/C = Z_0 = \sqrt{L/C}$

$L/C = t^2/C^2$

$LC^2/C = t^2$

$\sqrt{L \times C} = t$ per section.

Therefore, for '*n*' sections

$t = n \times \sqrt{L \times C}$ seconds.

This last factor is known as the 'one-way travel time'.

If the line is made up of '*n*' sections, each having identical values of L and C, then the time required to charge all the line sections is given by

$t = n\sqrt{LC}$ seconds (when basic units are employed)

therefore, the travelling waves of V and I will reach the end of the line in this time.

From this, the velocity can be deduced as follows:

Velocity = Distance travelled/Time

If the line is '*n*' sections long,

Velocity = $n/n\sqrt{LC}$

$$= 1/\sqrt{LC} \text{ units/second.}$$

DC applied to an infinite length of loss-free line

A hypothetical model will again be used for the purpose of illustration as it is not possible for an infinite length of wire to exist. In practice, however, it is possible to construct an artificial line which will possess the same characteristics as the model.

Referring to Fig. 5.5. When the switch S is closed, a voltage wave of V volts travels down the line from the input at a velocity of $1/\sqrt{LC}$ unit lengths per second. In step with the voltage wave is a current wave V/Z_0 amps. Waves of this nature, which travel along a line are referred to as Travelling waves. Travelling waves which move away from the supply are referred to as 'Incident waves'; thus Incident travelling waves of voltage and current move in step down the line.

If, for example $V = 100$ volts and $Z_0 = 200$ ohms, then the instant the switch is closed a travelling wave of 100 volts and a current of 0.5 amps move down the line. At any instant the voltage across the line over which the waves have passed will be 100 volts, and the current through the line will be 0.5 amps.

Since the line is assumed to be endless, the battery will continue to supply 100 volts at 0.5 amps as the travelling wave proceeds down the line. Because the incident voltage travelling wave continually 'sees' the impedance of the next section of line in front of it, the current from the supply will be constant at V/Z_0 amps.

DC applied to a finite length of loss-free line

When a more realistic finite length of loss-free line is employed consideration can be given to the termination of the line. In this respect, three cases will be considered, the first when the line is terminated in a load equal in value to the characteristic impedance ($RL = Z_0$ ohms), second, when the load is an open-circuit condition ($RL = \alpha$ ohms), and the third case where the load is a short circuit ($RL = 0$ ohms).

When $RL = Z_0$. Referring to Fig. 5.6: At the instant the switch S is closed, incident travelling waves of voltage and current move down the line with a velocity of $1/\sqrt{LC}$ unit lengths per second, all other operating conditions previously described being

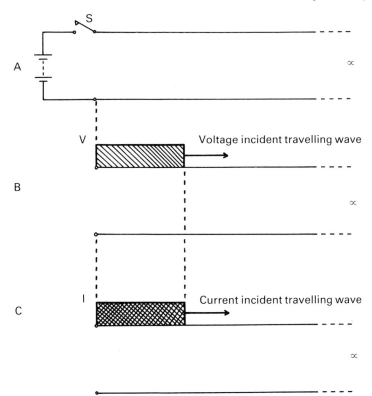

Fig. 5.5 DC applied to an infinite length of line

identical. After a time equal to $n\sqrt{LC}$ seconds the incident travelling waves arrive at the load, RL. The time interval between the instant the switch S was closed and the instant the energy arrived at the load is known as the Travel time, Delay time or Propagation time. Because the load is a perfect match for the line characteristic impedance the current flow will remain the same, and the load will dissipate the energy as heat (I^2R) as fast as it arrives, none of the energy being reflected back from the load.

In the second case, when the line is terminated in an open-circuit the initial sequence of events is identical to those previously described. However, after the one way travel time, the incident travelling waves of voltage and current arrive at the open circuit, and meet a mismatch condition, where the line characteristic impedance suddenly changes from Z_0 to infinity.

At any mismatch, all or part of the incident energy will be reflected back from the load end to the source end (known in transmission line terminology as the receiving end and the sending end respectively). Prior to arrival at the mismatch, the line capacitance had charged up to the supply voltage V, and a current equal to V/Z_0 amps

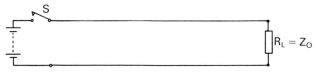

Fig. 5.6 DC applied to a line terminated in a matched load

was flowing along the line. At the instant of reflection both the voltage incident travelling wave and the current incident travelling wave are reflected back to the source, and become the reflected voltage travelling wave and the reflected current travelling wave. In addition to the reflection, one, but not both, of the travelling waves will undergo a phase reversal, which can be determined from the formula:

$$\frac{RL - Z_0}{RL + Z_0},$$

known as the reflection coefficient, and is also given by the ratio of Reflected voltage/Incident voltage.

This expression is used to determine the magnitude and the phase of the reflected waves for any value of termination.

$$\frac{Vr}{Vi} = \frac{RL - Z_0}{RL + Z_0}$$

which, by transposition becomes

$$Vr = Vi\left(\frac{RL - Z_0}{RL + Z_0}\right)$$

which indicates that the reflected voltage is equal to the incident voltage multiplied by the coefficient of reflection.

The coefficient of reflection is:

zero when the line is perfectly matched ($RL = Z_0$ conditions),

$\dfrac{\alpha - Z_0}{\alpha + Z_0} = 1$ when the line is terminated by an open circuit,

therefore, the reflected voltage $Vr = Vi \times 1$
$$Vr = Vi$$

which means that the reflected voltage is equal in magnitude to the incident voltage and of the same sign (phase or polarity). This in turn means that as the reflected voltage travelling wave is not phase reversed, the reflected current travelling wave must be. (If the incident current travelling wave is positive, the reflected current travelling wave is negative). The reflected travelling waves of voltage and current travel in step, and with the same velocity as the incident travelling waves.

The resultant voltage $= Vi + Vr = V + V = 2$ volts
The resultant current $= Ii + -Ir = Ii - Ir = 0$ amps.

By the time the reflected travelling waves of voltage and current arrive back at the source after twice the one-way travel time, the line conditions will be:

Voltage, equal to the supply (matched conditions exist between source and Z_0)
Current, equal to zero amps.

When the line termination mismatch is due to a short-circuit ($RL = 0$ ohms),

$$\frac{0 - Z_0}{0 + Z_0} = -1$$

Therefore $Vr = Vi \times -1$
$$Vr = -Vi$$

In this case the reflected voltage travelling wave is equal in magnitude to the incident voltage travelling wave, but is of the reverse polarity (if Vi was positive in sign, Vr will be negative). As the reflected voltage travelling wave has reversed polarity after reflection, the reflected current travelling wave has the same polarity as the incident (if Ii was positive in sign, Ir will also be positive).

The resultant voltage $= Vi + - Vr = Vi - Vr = 0$ volts
The resultant current $= Ii + Ir \quad = I + I \quad = 2I$ amps

Therefore, after twice the one-way travel time, the line conditions will be:

Voltage, equal to zero
Current flow, maximum value.

At any instant after reflection, the voltage and current on the line will be the sum of the incident and reflected travelling waves.

(The above reasoning is supported by the application of Ohm's Law: When an open-circuit condition exists the current flow is zero amps; and the voltage equals the supply: When a short-circuit condition exists the current flow is maximum and the voltage across a short-circuit is zero.)

AC operated loss-free transmission line

When ac operating conditions are considered, the physical length of the line has to be taken into account. For the purpose of simplification, the length of the line is taken as being one wave-length (λ) at the frequency of operation.

$$\lambda = c/f$$

where λ is the wave-length
c is the velocity of propagation
f is the operating frequency

All of the operating conditions established for the dc loss-free line remain the same, namely:

- Incident voltage and current travelling waves,
- Reflected voltage and current travelling waves,
- Coefficient of reflection,
- Characteristic impedance.

An appreciation of the basic operation of an ac line can best be related by a phasor (vector) representation. A phasor will rotate through 360° over one wavelength (λ), and therefore it will rotate 90° over $\lambda/4$. The direction of rotation being in a clockwise direction. The magnitude of the voltage and current is represented by the length of the phasors.

As the line is regarded as being loss-free, the length of the phasor remains unchanged throughout the two-way travel along the line. As with the dc operated line previously described, three termination conditions will be discussed; namely $RL = Z_0$, $RL = \infty$ (open circuit), $RL = 0$ ohms (short circuit).

When the load is a perfect match to the line characteristic impedance, as with the dc example, all of the energy will be dissipated by the load as fast as it arrives at the load end of the line, so no further explanation is necessary.

When the line is terminated by an open circuit, the instant the supply is made, the voltage and current phasors are shown as rotating 90° clockwise for every $\lambda/4$

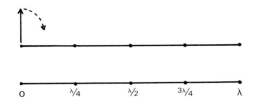

Fig. 5.7

travelled. Both phasors are shown together as it will be remembered that the voltage and current incident travelling waves travel down the line in step. When the incident waves reach the load mismatch a reflection of both voltage and current travelling waves will occur, but one of them will undergo a phase reversal. The coefficient of reflection will determine whether the voltage or the current travelling waves will be phase reversed in exactly the same way as in the dc example. When the load termination is an open circuit, the reflected voltage travelling wave remains unchanged, but the reflected current travelling wave will undergo a 180° phase shift. This is represented by the reversal in direction of the current phasor.

After reflection, both phasors continue to rotate clockwise, turning 90° for every λ/4 travelled back towards the supply. Following the elapse of the two-way travel time, that is when the reflected travelling waves have returned to the supply (sending) end of the line, the phasor sum on the line will produce a resulting wave pattern on the line of both voltage and current. The wave pattern which is established after the transit of the incident and reflected travelling waves is a stationary wave pattern, known because of this characteristic as a 'standing wave'. Figure 5.8 illustrates this.

When the load termination is a short-circuit ($RL = 0$ ohms), the incident travelling voltage and current waves proceed down the line as described for the open-circuit case. However, at the mismatch termination, the reflection coefficient dictates that

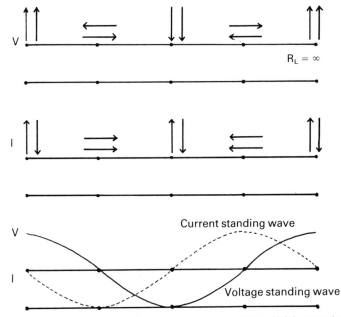

Fig. 5.8 The development of standing wave patterns on an a.c. operated line which is open circuit

the voltage reflected travelling wave is phase reversed and not the current (as in the open-circuit case).

The reversal of the reflected voltage travelling wave, and the non-reversal of the current travelling wave, using the same techniques as previously described, will give rise to a different standing wave pattern as illustrated in Fig. 5.9

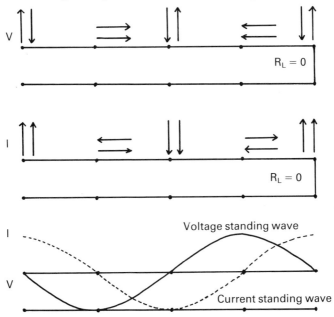

Fig. 5.9 The development of standing wave patterns on a short-circuited line

By using the standing wave pattern developed on the line, it is possible to determine, approximately, the impedance at points along the line as follows. When a point of zero current (a 'node') and voltage maximum (an 'anti-node') exist, the line at that point has an (ideally) infinite impedance—an open-circuit. Conversely, at voltage nodes and current anti-nodes the point will have zero impedance (short circuit). At all points inbetween, the impedance can be determined by observing whether the voltage or the current is lagging or leading. Where the current usually leads the voltage a capacitive reactance (XC) exists, and conversely, where the voltage leads the current an inductive reactance exists (XL). The reactance value is a smooth transition between, for example infinite impedance progressing from an inductive reactance whose value falls until zero impedance, after which a capacitive reactance will increase in value towards infinity. At points where the voltage and current standing waves 'cross over', the value of the capacitive or inductive reactance is equal to the characteristic impedance of the line (Z_0).

Remembering that it is the mismatched load which will determine the standing wave pattern, and therefore the reactance distribution, on the line, any reactance value presented to a generator (signal source) must be calculated by working away from the load end, back to the source. See for example Fig. 5.10.

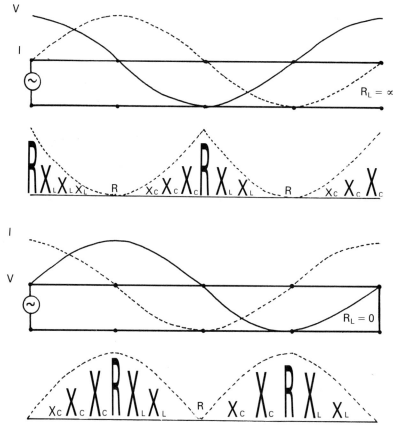

Fig. 5.10 Impedance distribution on mis-matched a.c. line

5.2   Artificial transmission lines

Open-wire feeders were introduced above, demonstrating how the distributed line inductance and capacitance can be 'lumped' together for the purpose of calculation. If the distributed values are now replaced by physical, discrete components, it is possible to construct a practical model of an open-wire transmission line which will behave in the same manner as a line of significant length. Such a model is known as an artificial line, and finds direct application in radar systems for time delays and pulse forming networks.

Artificial line used as a time delay

A network of inductors and capacitors, arranged in the form of an artificial line can be used to introduce time delays of the order of several microseconds to waveforms. An example of such application can be found in the timebase units, where the modulator sync pulse undergoes a time delay to ensure that the timebase starts its scan at the instant the radiated pulse leaves the scanner (at zero range), and not at the instant that the modulator pulse is applied to the magnetron. By so doing, the time taken by the rf pulse to transit the waveguide run is taken into account, and an accurate range measurement can be obtained.

A typical circuit employing an emitter follower and delay line is shown in Fig. 5.11.

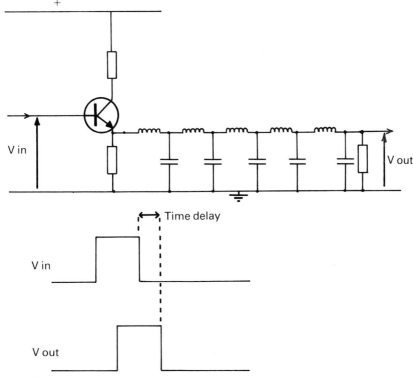

Fig. 5.11 Artificial line used to time delay a pulse

Example:
An artificial line is made up of 15 sections, each containing a series inductance of 20μ H, and shunt capacitance of 500 pF.

From this, it can be calculated that $Z_0 = 200\,\Omega$ and the time delay between inputting and outputting of the pulse would be 1.5μ seconds. To avoid distortion of the pulse the emitter resistance (Re) and the load resistance values would each have to be $200\,\Omega$

$$Z_0 = \sqrt{\frac{L}{C}} = \sqrt{\frac{20}{10^6} \times \frac{10^{12}}{500}} \qquad t = n\sqrt{L \times C} = 15\sqrt{\frac{20}{10^6} \times \frac{500}{10^{12}}}$$

$$= 200\,\Omega \qquad\qquad = 15\sqrt{\frac{1}{10^{14}}}$$

$$= 15 \times 10^{-7}\ \text{secs}$$

$$= 1.5\ \mu\text{s}$$

Artificial line used as a pulse forming network

The use of an artificial line as a pulse forming network constitutes the basis of the solid-state pulse modulator, the unit which supplies the magnetron with a rectangular, high-voltage dc pulse.

In considering this application, it is convenient to think of the line as initially being charged, that is to say, energy is stored on the line in the form of magnetic fields surrounding the inductors and electric fields between the plates of the capacitors. The charged line is connected in circuit with a load resistor whose value is equal to the line characteristic impedance ($RL = Z_0$) (see Fig. 5.12).

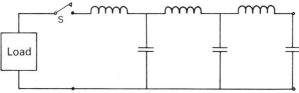

Fig. 5.12 Discharge of an artificial line into a matched load

Assuming the line is charged to V volts, then, at the instant the switch is closed, the matched load resistor is connected across the line, and the line commences to discharge. $V/2$ volts are immediately developed across the load, and a travelling wave of $-V/2$ volts travels along the line towards the open circuit end. After 't' seconds (the one-way travel time of the line), the travelling wave arrives at the open circuit. At this time, the line is discharged to $V/2$ volts, with $V/2$ volts across the load. Complete reflection takes place without phase reversal of the voltage wave, and the travelling wave of $-V/2$ volts travels back towards the load end of the line, reducing the line voltage from $V/2$ to zero.

't' seconds after reflection, and $2 \times$ 't' seconds after closing the switch, the reflected voltage wave arrives at the load end of the line, which is now completely discharged, and the voltage across the load drops to zero.

This process is the identical, but reverse process of what happens when an open-circuit line is charged from a dc supply.

For the duration of twice the one-way travel time a voltage, equal in magnitude to half the original voltage to which the line was charged is present across the load as illustrated in Fig. 5.13.

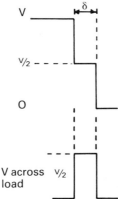

Fig. 5.13 Rectangular pulse produced across matched load

As the time during which the voltage across the load resistor was equal to half of the line voltage was determined by twice the one-way travel time of the line, it follows therefore, that if the line is increased in length (by the addition of more identical sections), the travel time will be increased, and the load voltage $V/2$ period will also increase. The converse will be true if the line is shortened.

These are the under-pinning concepts upon which the pulse modulator is founded.

6
The Modulator

Chapter 5 described how an artificial line terminated in an open-circuit can be used as the basis of a pulse modulator. This chapter will develop that concept and show the operation of a modulator which is typical of the type currently employed in marine radar.

In Chapter 2, it was noted that two trigger pulses from the prf generator are required for each complete cycle of modulator operation. The first trigger pulse being used to initiate the charging cycle of the artificial line, the second trigger pulse for the discharge action.

The supply from which the (artificial line) pulse forming network is charged is invariably a negative dc voltage, ranging from between 250–400 volts typically. The significance of the negative polarity will be more fully appreciated from the chapter dedicated to the magnetron.

In order to supply the magnetron with a high (typically 8 kV) voltage pulse it is necessary to charge the pulse-forming network to a voltage greater than that available directly from the power supply unit, and secondly to step-up the amplitude of the output pulse by means of a transformer.

The first stage in the process must be, therefore, to increase the initial charge on the pulse forming network (pfn) by some method other than by direct connection to the supply. This is done by a technique known as 'resonant choke charging'.

6.1   Resonant choke charging

This is a method whereby the pfn can be charged to a voltage higher than available from the power supply. The time interval between the application of a trigger pulse to initiate the pfn charging and the second trigger pulse to discharge the pfn is relatively long (see Chapter 1). Because of this, it can be said that the charging process takes place very slowly, and as a consequence, the inductors in the pfn can be regarded as being short circuited, taking no part in the action.

If the inductors can be imagined as shorted out, the pfn capacitors can be regarded as being in parallel, with the total capacitance value Ct being equal to the numerical sum of all the individual capacitors in the network. An additional inductor, the value of which is significantly different to those in the pfn is placed in series with the supply, and therefore in series with the total line capacitance Ct. The additional inductor is sometimes a 'choke', a coil wrapped round a laminated iron core, and is referred to as the charging choke Lc (Fig. 6.1)

The effect of the series combination of Lc and Ct is to form a resonant tuned circuit which will oscillate at a frequency of $1/2\pi\sqrt{Lc\,Ct}$ Hz. The action of the circuit with the addition of the charging choke is as follows. Immediately the switch $S1$ is closed, the charging process commences with C_t being initially uncharged. Due to the opposition offered by the back emf of Lc to current flow, the charging current rises slowly at first, and the voltage across Ct rises as shown in Fig. 6.2.

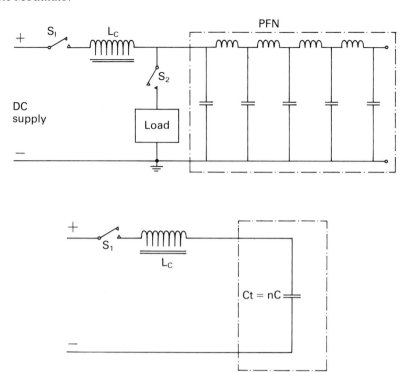

Fig. 6.1 Resonant circuit produced by charging inductor and pfn capacitance

The flow of current through the charging inductor Lc causes a magnetic field to build up around the inductor which, at any instant will store $\frac{1}{2}LI^2$ J of energy.

In the time period equal to one quarter period of natural oscillation, the pfn voltage rises to the supply. With the pfn capacitors now charged up to the supply voltage, the current from the supply falls. The fall of current in turn causes the magnetic field around Lc to collapse and return $\frac{1}{2}LI^2$ J to the circuit, boosting the charge on the capacitors (assuming zero losses) to twice the supply voltage.

The reasoning behind this is based on $Q = I \times t$ and $Q = C \times V$; the collapsing magnetic field causes the current (I) to flow for a period of time (t) increasing the charge (Q). Since $Q = C \times V$, as Q increases, and the value of capacitance (C) remains constant, the voltage (V) must increase. From this reasoning it can be seen that the pfn charges to twice the applied voltage in a time period equal to one half period of the natural oscillatory frequency.

To obtain maximum advantage from the circuit, it is essential that the pfn is discharged at the very instant the line voltage reaches $2V$, before the natural oscillatory action causes a voltage overswing as shown in Fig. 6.2.

To achieve this objective, the prf of the equipment would have to equal one half period of natural oscillation of the pfn. Such a restriction would be unacceptable, as it has already been seen that a switchable prf is required to accommodate operation on long and short ranges. (Having said that, some modern equipments do operate with a single, fixed prf, but use alternative techniques as explained later).

To enable a switched prf which is independent of the natural resonant frequency of the pfn to be used, some method has to be adopted which will enable the pfn to sustain a $2V$ charge until required. This function is provided by a 'hold-off' diode.

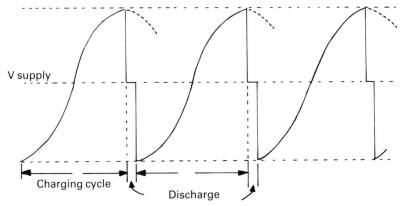

Fig. 6.2 PFN voltage during charge and discharge cycles

A conventional semiconductor power diode would be able to perform the function of 'hold-off diode', but in practice a thyristor is often used as it is able not only to act as a hold-off diode, but also take to the part of the switch *S*1. On the application of a trigger pulse from the prf generator to the gate electrode, the thyristor will conduct,

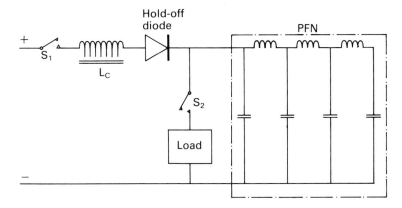

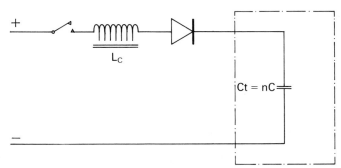

Fig. 6.3 Addition of hold-off diode

thereby initiating the charge on the pfn. The hold-off action of the diode comes about at the instant in the charging action when the charging inductor has returned its $\frac{1}{2}LI^2$ J of energy, and the pfn charge voltage is nearing twice the applied voltage. At this point, the pfn voltage on the diode anode is $2V$, and that on the cathode only V, causing the diode to be reverse biased by a voltage equal to the supply. As soon as the diode is reverse biased, the voltage to which the pfn has charged ($2V$) will remain on the line until it is required, the problem of voltage overshoot is eliminated, and the pfn can be used with more than one prf (Fig. 6.4).

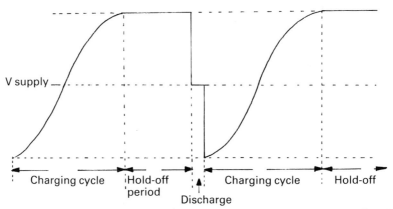

Fig. 6.4 PFN voltage during charge and discharge cycles modified by the addition of a hold-off diode

The discharge of the pfn occurs on receipt of a trigger pulse from the prf generator. Chapter 5 described the discharging of a previously charged pfn through a matched load. In a practical modulator, the matched load takes the form of a transformer, the primary winding impedance of which is made equal to the pfn characteristic impedance. The transformer will have a high step-up ratio, usually enough to ensure that the pulse delivered to the magnetron reaches somewhere in the order of 8 kV. To effect the discharge of the pfn a switch is required to connect the load across the pfn. Again a thyristor finds an application as upon receipt of a trigger pulse it will conduct, thereby completing the circuit. Unfortunately, the flow of current from the pfn to the load is usually of such magnitude that damage would be done to any thyristor used directly for this purpose. Time has to be allowed for the thyristor to be fully conductive before the full discharge current can be applied. This time delay is brought about by the addition of a saturable core reactor to the circuit.

A saturable core reactor is made by winding a coil on to a laminated former, but with the usual air gap omitted. As a consequence, once the current flowing through the coil reaches some designed value the core becomes magnetically saturated, and the flux ceases to change with increasing magnetic force. As a result, the impedance of the coil falls, and the voltage across it falls to almost zero—the same effect as when a mechanical switch is closed. To bring about a time delay the saturable core reactor may be biased by passing a dc current through a second winding which keeps the reactor biased to one end of its B/H characteristic (Fig. 6.5). As current starts to flow through the coil the operating point moves along the characteristic curve, taking a finite time to do so, until the core reaches saturation at the opposite end of the characteristic from which is started. At this instant the flux density is at maximum saturation point (B_{sat}), and any increase in magnetising force (H) (which is proportional to current flow), ceases to have any effect. The fall of impedance value

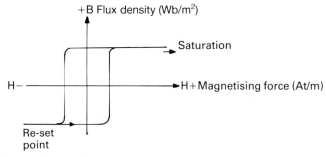

Fig. 6.5 Hysterisis curve of saturable core reactor

enables the winding to be considered as a short circuit, i.e. a closed switch. The instant at which the core saturates can be considered as the time when the matched load is connected across the pfn, by which time the discharge thyristor is fully conducting, and is able to carry the full discharge current—which may be in excess of 200–300 amps. The time delay introduced by the saturable reactor is normally in the region of $1\,\mu$–$1.5\,\mu$ seconds. During this time it is essential that the charge on the artificial line is not lost, and so some alternative source of energy is required to provide the reactor with current prior to saturation. This may be done by the use of an additional capacitor, or by a second, smaller, artificial line known as a priming network.

The action of a typical modulator circuit will now be described. Figure 6.6 shows a

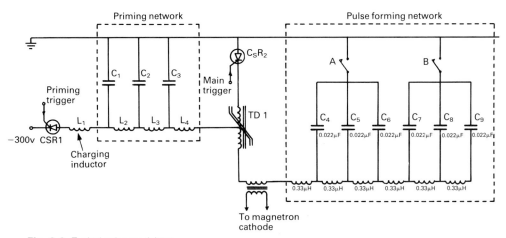

Fig. 6.6 Typical pulse modulator

pulse modulator capable of producing two pulse lengths. Pulse length switching is effected by the opening or closing of switch contacts A and B which would in practice be relay contacts. When long pulse is selected both contacts A and B would be closed, giving the line maximum length. When a shorter pulse is required contact B would open, disconnecting a part of the line, thus making it shorter. For the purpose of the description, long pulse operation is selected, and contacts A and B are both closed.

Charging cycle

A trigger pulse applied between gate and cathode of CSR1 initiates the charging cycle by causing CSR1 to conduct. With CSR1 conducting the −300 volts from the supply flows through the inductors of the priming network, charging the capacitors C1–C3 to the supply voltage; through the lower half of reactor TD1 and the inductors of the main pulse forming network C4–C9, also charging them to −300 volts. The relatively slow charging rate enables the inductors to be regarded as 'invisible' to the process. At this instant of time, the voltage charge on the modulator circuit equals the supply voltage, and the current starts to fall. As the flow of current falls, the magnetic field created around the charging inductor L1, by the initial flow of current, starts to collapse. The collapse of the magnetic field returns $\frac{1}{2}LI^2$ J of stored energy into the circuit, and the resonant choke charging action increases the voltage on the capacitors to twice the supply voltage (assuming zero losses). When the magnetic field has returned all the stored energy to the circuit the current falls to zero and no further charging is possible. At this instant, CSR1 has approximately −600 volts on its anode and −300 volts on its cathode, and is therefore reverse biased by 300 volts enabling CSR1 to act as a hold-off diode. The circuit will remain in this condition until the application of a trigger pulse to discharge the modulator.

Discharge cycle

The application of a trigger pulse to CSR2 starts the discharge cycle. With CSR2 conducting, the priming circuit C1–C3, L2–L4 and the top half of TD1 are connected in circuit, with the top half of TD1 forming a matched load to the priming network. As already noted, the purpose of the priming network is to cause a small current (about 20 amps) to flow in TD1 until CSR2 conducting surface is fully active and able to handle the large current flow of the main discharge. This small (priming) current flow will cause TD1 to saturate after a short time delay.

It is, however, essential that the main pulse forming network does not loose any of its charge during this delay. This is ensured by making TD1 a 2:1 step-up auto transformer, the action of which is as follows. At the instant CSR2 conducts and connects a matched load across the priming network, the voltage across the top half of TD1 will fall to half of the initial charge voltage of 600 volts. The 300 volts present across the top half of TD1 will, due to the 2:1 step-up ratio, ensure that the bottom half of TD1 winding remains at −600 volts and therefore keeps the main pfn at its fully charged value.

After the designed time delay, TD1 will saturate and act as a short circuit connecting the main pfn into circuit through the now fully conducting CSR2.

The main pfn has the primary winding of T1 as the matched load through which to discharge. 300 volts is developed across the primary of T1 for the two way travel time of the main pfn. With the values shown this would equal $12\sqrt{LC}$, approximately 1 μ second, twice the one-way travel time of the line; hence the figure of 12 in the formula for a six-section artificial line.

A current in the region of 200–300 amps will flow in the primary winding of T1 for the duration of the main discharge. Transformer T1 will step-up the line voltage to the several thousand volts required by the magnetron, and the current supplied will be in the order of 6–8 amps.

7
Magnetron

The purpose of the magnetron in a marine radar is to convert the dc pulse supplied by the modulator into radio frequency oscillations which last for the duration of the modulator pulse. The frequency of oscillation is very high; in the microwave band, and at such frequencies special techniques and devices have to be employed, the magnetron being just one example of such a device. Before examining the principles of the magnetron it would be beneficial to look briefly at the development of resonant cavities, around which the magnetron is designed.

A simple resonant circuit using the parallel connection of an inductor and a capacitor is well documented elsewhere, and is known to resonate at approximately $1/2\pi\sqrt{LC}$ Hz (ignoring all losses). To increase the resonant frequency of this circuit, the value of the capacitor, or the inductor or both, must be decreased. Following this reasoning through to its logical conclusion, a point will eventually be reached where the inductor is a single turn coil, and the capacitance consists of the distributed (stray) capacitance between the two sides of the coil. Such an arrangement is comparable to a Lecher line: a quarter wavelength section of open wire transmission line short-circuited at one end. This is shown in Fig. 7.1

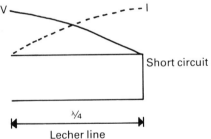

Fig. 7.1 Standing waves on Lecher line

With this arrangement there is capacitance between the two conductors and distributed inductance as shown. As has been explained, this circuit is equivalent to a parallel tuned circuit, and will have a resonant frequency corresponding to a wavelength four times the length of the Lecher line. For example, if the length of the Lecher line was 0.25 metre, the wavelength of the oscillation would be 1 metre, and the frequency 300 MHz.

When the Lecher line is used as a resonant circuit the frequency of oscillation can be increased by reducing the physical length of the line, since shortening the line means that it will be a quarter of a wavelength at a higher frequency. Unfortunately, as the line is shortened the damping losses attributable to skin effect and radiation losses increase very rapidly, causing a reduction in the 'Q' of the circuit. Eventually a point is reached when the losses become so great that the circuit ceases to oscillate. To restore the situation, the parallel connection of a second, identical section of Lecher line will halve the losses, preventing oscillation. The reasoning behind this statement is identical to the parallel connection of two, equal-value resistors producing a total resistance value which is half of the value of one of the resistors.

The resonant frequency of the combination of Lecher lines remains unchanged; the total inductance value will be reduced by the number of sections added, while the total capacitance will be increased by the total number of sections added. As progressively more Lecher lines are connected in parallel, the 'Q' of the circuit increases as the losses reduce, and eventually a situation will be reached whereby all the spaces between the lines are filled in, the result being a hollow cylinder, half a wavelength in

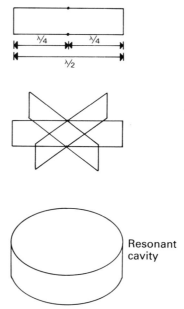

Fig. 7.2 The development of a resonant cavity from the Lecher line

diameter, with closed ends, which resembles an empty flat can (Fig. 7.2). This is known as a resonant cavity, and will resonate at a frequency which corresponds to a wavelength twice the diameter of the cylinder, and having a very high 'Q'—often in the region of tens of thousands.

The 'Q' factor of a resonant cavity is given by the general expression

$$Q = 2\pi f \times \frac{\text{maximum energy stored}}{\text{power loss}}$$

Since there is no radiation or dielectric losses, and the ohmic losses due to skin effect are small, the resulting Q factor is high.

In practice, resonant cavities take the form of enclosed metal chambers the shape of which is determined by manufacturing and tuning considerations. If energy is introduced into a cavity from a suitable source the cavity will respond by producing sinusoidal oscillations in the electric and magnetic fields in response to the excitation, behaving as an oscillatory device at a frequency determined by its dimensions.

Energy can be introduced to, or extracted from a resonant cavity by means of either a probe (acting as a $\frac{1}{4}$ wave antenna) placed parallel with the plane of the cavity electric field, or a loop positioned at 90° to the plane of the cavity magnetic field, so that the lines of oscillatory magnetic flux can 'thread' through the loop (rather like going through the eye of a needle) and cut the conductor at right angles, inducing a voltage into the conductor. Additionally, a cavity can be excited by an electron stream passing through a hole or aperture cut in the cavity wall.

The magnetron is a multicavity device, employing several resonant cavities, all operating at the same frequency, within a single module. The cavities, the dimensions of which determine the frequency of operation, are excited into oscillation by an electron stream passing over an open slot in the construction, and energy extracted from the magnetron by means of a loop, coupled into one of the cavities.

The magnetron is a thermionic device, having a heater, cathode and anode assembly. The anode and cathode are placed concentrically, and located between the poles of a magnet having a strong axial field (Fig. 7.3).

The resonant cavities (typically eight in number) are drilled equidistantly around the inner edge of a circular block of beryllium copper which constitutes the magnetron anode. Slots cut to join the holes to the inner edge of the block constitute the effective capacitor of the cavity, while the drilled hole constitutes the inductor. When viewed from the cathode, the anode surface consists of alternate segments and gaps. It can be seen, therefore, that the frequency of oscillation of the magnetron will be determined by the dimensions of the holes and slots within the anode block. As it is inevitable that, during manufacture, the machine cutting tools will experience some minute degree of wear, the dimensions of the holes and slots in any two magnetrons will never be the same. Consequently, each magnetron, as manufactured, will operate on a slightly different frequency within the designated radar band. It is this unique radar frequency aspect which, together with other attributes, enables military powers to identify, by radar 'fingerprint', any vessel operating a radar long before it becomes a visible target.

The magnetrons used in commercial marine radars cannot be tuned to change the frequency of operation, although tunable magnetrons are manufactured for other applications. Marine radar magnetron frequencies are, typically 9410 ± 30 MHz for 'X' Band, and 3050 ± 10 MHz for 'S' Band. During the initial warm-up period, slight expansion of the metal will cause the frequency to drift slightly, after which the frequency will remain reasonably constant.

The space between the anode block and the cathode is known as the 'interaction' space, and it is here that the electron stream imparts energy to maintain oscillation within the cavities as will be explained. The cathode is a conventional thermionic emitting surface, indirectly heated by an ac operated heating element. The ends of the cathode are fitted with end caps to confine the electron beam in a direction towards the cavities. The cathode and heater are joined together to obviate the necessity of insulating them as the cathode will be subjected to the high voltage modulator pulse, and the risk of breakdown between the low heater potential and the very high cathode potential is removed. Because of the very high voltages to which the cathode will be subjected, electrical connection is made by heavily insulated leads.

The copper anode block is kept at earth potential from a dc point of view which enables the metal waveguide run, to which it is connected, to be bolted directly to metal superstructures without the need for insulators. However, since the anode of the device is at earth potential, the cathode has to be driven negatively with respect to the anode, hence the necessity for the modulator to provide a negative-going dc pulse, and in turn, the need for a negative supply voltage to be provided for the modulator pulse forming network.

As already noted, rf energy is extracted from the magnetron by means of an inductive coupling loop inside one of the cavities, which couples with the oscillatory magnetic field within the cavity. The loop continues out from the magnetron to form a short metal probe which extends into a short section of integral waveguide, and acts as an antenna to radiate rf energy from the magnetron into the waveguide.

The anode, cathode, heater and loop/probe assembly are enclosed in an evacuated metal chamber, a technique identical to that used for other thermionic devices with the exception of the use of metal opposed to glass. The complete assembly is secured between the poles of a powerful permanent magnet so that the magnetic field runs axially through the interaction space between anode and cathode.

Because the magnetron is manufactured complete with its own magnet and integral short section of waveguide, it is of a type known as a 'packaged' magnetron (as opposed to others which are not supplied with magnets etc).

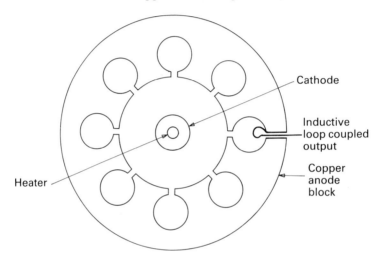

Fig. 7.3

7.1 Magnetron action

In considering the internal action of the magnetron, the omission of the effect brought about by the axial magnetic field will be of initial benefit.

It is assumed that the magnetron has a low voltage ac supply connected to the heater which in turn has already raised the temperature of the cathode up to emission temperature, and that a space charge of electrons is in the vicinity of the cathode.

In practice, these conditions are ensured to exist by means of a time delay imposed on the magnetron/modulator circuitry from switch-on. Depending on manufacture(r) and other criteria, a period of approximately three minutes is often experienced between the time of initial switch-on and the application of a modulator pulse to the magnetron. Failure to ensure this would result in the stripping of the cathode and destruction of the magnetron. After the initial time delay the radar can be switched between stand-by and run conditions without any further delay as the magnetron heater voltage is not removed during stand-by conditions.

The leading edge of the modulator pulse applied to the cathode causes an intense radial electric field to be established immediately between anode and cathode (anode at earth potential, cathode at $-8\,\text{kV}$ up to perhaps $-20\,\text{kV}$) causing the electrons to be drawn straight to the anode with considerable velocity. In the absence of the field from the permanent magnet that is all that would happen, with a sizable flow of current inside the magnetron in all probability causing irreversible damage (Fig. 7.4).

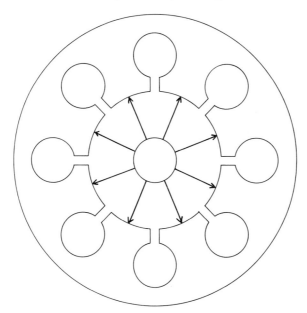

Fig. 7.4 Intense dc radial field in the absence of a magnetic field

When the effect of the magnet's field is considered the action is somewhat different. As before, the leading edge of the modulator dc pulse causes an intense radial electric field between anode and cathode, drawing the electrons towards the anode. However, as soon as electrons start to move they, by definition, constitute an electric current which is seen to be flowing at right-angles to the magnetic field. Interaction between the electrons and the magnetic field, in accordance with Fleming's rule, results in the electrons being deflected in a direction which is at right-angles to their motion and the magnetic field, see Fig. 7.5.

The lines of magnetic flux from the permanent magnet are shown flowing from the North pole which is coincident with the reader's eye down through the page to the South pole. This is represented by the crosses signifying the tails of arrows by normal convention. The electrons, in their attempt to flow directly, in a straight line towards the anode are caused to follow a clockwise curved path as shown. Assuming that the cavity rf oscillations are frozen at a particular instant in time, producing the fields as shown in Fig. 7.5.

An electron leaving the cathode of point 'A' would be accelerated outwards by the dc eht field produced by the modulator pulse, from which it extracts energy. It is deflected to the right (in accordance with Fleming's Left Hand Rule, remembering that an electron flow corresponds to a conventional current flowing in the opposite direction) by the magnetic field, and comes under the influence of the cavity oscillatory electric field at an instant when the cavity field is in a direction to impart further acceleration velocity. In this example, the electron has extracted energy from the cavity, and has not provided any work. However, its increase in velocity is accompanied by an increase in the bending effect, due to the force of the magnetic

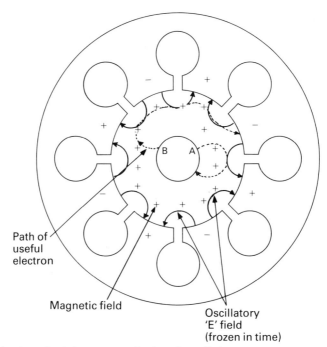

Fig. 7.5 Paths taken by emitted electrons to maintain cavity oscillations

field which causes it to bend back towards the cathode. Such electrons are removed from the interaction space after one short radial excursion, and extract no more energy from the oscillatory field. The electron would be subsequently re-emitted.

An electron leaving the cathode at point 'B' is accelerated outwards by the intense radial field, gaining velocity all the time, and bending under the influence of the magnetic field. As it passes through the rf field as shown, it is retarded, thus giving up some of its own kinetic energy to the cavity field. Once it has been slowed down, it is less influenced by the magnetic field and therefore commences moving outwards towards the anode, once more acquiring energy from the dc field which can be imparted to another cavity. Figure 7.6 shows electron paths.

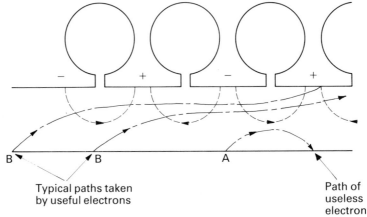

Fig. 7.6 Simplified drawing showing electron paths

In practice, the fields shown across the mouths of the cavities are oscillating, and the time taken by an electron to pass from one cavity mouth to another will be coincident with the retarding of the electron so that each cavity is 'fed' with energy. Oscillations can be sustained in the magnetron because the electrons which find themselves in an accelerating field are quickly removed from the interaction space, whereas those which encounter a decelerating field are able to remain in the interaction space for a longer period, and are able to transfer appreciable energy from the dc field to the rf field before finally reaching the anode and returning via the power supply back to the cathode.

To bring about this effect requires careful design of all aspects of the magnetron, especially the strength of the magnetic field, which if too strong will cause all electrons to return to the cathode before they have done any work. Reducing the field strength to produce a 'cut-off field' will cause the electrons to graze the anode before returning to the cathode. It follows, that for a given magnetic field there is a critical cut-off voltage between anode and cathode, below which no electrons can reach the anode. This is known as the Hull cut-off value (named after its discoverer. Therefore, to bring about oscillations in a multicavity magnetron requires the modulator dc pulse to be of the correct value for a particular design of magnetron.

The electrons in the interaction space circle on a cycloidal path, almost grazing the cavity mouths; the overall space charge pattern resembling the spokes of a wheel as the electrons bunch together, the number of spokes being half the number of segments. Electrons returning to the cathode strike it with considerable velocity, causing further electrons to be emitted (secondary emission) by bombardment, and care must be exercised to prevent the cathode from overheating. The increase in cathode temperature due to being struck by returning electrons is known as back-heating, and enables the magnetron heater voltage to be reduced after an initial warm-up period, or when switching to pulse lengths which demand greater magnetron power. To ensure that all cavities oscillate in the same mode alternate anode segments are strapped together with short copper wires, a technique known as 'strapping' (Fig. 7.7).

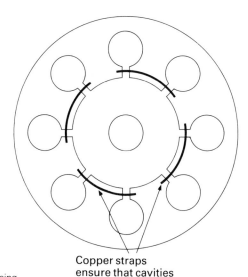

Fig. 7.7 Magnetron strapping

Copper straps
ensure that cavities
oscillate in a stable mode

The working life of a magnetron can be regarded in terms of years rather than months as, due to the duty cycle of operation, the magnetron is only active for a comparatively short period of time as opposed to a device which is continuously active. A typical life expectancy would be at least 10 000 hours (8760 hours = 1 year). Indications of a magnetron nearing the end of its life are a gradual fall-off of long-range echoes, a reduction in performance monitor length; occasionally noise rings appear on the display.

When the magnetron has failed completely this fact may be indicated by all the energy in the modulator pulse being dissipated in a corona discharge, often accompanied by tracking over the insulation.

8
Waveguide

In essence, waveguide is the feeder used to connect the transceiver with the antenna. It is, almost without exception, found in all 3 cm installations, and occasionally in some 10 cm installations where distance and cost are not excessive. The alternative for 10 cm installations is the use of a high-grade, low-loss coaxial cable. Initial inspection of a section of waveguide reveals a hollow rectangular pipe, often made from copper or brass.

In Chapter 5 open-wire transmission lines were discussed, together with their operation under ac conditions using resonant lengths. A $\lambda/4$ section of open wire line with a short-circuit load termination will reflect an open-circuit condition back to the sending end terminals. Such a section of line can, therefore, be used to support an open-wire feeder, employing the $\lambda/4$ section as a 'quarter-wave metallic insulator', utilising the fact that a physical short circuit will reflect an open-circuit at the point of support, see Fig. 8.1.

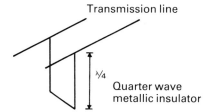

Fig. 8.1 Metallic insulator supporting a transmission line

If an 'infinite' number of identical $\lambda/4$ metallic insulator sections were placed side-by-side, above and below the original open wire feeder, to join all the spaces between them, the result would be a rectangular, hollow metal pipe: waveguide. See Fig. 8.2

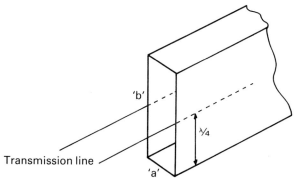

Fig. 8.2 The development of waveguide from the metallic insulator concept

The two dimensions of the waveguide are determined as follows. The narrow, or 'a' side dimension is the governing factor in determining the power carrying capacity of the waveguide. Basically it must be broad enough to prevent 'flash-over' inside the pipe. The broad, or 'b' side is in practice approximately $0.707\,\lambda_g$, where λ_g is the 'guide wavelength'—'the electro-magnetic radiation wavelength inside the waveguide which is modified from that in open space, hence the different terminology which will be explained.

The energy extracted from the oscillatory magnetic field of the magnetron cavities by an inductive loop are coupled into the waveguide by means of a probe. The probe, which acts as a quarter wave antenna penetrates the 'b' side of the waveguide, and is located $\lambda_g/4$ from the closed end of the waveguide section integral with the magnetron. If the output frequency of the magnetron is 10 GHz (10 000 MHz), the wavelength is 3 cm, therefore, at this frequency a probe $\frac{3}{4}$ cm long can act as an antenna. This is shown in Fig. 8.3.

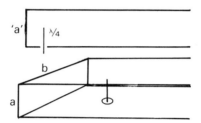

Fig. 8.3 Probe coupling

A vertical antenna will radiate electromagnetic energy with the plane of the electric field corresponding to that of the antenna. If, as in this example, the antenna is vertical, then the electric field radiated from the antenna must also be vertical, and its associated magnetic field will be horizontal. Such a wave configuration is known as a transverse electromagnetic wave, and is shown in Fig. 8.4.

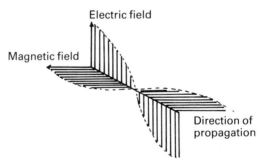

Fig. 8.4 Transverse electro-magnet wave

Placing the probe within the confines of the waveguide produces the field shown in Fig. 8.5

As the probe radiates, an electromagnetic wave which strikes the conducting surface of the waveguide the wave will be reflected. If two separate rays only were considered the general effect of the propagation mechanism can be appreciated. Ray 'A', radiated to the right but moving upwards, soon strikes the upper wall of the guide, from where it is reflected, and continues to bounce along in a zig-zag manner as

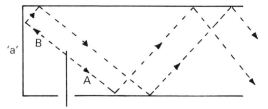

Fig. 8.5 Radiating probe inside waveguide

shown. Ray 'B', radiated to the left, strikes the reflecting surface at the end of the guide before being reflected to the right as shown.

Because the electromagnetic wave bounces along the guide walls as described, as opposed to travelling a straight line, the velocity of the wave in the guide is less than the velocity in free space. The speed at which the energy travels along the guide is called the 'Group velocity', and is always less than the velocity would be in free space. In the space between the guide walls the electric and magnetic fields combine to produce a field pattern, or mode, which travels at a greater velocity than the free space velocity. This is known as the 'Phase velocity'. Because of this, it is usual to refer to λ_g, the guide wavelength as opposed to λ, the wavelength in free space, as the wavelength must differ if the speed of propagation differs. (Velocity $+ \lambda \times F$, where λ = wavelength and F = frequency.)

Various configurations of the electric and magnetic fields can exist within a waveguide: they are called 'modes'. In the rectangular waveguide used for 3 cm marine radar, the predominant mode is known as the TE01 mode. The letters TE refer to the electric field being transverse (across) the direction of propagation, whereas the subscripts 01 refer to the pattern of the fields. Zero is the number of half cycles along the 'a' side of the guide, the figure one indicating one half cycle of pattern along the 'b' side. This is shown in Fig. 8.6.

An appreciation of the electric and magnetic field patterns inside the waveguide enables the current distribution pattern in the waveguide walls to be developed, the application being the slotted waveguide scanner. The current flow in the narrow side walls of the waveguide is vertical, converging towards point 'A' on the broad side and diverging from 'B', points 'A' and 'B' being spaced $\lambda_g/2$ in accordance with the mode being propagated. This distribution is shown in Fig. 8.7.

Waveguide, as with both coaxial and open wire feeders, has to be impedance matched to the source and load, although the term impedance is not quite so obvious for waveguide as it has no terminals between which voltage and current can be measured. There are three ways by which the impedance may be calculated:

first: $\quad Z_g = \dfrac{\text{Strength of electric field in guide}}{\text{Strength of magnetic field in guide}}$

second: $\text{Power} = \dfrac{(\text{volts})^2}{\text{Resistance}}$

which, for H waves in a rectangular guide gives

$$Z_0 = \frac{2b}{a} \times \frac{120\pi \, \lambda_g}{\lambda f} \text{ ohms}$$

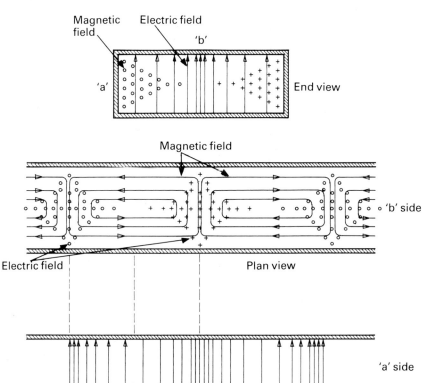

Fig. 8.6 TEO1 mode. Electric and Magnetic field patterns inside waveguide

where a and b are the narrow and wide dimensions of the guide, λ_g the guide wavelength, and λf the wavelength in free space.

third: $Z_0 = \dfrac{\text{Volts}}{\text{Current}}$

which leads to

$$Z = \frac{\pi b}{2a} \times \frac{120\pi\,\lambda_g}{\lambda f} \text{ ohms}$$

Unfortunately, the three methods each produce separate answers which, in the case

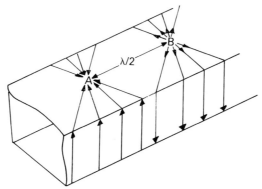

Fig. 8.7 Current distribution in waveguide walls

of 3 cm waveguide: the first method 498 Ω, the second 443 Ω and the third 366 Ω, but in practice a figure of approximately 600 Ω is considered to be acceptable.

Waveguide is manufactured and supplied in straight lengths of approximately 5 metres which, therefore, means joining sections together in order to complete the run. This process is sometimes referred to as plumbing, since the tools of the two trades are identical, namely hacksaw, wire-wool, flux, solder and blow lamp. The joints between two lengths of waveguide are made by brazing flanges on to the ends of the main guide. Two joints are commonly used: the simple flange joint and the choke joint, both of which offer electrical continuity of the guide whilst at the same time offering physical separation of the two sections, to allow for expansion and contraction with temperature changes. Electrical continuity is maintained despite the physical separation of the sections by using transmission line techniques.

Referring to Fig. 8.8, the open circuit at 'A' reflects back as a short circuit at 'B'

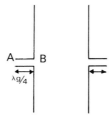

Fig. 8.8 Flange joint

providing the distance between the two points is kept an odd-number of $\lambda_g/4$ apart ($\frac{1}{4}$, $\frac{3}{4}$, $1\frac{1}{4}$ etc). The guide is effectively continuous despite the mechanical break. The watertight integrity of the waveguide is maintained by placing a neoprene sealing ring between the two sections. Bolts placed through the two flanges hold the joint together.

Figure 8.9 shows the choke joint variation. Here a $\lambda_g/4$ deep groove is cut into the flange piece, located $\lambda_g/4$ from the inner wall of the guide. The groove, being cut into a metal block, can be thought of as a section of short-circuited transmission line. The metal block which provides the end termination will reflect an open circuit impedance at the point where the two flanges meet. However, as this is also $\lambda_g/4$ from the inner wall, it in turn will reflect an electrical short circuit at the guide wall, again providing continuity without a physical connection. The joint is sealed and secured in the same manner as that used for the flange joint.

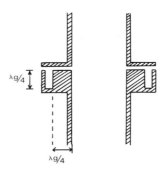

Fig. 8.9 Choke joint

Bends are manufactured as, unlike copper pipe, waveguide cannot be successfully bent. The bends are made in the plane of either the electric or the magnetic field, and consequently are known as either E or H plane bends. Occasionally people think of the E and H as meaning Easy and Hard—referring to the most obvious and least obvious ways of bending a malleable rectangular section bar.

It is apparent that at some point in the waveguide run provision must be made for a rotating joint to be incorporated to enable power to be delivered to the scanner. This is normally effected by incorporating a short section of circular waveguide between two sections of rectangular guide as shown in Fig. 8.10.

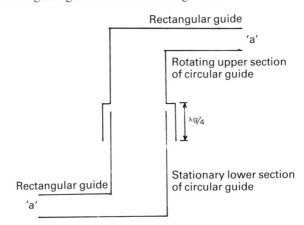

Fig. 8.10 Rotating joint

The use of the choke joint principle enables electrical continuity to be maintained between the two rotating sections. Inside the joint the H field of the rectangular guide is converted into an E field (TM01 mode conversion) during the transit of the circular guide, and back into an H field when it rejoins the rectangular guide.

Certain sections of the waveguide linking the transceiver to the scanner often require the use of a length of flexible waveguide, particularly the section which links the scanner to the main waveguide run, or on vessels where excessive vibration occurs at critical propeller/engine speeds would cause undue strain on rigid guide. Flexible waveguide is manufactured from a continuous, rectangular shaped, interleaved spiral of copper/bronze, integral with flanges preformed at each end and protected by a heavy duty rubber coat along the length.

The use of thin metal shims, located at joints in the waveguide run, and known as 'reactance diaphragms' can be used to reduce or eliminate standing waves due to reflections within the guide.The shims, which are of similar dimensions to a razor blade, are available as inductive, capacitive or resonant insertions. The inductive shim compresses the lines of magnetic flux of the field pattern in the guide by protruding across the broad side of the guide; whereas the capacitive shim compresses the lines of electric force by protruding across the narrow side; and the resonant shim, which protrudes across both broad and narrow gives the effect of a parallel tuned circuit.

Windows, made from ptfe, and transparent to electromagnetic radiation are placed at joints in horizontal sections of guide after any transition between an interior and exterior on the run. The waveguide, when passing from the interior of the vessel to the exterior, will be subject to a thermal gradient, most noticeably in tropical areas with an air conditioned vessel. The effect of this is to induce condensation to form on the inside of the waveguide, which would trickle down over a period of time. If provision was not included to block the moisture it would run down to the rf head and prevent the operation of the equipment. It is important that the windows are placed in horizontal sections as any vertical position would cause the moisture to puddle across the guide and act as a block to rf radiation.

Moisture must be kept out of the waveguide at all times, and it is imperative that all joints are securely made, and that sealing rings are carefully positioned during installation. Some (usually military) installations operate a pressurised waveguide system where normal dry air keeps the guide at a pressure slightly higher than atmospheric. Should any hole or potential leak develop in the waveguide, the venting of the air (normally fed from a reservoir gas bottle) from the hole would prevent the ingress of moisture into the guide, and the fall of gas pressure from the reservoir would signal that the guide had been penetrated.

9
Scanner

In Chapter 1 it was established that a requirement existed for a scanner capable of radiating energy in the form of a fan-shaped beam. The beam requirements are for a very narrow horizontal beam, in order to provide optimum bearing discrimination, and at the same time a broad vertical beam, for optimum minimum range operation and also to keep close-range targets in the beam when the observing vessel is rolling.

Scanners are manufactured in several different forms, but by far the most common in non-military radar systems is the slotted waveguide scanner. This uses a horizontal length of rectangular waveguide, rotated about a point midway along its length and radiating energy from a series of slots cut into the narrow side of the guide. The scanner is a continuation of the normal rectangular guide carrying the TE01 mode from the upper section of the rotating joint coupled to the stationary waveguide run.

A radiating slot antenna in its simplest form consists of a sheet of metal into which a slot, approximately $\lambda/2$ long has been cut. The slot is excited by an open wire transmission line connected midway along the slot length. The behaviour of the resonant slot is very closely related to $\lambda/2$ dipole formed by the piece of metal which was initially removed from the sheet to form the slot being excited with the same current. The shape of the polar diagrams for both the slot and the $\lambda/2$ dipole are the same, but the direction of the electric and magnetic fields of the radiated energy are interchanged. Whereas a vertical $\lambda/2$ dipole radiates vertically polarised waves, a vertical slot will radiate horizontally polarised waves. The space of the slot may be filled with a good dielectric material without affecting its radiating properties. Horizontally polarised radiation is desirable in marine radar applications as it has been found that better echo responses are obtained if the major plane of the target lies in the same direction as the radiated electric field. In marine radar the majority of all targets offer a greater dimension horizontally than vertically, and as such respond better to horizontally polarised radiation.

Figure 8.7 shows the distribution of current flowing in the walls of the waveguide. If the waveguide wall was perforated by a slot cut in such a way as to disturb the current flow in the wall, a potential difference would be set up at opposite sides of the slot and, as the current and voltage are both alternating at radio frequencies, the slot would radiate energy.

Figure 9.1 shows two $\lambda/2$ slots cut in the narrow wall of the waveguide. Slot 'A', cut parallel to the direction in which the wall current is flowing does not interrupt the current flow, and as a consequence does not radiate any significant energy. Slot 'B', which has been cut horizontally, cuts the line of current flow at right angles, noticeably disturbing the flow and therefore radiating significant energy.

As has previously been noted, the slot antenna radiation characteristics have similarity with those of the $\lambda/2$ dipole antenna. Because of this it is possible to use the dipole antenna to explain the formation of the scanner's radiated beam shape. A single $\lambda/2$ dipole mounted in free-space will have a radiation pattern as shown in Fig. 9.2.

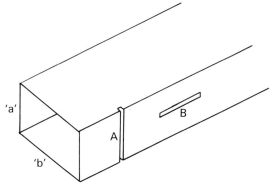

Fig. 9.1 Slots cut in waveguide wall

As can be seen from Fig. 9.2, the radiation pattern in the horizontal plane is omnidirectional. If an array of several λ/2 dipoles, each spaced λ/2 apart with each

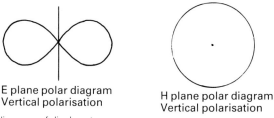

E plane polar diagram
Vertical polarisation

H plane polar diagram
Vertical polarisation

Fig. 9.2 E and H polar diagrams of dipole antenna

dipole being fed in phase, was employed the radiation pattern would be modified as shown in Fig. 9.3.

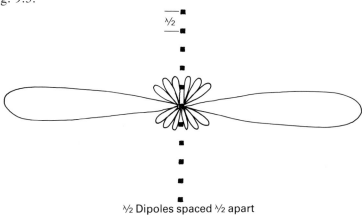

λ/2 Dipoles spaced λ/2 apart

Fig. 9.3 Array of λ/2 dipoles to produce directional radiation

From Fig. 9.3 the following can be seen:

1 Maximum radiation takes place at right angles to the array.
2 The field strength in the direction of maximum radiation increases in proportion to the number of dipoles in the array.

3 The width of the main beam decreases as the number of dipoles in increased.
4 Subsidiary 'side lobes' are produced.

The beam width is measured as being the angle subtended between the points on the main lobe where the field strength is 0.707 (half power, or −3 dB points) of maximum. The width of the beam may be calculated using the formula:

$$\Theta = \frac{\lambda}{N \times D} \text{ radians}$$

where N: the number of dipoles in the array
  D: the distance the dipoles are apart in terms of λ
  λ: the wavelength (cm)

To convert radians to degrees multiply the answer by 57.3.

An antenna array having 70 dipoles spaced 0.5 λ apart, operating at 10 GHz (3 cm) will produce a horizontal beam width of approximately 1.6°.

An 'S' Band (10 cm) scanner would have to be physically almost three times longer than that used in the 'X' Band (3 cm) to achieve the same horizontal beamwidth.

As can be seen from Fig. 9.3, radiation occurs at right angles from both sides of the array. To restrict the radiation to one direction only it would be possible to place a parasitic array of dipoles λ/4 behind the active (driven) dipoles, using a well established technique, or, as in the case of the radar scanner, a reflector.

The slotted waveguide scanner has to be fed with energy at the end which connects with the rotating joint and is, therefore, end-fed. As is already known from basic antenna theory, to achieve the effects described, it is essential that all antennas (or slots in the case of the scanner) radiate an equal amount of energy. Because the scanner is end-fed, it would be logical to presume that the power radiated from the slots diminishes the further away from the feed point they are. This reasoning is based on the fact that, given an initial finite amount of power, the radiating slots will subtract from this leaving progressively less for subsequent slots, and so on.

The two slots shown in Fig. 9.1 provide the solution to this problem. As slot 'A' did not radiate, while slot 'B' produced maximum radiation, it follows that if slots were cut at a skew angle of somewhere between a fraction of a degree and several degrees, it would be possible to control the amount of power radiated by the slots. At the feed end of the scanner, where maximum power is fed into the guide, the skew angle is only a few minutes, such that it is almost vertical, while slots cut at the opposite end of the scanner will have a skew angle of several degrees. For example, if the scanner comprised a total of ten slots, and the maximum power available was 1 kW, the skew angles would have to be cut so that the first, and all other subsequent slots, all radiated 100 watts of power so that by the time the last slot is reached, 900 watts of power will already have been radiated, and the last slot, with the greatest skew angle, is able to radiate the remaining 100 watts.

If all the slots were to be cut with either an all-clockwise skew or an all-anticlockwise skew the result would be to twist the plane of the radiated electric field away from the desired horizontal plane. To counter this, the slots are cut with alternate clockwise and anticlockwise skew angles; and with adjacent slots having almost identical skew angles, the result is for any electric field twist in a clockwise direction to be counteracted by an opposite and almost equal anticlockwise direction. Refer to Fig. 9.4 (a).

In theory, all the input energy to the scanner will be dissipated by radiation from the slots. However, in practice this is not necessarily so and some method is needed of

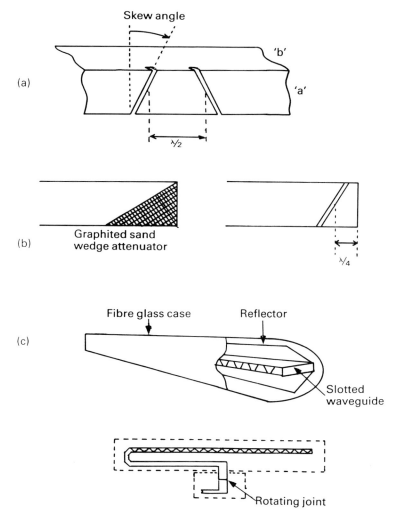

Fig. 9.4 Scanner construction

ensuring that any unradiated energy is not reflected from the closed end of the scanner as an interfering wave. One possible is to terminate the end of the waveguide with a short circuit placed $\lambda/4$ beyond the last slot. Any unradiated energy in the incident wave would then be reflected by the short circuit in such a way that its phase reinforces the incident wave at the slots. A slotted waveguide antenna having this type of termination is known as a 'resonant scanner'. A more popular solution to the problem is to use a non-resonant termination in which a dissipative attenuator is placed inside the guide after the last slot. Any energy not radiated by the slots would be absorbed by the attenuator and dissipated (as heat), so preventing any reflection, see Fig. 9.4 (b).

The reasoning used so far to produce a narrow horizontal beam is based on the accurate $\lambda/2$ spacing between adjacent slots. However, the spacing dimension of $\lambda/2$ is based on one frequency only, any other frequency producing a different dimension in accordance with the corresponding wavelength. In Chapter 1, the 'X' and 'S' radar frequency bands were defined, and the maximum and minimum frequencies within each band were also shown. Chapter 7 briefly introduced some of the factors which determined the output frequency of a magnetron. Combining both of these demonstrates the impracticality of attempting to tie any radar transmission to an exact wavelength, and the resultant spacing dimension between adjacent slots. The end result of using a scanner the slot spacing of which does not correspond exactly to the wavelength of the transmission is to cause the beam to be radiated: firstly not exactly from 'dead-centre' of the scanner, and secondly not exactly at right angles to the scanner. The scanner is said to 'squint', with the main lobe being slightly offset from what might otherwise be expected. This has serious implications in so far as the accuracy of target bearing information is concerned, and the necessity for the accurate alignment of the scanner heading marker switch contacts and bearing transmission system in general are highlighted.

It should also be noted that when a magnetron has been changed, its frequency will be slightly different from its predecessor and the squint angle will be different. For this reason the accuracy of the heading marker should be checked whenever a magnetron has been replaced. A parabolic reflector, or an asymptote of a parabola is placed on the opposite side of the waveguide to where the slots have been cut. This has the effect of both controlling the vertical beam width of the scanner and also reducing to zero any back radiation which may emanate from the guide.

The effects of the array of slots and the reflector combine to produce the required beam shape, focusing the radiation from what was originally an omnidirectional radiation pattern as in Fig. 9.2. In Chapter 4, the concept of antenna gain was introduced and defined. In the case of a radar scanner, the gain can, as a rule of thumb, be calculated from:

$$\frac{32\,000}{\Delta\Theta° \, \Delta\Phi°}$$

where $\Delta\Theta°$: horizontal beam width (radians)
        $\Delta\Phi°$: vertical beam width (radians)

and the power gain when typical losses are included:

$$\frac{25\,000}{\Delta\Theta° \, \Delta\Phi°}$$

The gain of a scanner is proportional to the size of the aperture and inversely proportional to wavelength.

A comparison between two commercial 'X' Band scanners of different physical lengths is shown below:

Length	1.8m	2.4m
Horizontal beamwidth at −3 dB	1.2°	1.0°
Vertical beamwidth at −3 dB	20°	20°
Gain	28 dB	33 dB

The scanner assembly is completed by enclosing it in a fibreglass radome which not only provides protection against moisture entering the open slots in the waveguide, but also aids the aero-dynamic properties, see Fig. 9.4 (c).

To comply with type approval specification, the scanner must be capable of starting and continual rotation in a 100 knot wind, hence the need for some attention to its shape if the drive motor dimensions are to be kept to sensible proportions. The scanner is rotated at a rate somewhere between 20 to 30 rpm through a gearbox assembly in which the prime consideration is the absence of backlash in the gear train. Helically cut gear wheels or toothed synthetic drive belts ensure the minimum of free play which, if of significant proportions, would affect the accuracy of target bearing information.

When installing a scanner, consideration must be given to the needs of servicing it in all weathers, and the provision of a platform with guard rails must be included if the scanner is above head height. The chosen location for the scanner should ideally be higher than any part of the ship's structure, to minimise blind or shadow sectors and give maximum freedom from indirect echoes. Fouling of the scanner by ropes, bunting etc should be avoided, but where these hazards are unavoidable, the provision of a single metal hoop placed over the scanner will offer some protection, while totally enclosing the scanner in a fibreglass radome offers even greater protection on small craft.

General maintenance of the scanner and antenna drive unit involves keeping the scanner face clear of dirt and salt accumulation by washing with a non-abrasive cleaning solution (the scanner should never be painted with anything other than special, lead-free scanner paint supplied by the scanner manufacturer, and only then in extreme circumstances); checking for the ingress of moisture into the waveguide assembly; checking the level of oil in the gearbox and replacing at intervals as suggested by the manufacturer; and checking the tightness of all nuts, bolts and electrical connections and the drive motor slip rings, commutator, brushes etc as applicable.

The type approval specification for scanners requires them not only to start and run in wind speeds of up to 100 knots, but also to rotate clockwise (when viewed from above) at speeds not less than 20 rpm for ranges up to 6 miles, and not less than 12 rpm for higher range scales. The main lobe specification requires the beam to be inside $\pm 1°$ at -3 dB (half power) relative to the main beam, and inside $\pm 2.5°$ at -20 dB (1/100 power). Side lobes inside $\pm 10°$ have to be -23 dB (1/200 power) down on the main lobe, and outside $\pm 10° - 30$ dB (1/1000 power) down.

Integral with the scanner assembly is the heading marker switch, the device which initiates the operation of the circuit, producing a visible line on the display whenever the main lobe radiated from the scanner passes dead ahead. The switch, depending on the manufacturer, may be a microswitch the contact of which is closed by a metal pin forming part of the rotating section of the scanner; or alternatively a glass capsule reed switch, closed by the passing of a small permanent magnet which rotates with the scanner. Regardless of type, the switch is mounted on a moveable plate, calibrated in degrees and aligned against a datum marker. The switch plate is adjusted so that when visual and radar bearings taken of the same target are coincidental the heading marker on the display aligns with 000° on a ship's head up presentation.

10
Power monitor

The power monitor, as its name suggests, enables the radiated power level to be monitored by means of a visible indication on the radar display. The sensor of the power monitor is mounted externally on the scanner drive unit where it can be illuminated by microwave radiation every time the scanner beam passes over it. Invariably, the sensor is a neon bulb, housed in a fibreglass capsule, and very often mounted on the end of a boom arm. The circuit of a power monitor is shown in Fig. 10.1.

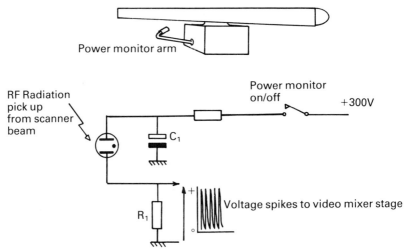

Fig. 10.1 Power monitor. Simplified circuit of power monitor

A switch, normally on the display control panel, enables the power monitor to be switched on when required. A dc supply of approximately 300 volts is used to energise the neon lamp. On exposure to a short series of rf pulses as the scanner beam passes overhead the neon ionisation increases, causing the lamp impedance to decrease momentarily, and a surge of lamp current. The surge is drawn from capacitor C1, and passes through the neon to produce across R1 a positive-going voltage pulse. The voltage pulse is subsequently amplified and fed via the video mixer and amplifier to the display. The visual appearance of the power monitor takes the form of a 'plume' of bright-up, composed of a series of consecutive pulses which increase in length as the scanner beam approaches the sensor, reaching a maximum when the beam is directly over the sensor, and then decaying as the beam moves away. The duration of the monitor pulse and the length of the plume on the display is determined by the time taken for the neon to de-ionise back to its original level. This time depends on the intensity of illumination of the neon caused by the rf pulses, and hence on the radiated mean power level. A fall-off in radiated power, which may be due to the transmitter, waveguide run, or scanner would result in a reduction in the length of the plume when measured by the variable range marker. At the time of installation, when the equipment is known to be correctly adjusted and in full (optimum) working order, the length of the power monitor plume is measured, using the variable range marker (vrm), and recorded in the radar log-book for future reference. See Fig. 10.2.

To increase the visibility of the plume, and to enable its length to be measured easily at al' times, the power monitor boom is normally secured in a position such that

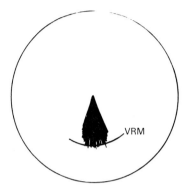

Fig. 10.2 Power monitor indication on PPI screeem

the plume is produced in a blind sector of the display. It is usual for the power monitor to be used in conjunction with an internal performance monitor device, normally mounted at the bottom of the waveguide run, either at the transceiver output port, or integral with the rf head assembly.

The performance monitor takes the form of a resonant cavity, coupled to the waveguide run by an aperture common to both the waveguide wall and the cavity wall. This enables the electromagnetic fields to enter and excite the cavity during the transmission of pulses, and allows for the return of energy from the cavity back into the waveguide during reception. Because of the coupling technique employed it means that the performance monitor is permanently connected into the radar system, and some method has to be employed to nullify any response from the cavity when not in use. As it is known that the physical dimensions of a resonant cavity determine its frequency of oscillation, a relay operated detuning plunger or piston is incorporated into one end of the cavity. When the relay is deactivated, a return spring pushes the plunger into the cavity, causing it to be resonant at a frequency outside of the normal radar operating band. Conversely, when the performance monitor is required the relay pulls the plunger out of the cavity, allowing it to oscillate at the frequency to which it has been tuned. The cavity has to be manually tuned to the same frequency as the radar's magnetron by means of a lockable tuning knob. An alternative approach is to employ a tuning 'paddle' driven by a small electric motor via an eccentric cam. The cam action causes the paddle to be moved quickly in and out of the cavity space, thereby sweeping the cavity resonant frequency of the cavity as it does so. At regular intervals the resonant frequency of the cavity will, therefore, coincide with the magnetron frequency, and the operation will be as for a manually tuned monitor.

In operation, oscillations build up exponentially inside the monitor cavity during the transmission of a pulse as energy couples through the aperture and excites it. As the cavity dimensions have been tuned to resonance at the magnetron's frequency, oscillations start to build up. The amplitude of the oscillations is dependant on the

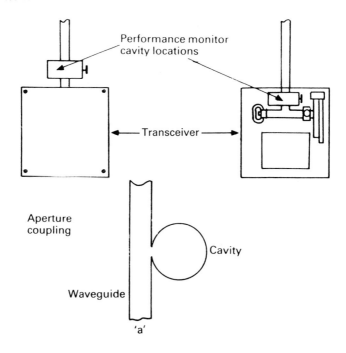

Performance monitor
cavity locations

Transceiver

Aperture
coupling

Cavity

Waveguide

'a'

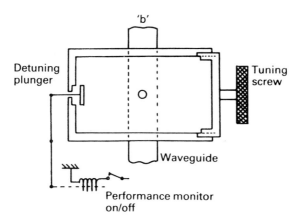

'b'

Detuning
plunger

Tuning
screw

Waveguide

Performance monitor
on/off

Fig. 10.3 Internal performance monitor

power in the transmitted pulse and the pulse duration. The amount of power lost to the cavity from the waveguide is an insignificant portion of the total. The termination of the transmitted pulse means that there is no longer any way of maintaining the oscillations inside the cavity, and they begin to decay exponentially. The energy which had built up inside the cavity during the transmission period is returned, through the coupling aperture into the waveguide and to the receiver. The receiver detects the cavity oscillations which are at the same frequency as an incoming echo pulse would be. As the oscillations decay there will come a point where their amplitude falls below the detection level of the receiver, a point usually determined by the noise floor of the receiver, and they can no longer be displayed. The time interval between the end of the transmission and the time the amplitude of the cavity oscillations fall below the receiver threshold level is known as the 'ringing time'. The next transmission pulse builds up oscillations inside the cavity once again and the whole process is repeated.

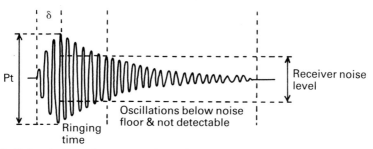

Fig. 10.4 Oscillations inside performance monitor cavity

Each transmission pulse will produce a visual indication on the screen, and as the screen timebase is rotated each visual indication is joined together to produce a single pattern comprising of several thousand individual indications (if prf is 1000 pps, and scanner rpm is 20, in one revolution there will be 3000 visual indications displayed on the screen). As the response from the cavity is independent of the scanner position the pattern which is displayed resembles a sun burst, the radius of which can be measured on the screen by use of the variable range marker.

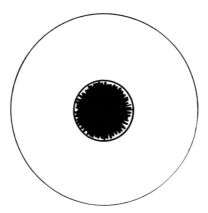

Fig. 10.5 Sun burst pattern

Because of its location in the system, the performance monitor visible response could be shortened because of substandard performance of either the transmitter or the receiver. However, by switching between the power monitor plume response and the performance monitor sun response it is possible to check a radar's performance and crudely diagnose a fault area. Because the performance monitor receives its excitation at the transceiver and feeds its oscillatory energy directly into the receiver; whereas the power monitor samples the radiated energy level and feeds the result into the video amplifier, the following deductions are quite valid:

- Sun and plume responses satisfactory, so the equipment is working normally.
- Sun correct, plume incorrect: transmitter/receiver satisfactory, but there is a loss of power in either the waveguide run or the scanner (assuming the power monitor amplifier is not defective).
- Sun incorrect, plume correct: the receiver performance is below normal.
- Sun incorrect, plume incorrect: substandard transmitter performance or substandard performance by the video amplifier in the display.

A third method of monitoring the performance of a radar is to use an externally mounted 'echo box' as an 'overall performance monitor'. The echo box would be mounted on some part of the ship's superstructure which causes a blind sector, (possibly the funnel), and at a height corresponding to that of the scanner.

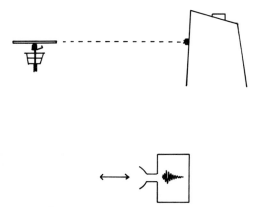

Fig. 10.6 Overall performance monitor

As before, the dimensions of the cavity have to be manually adjusted to cause its resonant frequency to be that of the magnetron in use. The echo box is excited into oscillation on receipt of a sample of the pulse radiated by the scanner, and returns the oscillations back to the scanner during the reception period. The oscillations inside the echo box build up and decay exponentially in the same manner as those already described for the internal performance monitor. The ringing time response of the echo box will determine the length of the visual indication which, because the echo box is being scanned by the rotating radar beam, will be a 'plume' rather than a sun pattern. Unfortunately, with this method it is only possible to check the 'overall' performance of the radar, and any shortening of the plume length could be due to a transmitter, or a receiver, or a waveguide, or a scanner fault as any one could bring about the same effect. Because of these relative shortcomings the overall performance monitor does not find much popularity in modern equipments. The echo box may be deactivated when not required by means of a relay operated device which blocks the entry/exit port of the box. The type approval specification requires that a reduction in performance of 10 dB or more to be clearly identifiable from the performance monitor responses.

11
Bearing Transmission System

The bearing transmitter, the sending end of the bearing transmission system, is housed within the scanner assembly, while the bearing receiver is situated in the display.

Modern radars may employ either of two bearing transmission systems, both of which are described. In the first system two small 3ϕ machines, having almost identical electrical characteristics are connected together as shown in Fig. 11.1.

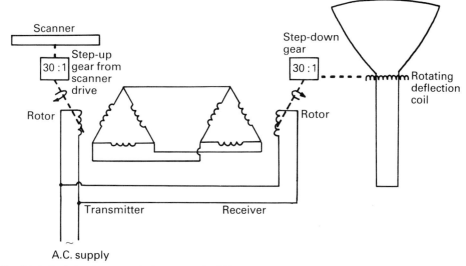

Fig. 11.1 Basic bearing transmission system for PPI display using rotating deflection coils

The stator windings are connected in delta, and interconnected between transmitter and receiver as shown. The rotor of the bearing transmitter is driven by a step-up gear ratio, typically 30:1 by the scanner turning mechanism. The gear train serves to improve the mechanical resolution of the system and hence the accuracy of target bearings. An ac voltage is fed via slip rings to the rotor of the bearing transmitter which, as it turns, produces an alternating complex induced emf into the three stator windings. The windings, being physically displaced by 120°, produce a standard 3ϕ output, the respective amplitude and phase of which relate to the angular position of both the rotor and, in turn, the scanner which is turning it. The interconnection between the two machines causes current to flow around the closed loops, creating magnetic fields around the stator windings of the bearing receiver. As the voltages induced in the transmitter stator windings vary in amplitude and phase in accordance with the angular position of the scanner, so the magnetic fields around the receiver stator windings produce a rotating magnetic field. The rotor of the bearing receiver is connected to the same supply as that fed to the rotor of the bearing transmitter, again using slip rings. As a consequence a magnetic field surrounds the receiver rotor. Interaction between the magnetic field of the rotor and the rotating magnetic field of the stator windings causes the bearing receiver rotor to align automatically with that of the rotating field, and turn in the same direction and at the same speed as the driven rotor of the bearing transmitter. As a consequence the two rotors turn in synchronism and earn the system the name of a 'synchro'. A step-down reduction gearing, identical in ratio to that employed at the scanner, provides adequate driving torque to turn the deflection coil assembly and to restore the rotation rate back to that of the scanner itself. In this way, information relating to the bearing of the main lobe of the transmitted energy is sent to the display.

The system described, although sound in principle, has the disadvantage of requiring the rotation of the deflection coil assembly round the neck of the picture tube. An improvement on this is a system using stationary deflection coils into which a rotating timebase, resolved into sine and cosine components, can be fed directly.

Figure 11.2 shows a system for use with stationary deflection coils. The timebase

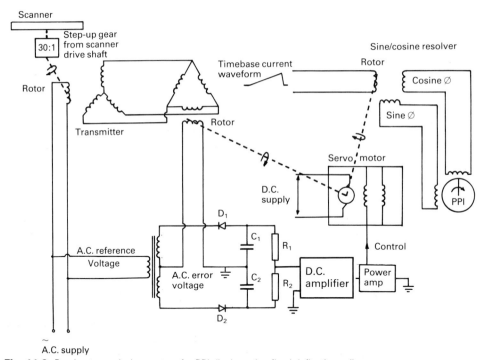

Fig. 11.2 Bearing transmission system for PPI display using fixed deflection coils

waveform is fed to the rotor of a sine/cosine resolver. The induced emfs in the stator windings are fed directly to the horizontal and vertical deflection coils having been resolved into sine and cosine components. The name 'sine/cosine' is given to the device as the two stator windings are physically displaced by 90° from each other in the same way that sine and cosine waves are electrically 90° out of phase see Fig. 11.3.

The rotor of the sine/cosine resolver is driven by a small servo motor which also turns the rotor of a three-phase synchro control transformer (and provides drive to the electronic bearing indicator contacts). In operation, the rotor of the synchro transmit-

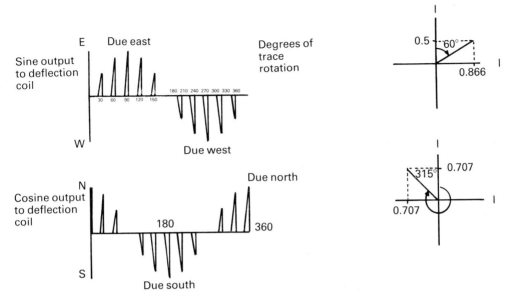

Fig. 11.3 Timebase current output from sine/cosine resolver

ter is turned by the scanner drive as before, and the ac supply fed to the rotor induces emfs in the three stator windings of the synchro transmitter. At the display, the current flowing in the stator windings of the control transformer will induce emfs into the rotor by conventional transformer action, the magnitude of the emfs depending on the angular displacement between the rotor and the stators. The voltage output from the rotor is used as an error voltage for a phase conscious rectifier unit.

The ac supply fed to the synchro transmitter rotor is also used as a reference voltage, supplied to the transformer primary winding of the phase conscious rectifier. In the absence of an ac error voltage the output from the phase conscious rectifier would be zero, as top and bottom halves of the circuit provide equal and opposite voltages at the junction of R1 and R2.

The output from the phase conscious rectifier is fed via a dc amplifier to the power amplifier which provides current for the field windings of the servo motor. The power amplifier is of a differential configuration which, depending on the polarity of the dc voltage fed out from the phase conscious rectifier, will produce a rising value of current in one of the field windings, and a falling value in the other. As the field windings are wound in opposition to each other the dc voltage supplied to the servo motor armature will cause the servo motor to turn in either a clockwise or an anticlockwise direction. Should the ac error voltage output from the synchro control transformer be zero, there will be zero output from the phase conscious rectifier; the two field windings will have equal and opposite values of current flowing in them, thus causing their associated magnetic flux to cancel out, and the servo motor to remain stopped.

However, as the scanner drives the synchro transmitter rotor round, the angular displacement between the synchro control transformer rotor and the stators will induce an emf into the rotor as the magnetic field of the stators starts to rotate. The output from the rotor is applied to the phase conscious rectifier and, depending on phase (polarity) and magnitude, will upset the balance of the circuit. If the error voltage starts to rise in a positive direction D2 will conduct more and D1 less, and the output of the phase conscious rectifier will rise in a positive direction. Had the error voltage been negative D1 would have conducted more and D2 less, and the output would have fallen negatively. The loss of balance which causes the phase conscious rectifier to produce an output will cause the servo motor to turn in one direction or the other, depending on the polarity of the original error voltage, due to the current in the field windings no longer being equal and opposite. The servo motor turns the rotor of the synchro control transformer in an attempt to reduce the ac error voltage back to zero. If this situation was ever achieved the servo motor would stop once more. However, the scanner itself continues to turn the rotor of the synchro transmitter round and maintains an error voltage out from the synchro control transformer rotor; the servo motor chases round, continually trying to reduce the error to zero, and never succeeding. Consequently, the servo motor continues to turn at the same speed, and in the same direction as the scanner—the two are electrically locked together by means of the small error voltage which has to exist to keep the system turning.

Recent developments in marine radar have seen the bearing transmission system changed from the traditional electromechanical system to ones employing microprocessor control.

Scanner bearing information can be produced initially in analogue form by a sine/cosine resolver, and the sine and cosine components converted into digital form before being fed to the microprocessor. A reference voltage is fed to the rotor of the sine/cosine resolver which is turned by the scanner, inducing emfs into the stators as a voltage whose magnitude is the Reference value multiplied by Sine of the scanner bearing (angle) referenced to 'dead-ahead', and the Reference value multiplied by Cosine of the scanner bearing (angle), also reference to 'dead-ahead'. The microprocessor calculates from these digitised values the corresponding values of 'X' and 'Y' deflection current required to deflect the spot in the direction corresponding to the scanner bearing. Two digital-to-analogue converters at the processor output provide a pair of current driver stages with the information relating to the value of the current.

Alternatively, a spot of light produced by a semiconductor device provides pulses of light to a photo sensor when the beam is interrupted by a rotating, segmented optical encoder turning in synchronism with the scanner. A typical optical encoder will produce 2048 light pulses for every revolution made.

The light pulses are fed to a binary counter which, for every 360° of azimuth gives a count of logic level '1', corresponding to a denary count of:

1	1	1	1	1	1	1	1	1	1	1	1
2048	1024	512	256	128	64	32	16	8	4	2	1

4095 when all the numbers corresponding to logic '1' are added up.

If, for example, the pulses provided a system count of;

1	1	1	0	0	0	0	0	0	0	0	0
2048	1024	512	256	128	64	32	16	8	4	2	1

which in denary adds up to 3585,

it would correspond to a bearing of:

$$\frac{3585}{4095} \times 360° = 315°$$

The Heading line azimuth pulse at 000° is used to reset the counters back to zero, from where the count restarts. The bearing transmission systems described provide the minimum requirement for a display presentation of the 'unstabilised', Ship's head up type. All other display configurations and associated bearing transmission systems will be covered in Chapter 17.

12
Duplexing

To facilitate the use of a single scanner for both transmission and reception functions some form of transmit/receive switch must be incorporated into the rf head assembly. The requirement is that the switch connects the transmitter to the waveguide run during the period that a pulse is being radiated, and that the receiver be as completely isolated as is possible during transmission; while during the transmitter resting period the waveguide is connected to the receiver, enabling returning echoes to be detected. The physical constraints which accompany these requirements are: firstly, the switching change-over process must occur at high repetition rate (the same as the prf in use; i.e. possibly up to 4000 times per second).

Secondly, the accuracy of the switching process must be both high and reliable; any delay in isolating the receiver during transmission will damage the sensitive receiver, certainly destroying the crystals. At the very least, assuming that no damage occurred, the receiver would be paralysed to such an extent that it would be inoperable when echoes returned. Any delay in switching in the receiver immediately after transmission will result in the loss of close-range echoes. Any 'missed' switching cycle would either damage the receiver or cause the loss of echo returns from the preceding transmitter pulse.

Thirdly, an electronic switch must be employed as any physical/mechanical switch would be unsatisfactory if not impossible to engineer.

The device which meets this criteria employs the principle of a spark-gap, and is known as a T-R cell. By placing the cell in the waveguide across the entrance to the receiver, the path can be blocked to powerful microwave pulses. The cell consists of a short section of waveguide, sealed at both ends with windows of either glass or ceramic which are transparent to rf energy. The windows are matched with inductive irises to increase the bandwidth of the device. Inside the cell, spaced a quarter of a wavelength away from the window, two, truncated metal cones extend across the narrow dimension of the guide to form a spark-gap (Fig. 12.1). In the presence of a powerful pulse of microwave energy from the transmitter the cell ionises, and an arc is struck between the cones. As the arc is across the waveguide it is in effect short-circuited by the low impedance path afforded by the arc. When the transmitted pulse ceases the cell de-ionises, the arc is extinguished, and the short-circuit removed.

However, the gap would require regular adjustment as the arcing action erodes the cone surfaces, and its operating characteristics would change with time. By operating the spark-gap within a cavity the performance of the device can be improved. The sealed envelope is partially evacuated and filled with a low pressure gas of hydrogen, a halogen, or water vapour which ensures that the voltage at which the device operates can be reduced. It is imperative that the cell ionises and de-ionises as quickly as possible.

To speed up the ionisation process an additional source of electrons within the cell is required. This can be effected by the introduction of a radioactive isotope, or, more popularly, by the use of an auxiliary spark discharge from an additional electrode. The additional electrode, which takes the form of a short metal rod, introduced inside one of the truncated cones the end of which has been left open. By applying a 'keep-alive' voltage of approximately 1 kV to the electrode a small, permanent electrical discharge occurs in the vicinity of the cone tip. The discharge naturally generates noise, and the intensity of the discharge must be controlled such that the noise level does not become sufficient to degrade the sensitivity of the receiver. T-R cells employing radioactive isotopes naturally do not suffer from this problem. It is a well known fact that the voltage in a tuned circuit peaks when the circuit is at resonance. By placing metal baffles alongside the truncated cones to act as inductive elements, and employing the capacitive effect already brought about by the placement of the cones within the waveguide, a resonant filter can be produced. The effect of the filter is to increase the strength of the electric fields in the vicinity of the cones, which will further speed up the ionisation process.

By employing a second pair of truncated cones within the cell, this time without a 'keep-alive' electrode, a greater bandwidth can be produced than would be possible by the use of only a single pair. The second pair of cones is also supplemented with inductive matching irises to improve the bandwidth, and the assembly placed at the window nearest to the transmitter.

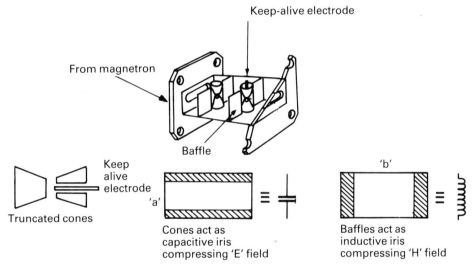

Fig. 12.1 TR cell

When subject to the high-power transmitter pulse, the gap with the 'keep-alive' electrode breaks down first, followed by the main discharge across the second pair of cones nearest to the transmitter. The combined attenuation provided by the T-R cell can be in the order of 80–100 dB.

The T-R cell is not a perfect switch, and a finite time must elapse between it being subjected to a transmitted pulse and the time it ionises. During this period a 'spike' of energy leaks through into the receiver, followed by a constant, very low level 'flat' portion. To minimise the effect of the leakage, a varactor diode limiter is incorporated into the waveguide at the receiver entrance. The varactor diode also offers protection to the receiver crystals when the equipment is switched off. In radars employing a 'keep-alive' voltage type T-R cell, the absence of the voltage renders the receiver crystals vulnerable to damage from high power pulses from adjacent radars, as in a congested anchorage for example. The varactor diode limits the amplitude of such pulses to within safe limits and no damage occurs. A small portion of the energy in the transmitted pulse is absorbed by the T-R cell discharge; typically 0.5–1 dB.

During the reception of echoes, the cell is de-ionised, the rf strength of the echo returns being far too weak to activate the cell. Although operating as a wide-band tuned circuit, the presence of the T-R cell in the waveguide does slightly attenuate the in-coming echoes due to an 'insertion loss' of between 0.5–1 dB. The working life of a T-R cell is in the region of several hundred hours, and is usually considered to be unsatisfactory when it no longer affords sufficient protection to the receiver crystals. On cells employing a 'keep-alive' voltage, the condition of the cell can be monitored by measuring the 'keep-alive' current. A cell in good condition would draw approximately 100μ amps.

Although it has been said that the T-R cell is placed across the waveguide which forms the entrance to the receiver, it is essential that the position of the cell does not interfere with the normal operation of the rf head by causing reflections in the guide when the cell is ionised.

Although open-wire feeders are not employed in marine radar they serve a purpose for the explanation of the principles of duplexing, and so will be referred to as such. The commonality between an open wire feeder and waveguide is illustrated in Chapters 5 and 8. The waveguide configuration can be arranged for either series or shunt duplexing. When shunt duplexing is employed the T-R cell is placed in parallel with the transmission line, and when series duplexing is used the T-R cell and receiver are connected as shown in Fig. 12.2.

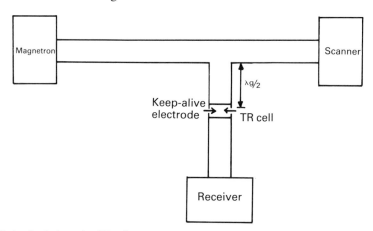

Fig. 12.2 Series Duplexing using TR cell

The distance between the T-R cell and the mouth of the receiver branch has to be calculated in odd multiples of $\lambda/2$, i.e. $\lambda/2$, $3\lambda/2$, $5\lambda/2$ etc. The use of $\lambda/2$ as such in 3 cm system would produce an unworkable dimension of 1.5 cm, hence the use of multiples. For the purpose of explanation, however, $\lambda/2$ will be employed. During the transmission of a pulse, the rf energy, assisted by either the radioactive isotope or the 'keep-alive' voltage, causes the T-R cell to ionise, producing a short-circuit across the waveguide. The short-circuit across the receiver input terminals ensures that nothing other than rf leakage through the switch enters the receiver (transmission breakthrough). The short-circuit, occurring $\lambda/2$ away from the entrance to the receiver branch, reflects a short-circuit across the entrance of the branch. Rf energy leaving the transmitter, therefore, 'sees' an electrically continuous path all the way to the scanner.

At the end of the transmitted pulse, the T-R cell de-ionises, opening the receiver branch in readiness for returning echoes. Although provision has been made in the design of the cell for a bandwidth, sufficiently wide to encompass all transmissions within the band, some T-R cells are manufactured with a tuneable cavity dimension. In either case, during the reception period, the T-R cell acts as an acceptor circuit to the in-coming echo returns.

(Tunable T-R cell; if this is incorrectly adjusted, long-range target returns will be lost. Such echoes would be considerably weaker than those from close-range targets, and would be lost if the cavity was not exactly on tune.)

Some thought has to be given to the routing of returned echoes to ensure that all their energy is directed into the receiver, and is not wasted travelling down the transmitter branch towards the magnetron. Two alternative approaches can be employed: the first is the use of a second cell; a T-B, or 'transmit block' cell, the second is the use of a 3-port circulator.

The T-B cell is similar in construction to the T-R cell, but differs in so far as it does not have a 'keep-alive' electrode or supply. The series duplexer shown in Fig. 12.2 could be modified to include a T-B cell as in Fig. 12.3.

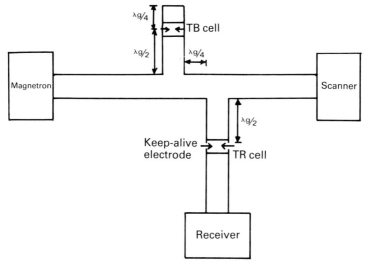

Fig. 12.3 Series Duplexing using TR and TB cells

During the transmission period both the T-R and the T-B cells ionise and reflect a short circuit λ/2 away at the entrances to the T-B and receiver branches of the waveguide. As before, electrical continuity is ensured between transmitter and scanner, and the receiver is protected.

It is during the reception period that the T-B aspect is employed. The intention is to place a block on the section of waveguide beyond the receiver branch, so that all echo energy has no alternative path other than the direct one into the receiver. With the T-B cell in a de-ionised state it can be disregarded. The physical short-circuit at the distant end of the T-B branch lies 3λ/4 away from the open mouth of the T-B branch, and thus reflects back as an open-circuit at the T-B branch mouth. However, the dimension between the T-B branch mouth and the receiver branch mouth is λ/4. The open-circuit reflected from the distant end of the T-B branch appears across the main waveguide run as a short-circuit due to the extra λ/4 distance involved. The reflected short-circuit is almost like a road block, leaving in-coming energy only one possible path, and ensuring that none of the energy is dissipated in the transmitter branch.

The second alternative method of performing this task is the use of a 3-port circulator, illustrated in Fig. 12.4.

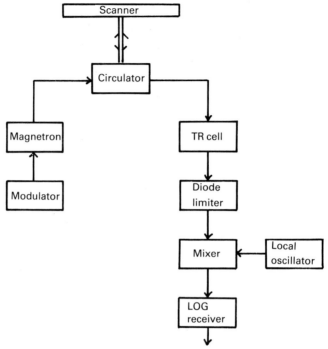

Fig. 12.4 The use of a circulator in duplexing

The circulator employs yttrium-iron-garnet ferrite, operating under the influence of magnetic field produced by a permanent magnet. The ferrite, being a dielectric, supports the propagation of electromagnetic energy, while the magnet provides a bias, the effect of which is to bring about a predictable gyroscopic precession of the electrons in the signal. The circulator has three ports, each spaced 120° apart. Energy entering port 1 is forced to leave only at port 2 due to the precession effect, and similarly energy entering port 2 leaves at port 3 only. By connecting the transmitter to port 1, the scanner to port 2 and the receiver to port 3, the transmitter branch and the receiver branch can be separated. In-coming echoes enter the circulator at port 2, and have no alternative but to leave at the next available exit port, i.e., into the receiver.

A T-R cell is still employed in the receiver branch as before.

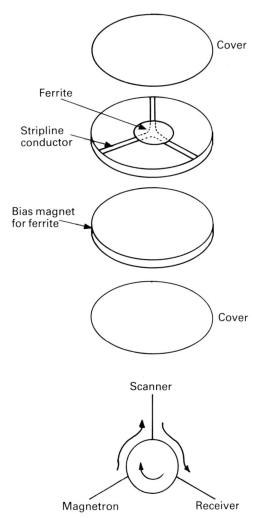

Fig. 12.5 Construction of a YIG circulator

13
Mixer Stage

Returned echoes are on the same frequency as that used for transmission by virtue of the echo being a reradiation of the transmitted pulse which, in 3 cm radar, is approximately 10 GHz. In a communication receiver, one of the first stages in the system is a radio frequency amplifier which, as well as performing more important tasks, prepares the signal for subsequent processing by providing a small amount of amplification.

Amplification at 10 GHz is possible, but is costly and somewhat complicated, i.e. cooled parametric amplifiers; hence in marine radar receivers the first stage is a mixer. The mixing process down-converts the echo frequency to one which can be amplified more easily by conventional techniques.

The rf echo and the frequency produced by a local oscillator are both fed to the mixer. For a mixing process to take place a non-linear device has to be employed as the mixer. A diode exhibits a non-linear resistance characteristic, and at frequencies in the 10 GHz band low capacitance, point contact, *p-n* junction crystal diode mixers are used, with additive mixing occurring due to the square law current/voltage characteristics. Multiplicative or additive mixing is not possible using transistors due to the transient time being too great, in addition to the excessive noise which would be introduced by them. Crystal diodes are normally constructed using silicon, polycrystalline doped with aluminium and a tungsten whisker, alternatively a titanium whisker may be used with N type germanium. The crystals may be encapsulated in cartridge, coaxial or capsule form as shown in Fig. 13.1, together with their mountings. A serviceable crystal should exhibit a back-to-front resistance ratio of at least 6:1. A low back-to-front resistance ratio will increase the noise level.

The rf echo and the local oscillator are frequency brought together in the mixer stage as separate frequencies which combine to produce at the output the 'sum' of the input frequencies and their 'difference' frequencies. If, for example, the echo frequency was that of a magnetron oscillating at a frequency of 9400 MHz (9.4 GHz), approximately in the middle of the 3 cm band, and the local oscillator frequency was slightly below this at 9340 MHz, the mixing process would produce a 'sum' frequency of 18 740 MHz (18.74 GHz) and a difference frequency of 60 MHz (0.6 GHz). As can be seen from this example, the 'sum' frequency is almost double that of the original frequency which itself was too high to process easily, whereas the 'difference' frequency of 60 MHz is sufficiently low to be amplified using devices and techniques commonly used in vhf equipment.

The 'difference' frequency of 60 MHz is known as the 'Intermediate frequency' (IF), and is of a value which has been adopted almost as a standard for the majority of marine radars. A third product is produced by the mixing process: a dc component, which is normally used to monitor the crystal current as an indication of mixer efficiency. One method of introducing the echo and the local oscillator frequencies is illustrated in Fig. 13.2.

A directional coupler is employed to bring the two inputs together. The directional

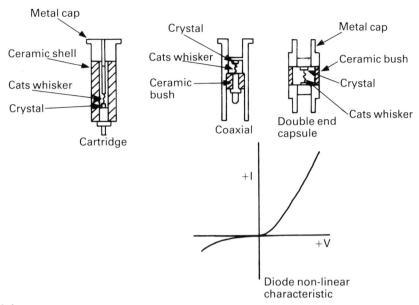

Fig. 13.1 Crystal diodes

coupler is formed by manufacturing two sections of waveguide joined together with a common broadside wall. Two apertures are drilled along the centre line, λ/4 apart. A signal propagating along the lower section of waveguide from left to right; some of which would enter the upper section of waveguide via the first aperture, the rest of the signal propagating towards the right. λ/4 later, part of the signal would couple into the upper section via the second aperture. Signals which have been propagating to the right will be in-phase when the signal coupling through the second aperture meets with that propagating in the upper section. The two signals combine and carry on propagating towards the mixer crystal. On the other hand, any signal which couples through the second aperture and propagates to the left will have travelled λ/2 by the time that it reaches the aperture on the extreme left and will be approximately equal in amplitude and 180° out of phase with the signal coupling through this aperture, and will thus cancel.

By using such a device the local oscillator output is prevented from reaching the scanner and being radiated, and conversely the echo does not pass down to the local oscillator thereby minimising the risk of frequency pulling. The use of automatic frequency control (afc) of the local oscillator would further minimise the risk of frequency pulling. The amplitude of the local oscillator output can be adjusted by

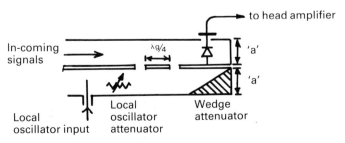

Fig. 13.2 Mixer stage

means of a variable attenuator to the required level, and any local oscillator signal which is not coupled up into the mixer chamber is dissipated by means of a wedge of graphite sand or a similar substance.

As the mixer is the first stage in the receiver, any noise it may produce has a very significant effect because of the subsequent amplification in the IF and video amplifiers. The noise at the mixer output is increased by the presence of noise originating in the local oscillator, which supplies to the mixer not only the desired sine wave of large amplitude, but also noise components of small amplitude in a broad band surrounding the oscillator frequency. Noise components at the signal and image frequencies are converted by the mixer into IF noise.

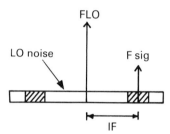

Fig. 13.3 Local oscillator and signal noise

The noise of a crystal mixer will increase as the rectified current produced by the local oscillator becomes greater. Therefore, for minimum noise temperature of the crystal, the local oscillator output and hence the crystal current should be at a minimum. However, the conversion gain (or efficiency) of a crystal mixer increases with the crystal current. This may be more easily shown against the increase in noise temperature with crystal current, by showing the variation of conversion loss (the reciprocal of conversion gain) with crystal current in Fig. 13.4. This shows that there is an optimum setting for the crystal current.

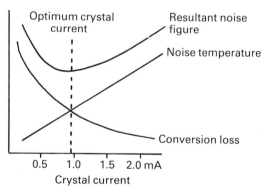

Fig. 13.4 Crystal current setting

13.1   The balanced mixer hybrid ring or rat race

The main advantage of the balanced mixer over the single ended mixer is a reduction of local oscillator noise fed to the IF amplifiers. This is brought about by the use of two crystal mixers, spaced λ/2 apart, which cause the local oscillator noise to appear anti-phase and thereby cancel.

A transmission line of a type known as 'stripline' is used to form a hybrid ring, sometimes known as a 'rat-race'. The stripline is a photo-etched printed circuit encapsulated between two layers of insulation, the whole being sandwiched between two brass plates. The complete triplate arrangement exhibits the normal transmission line characteristics (Fig. 13.5).

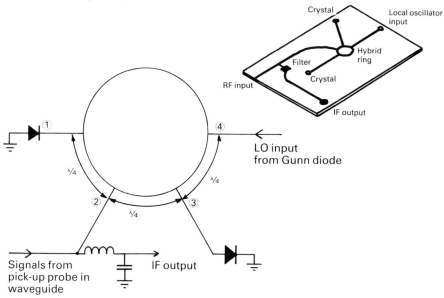

Fig. 13.5 Hybrid ring balanced mixer

The rf (echo) signal is fed in to the ring at arm 2. The energy divides on entry to the ring, one half proceeding in a clockwise direction, the other half anticlockwise. At arm 1 the voltages will be in phase and a standing wave antinode will occur; the same occurring at arm 3. At arm 4 the path length difference is $\lambda/2$, hence there will be a voltage node. From this it can be seen that the signal frequency appears at arms 1 and 3 in phase, but cancels at arm 4. This ensures that the echo signals do not enter into the local oscillator. The local oscillator energy from arm 4 sets up standing waves in a similar manner, and appears at arms 1 and 3 in anti-phase (voltage antinode). Furthermore, the noise appearing at these two points is also anti-phase. This relationship is shown in Fig. 13.6.

At the much lower IF of typically 60 MHz produced by the diodes the stripline acts as an ordinary conductor, since the wavelength at this frequency is very much greater than the dimension of the stripline. The detected signals applied to the conductor are in phase and add together, providing the IF output via an L/C rf filter. The local oscillator noise signals are in anti-phase and subtract resulting in a very much improved noise figure when compared with the single ended mixer.

For many years low-power versions of the reflex klystron were employed as the local oscillator in marine radars, but their inherent high noise level proved a problem. The development of the Gunn device as a solid state replacement offered a low noise alternative which is now almost universally employed (Fig. 13.8). The Gunn device (usually referred to as a diode because it is a two-terminal device), is a gallium arsenide semiconductor (GaAs) device which produces a train of current pulses at a repetition rate determined by the physical dimensions of the diode. The current pulses

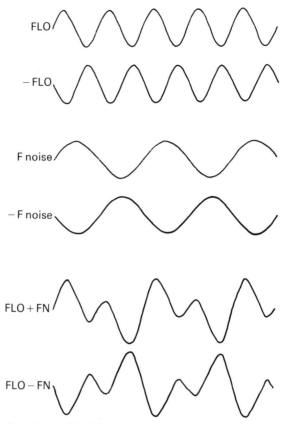

Fig. 13.6 Noise cancellation in a double mixer

are formed by electrons travelling as a bunch across the diode junction from cathode to anode when a threshold voltage (typically 7.2 volts) is applied across the junction.

The make up of the device employs different energy bands across which bunches of electrons, known as domains, move with a constant velocity of 10.7 cm/s when subjected to a field from a low voltage supply. The prf of the device is determined

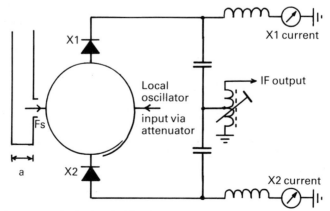

Fig. 13.7 Crystal current monitoring in a double mixer

primarily by the distance between cathode and anode, with a separation of 10 microns producing pulses at 10 GHz. By placing the device inside a resonant cavity it is possible to build up oscillations by supplying current pulses from the diode. The rf oscillatory voltage in the cavity alternately adds and subtracts from the dc supply (bias) voltage. On negative-going swings the voltage drives the diode below threshold level and delays the production of the next current pulse until the elapse of the transit period.

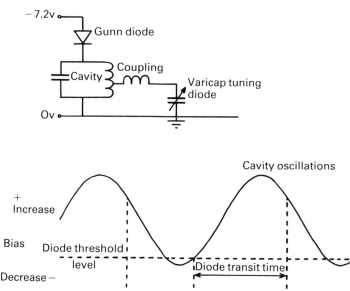

Fig. 13.8 Gunn diode local oscillator

The frequency of the Gunn assembly can be varied by incorporating a varactor diode within the cavity giving a tuning range of approximately 80 MHz. The varactor diode bias voltage is variable by adjusting the front panel 'tune' control. By adjustment of this control the local oscillator frequency can be made to differ from the magnetron frequency (which cannot be changed) by an amount which is equal to the exact IF frequency. Because the radar employs a tuned receiver, any other frequency combination produced by the mixer other than the correct IF will not be accepted, and the display will contain only noise (grass) and no targets. The use of an automatic frequency control (afc) circuit to adjust the varactor tuning voltage will keep the local oscillator apart in frequency (equal to the IF) from the magnetron as the magnetron frequency changes: during initial warm-up, and with age. It should be noted that constant necessity for readjustment of the tuning control to maintain the presence of long range targets may be indicative of possible magnetron failure. Course tuning of the cavity can be effected by means of a pre-set (factory aligned) inductive screw penetrating the cavity so as to compress the oscillatory *H* field inside. The cavity is coupled to a short section of waveguide through an aperture, or probe to deliver power, in the region of 2 mW, to the mixer.

14
Receiver

14.1 Noise and bandwidth considerations

The echoes returned from long range targets will, naturally, be very weak and therefore a high sensitivity receiver is required to pick them up. The sensitivity of a radar receiver will, therefore, contribute to determining the maximum range of the equipment. Selectivity, which is a problem in communication receivers, does not become a problem in radar receivers because the radar is a time-measuring device, spending most of its time in the quiescent state. It is virtually impossible for one ship to display the echoes of another ship's radar, and only limited interference is experienced from their transmissions. The overriding consideration is that of noise, for it is the level of the noise floor which will determine whether or not an echo can be detected. If the noise floor is high the echo will be lost, if it is low the same echo will be detected. Unlike a communication receiver a microwave radar receiver is unaffected by atmospheric noise, but suffers from internally generated noise or noise induced into it from adjacent machinery.

Noise comes from many sources:

Thermal agitation

The random movement of free electrons in a conductor averages out at zero. However, if random movement is studied at a particular instant it is likely that there will be a greater number of electrons moving in one direction than in the other. This constitutes a tiny current which flows through the internal resistance of the conductor and sets up small voltages called noise. Analysis of noise generated in this way shows that it is composed of frequencies which lie across the whole spectrum. An increase in temperature aggravates the random noise, and the voltage is increased. Thermal noise can be minimised by good ventilation and by keeping all conductors as short as possible.

Shot effect

This is particularly troublesome in amplifiers, and is caused by tiny variations in the number of charge carriers crossing the device. If the quiescent current through an amplifier is measured it will appear to be steady. However, if this current was magnified it would be found to have minute fluctuations which constitute noise. The fluctuations of current flow through the amplifier load resistor and develop small voltages across it which are then passed on to the next stage and thus amplified. Reduction of shot noise is mainly a function of production cost; i.e. the design of special components such as transistors in which the impurity doping atoms are evenly distributed throughout the semiconductor material.

Unsuppressed electrical machinery

Such equipment will radiate noise which may affect the power cables supplying the equipment. All cables interconnecting with the radar should have L/C noise filters fitted. Insufficient screening of sensitive areas in units and inadequate decoupling will permit the direct pick-up of noise. Noise generated in the first stage of the receiver is the most troublesome as it will receive the maximum amplification afforded by the receiver.

The background speckle seen on analogue displays is composed mainly of noise which has been generated in the early stages of the receiver. Noise generated in later stages does not receive as much amplification and is, therefore, not as big a problem.

During the design of a radar, the following steps are normally taken to minimise inherent noise in the receiver:

1 The radiation resistance of the scanner is carefully matched to the waveguide, and the input impedance to the mixer stage.
2 Local oscillator noise cannot be suppressed at source, but, by using a balanced mixer in which there are two crystals back-to-back, in a hybrid ring, it is possible to reinforce the echo content from each crystal whilst cancelling out the noise content. The use of a Gunn device as the local oscillator produces less noise than a reflex klystron.
3 The first IF amplifier following the mixer is very often a cascode configuration, in which a pair of amplifiers are connected to give twice the gain but without any significant increase in noise.

   Only in recent years have transistors, suitable for use in 'X' Band pre-amps become available, these being low-noise, dual gate FETs.

   All interconnections are short and direct. Parallel runs of sensitive wires are avoided, and layout is arranged to limit the direct coupling between wires. Each stage is independently screened with its own earth point to chassis.
4 In general, all noise sources produce frequencies of a very wide spectrum, hence a very narrow bandwidth will reject most of them and thus improve the signal:noise ratio. The s/n ratio is a measure of signal power compared to noise power at any point in the receiver. It must always be better than unity for an echo signal to be clearly painted on the display. If the s/n ratio at the output of the receiver is compared with the s/n ratio at the input, then the ratio of output/input is called the Noise figure;

$$\text{Noise figure (overall)} = F1 + \frac{F2 - 1}{G1} + \frac{F3 - 1}{G1\ G2} + \frac{F4 - 1}{G1\ G2\ G3} \text{ etc.}$$

Example:
If three identical cascaded stages, each have a gain of 10, and a noise figure of 3, then the overall noise figure would be

$$3 + \frac{3 - 1}{10} + \frac{3 - 1}{10 \times 10} = 3.22$$

This shows the importance of ensuring a low-noise first stage in the amplifier chain.

The expression for the overall noise of a multistage amplifier indicates that provided the gain of each stage is high, then the majority of the noise in the output is contributed by the first stage. Radar receivers, therefore, pay particular attention to the design of the early stages. These features, as well as those already noted, included mounting the first IF amplifier as close to the mixer crystal as possible, and making the head amplifier part of the crystal mixer/local oscillator assembly.

14.2   Bandwidth

Noise consists of frequencies spread right across the spectrum. The effects of noise can be minimised by keeping the bandwidth of the amplifiers as narrow as possible. Unfortunately, the rectangular pulses offered to the receiver as echoes are composed of many sine waves, and in order to ensure the pulse shape and presentation accuracy the shape of the pulse must be maintained. This requires an increase in the receiver bandwidth to accommodate the 'infinite' number of sine waves, known as harmonics (mainly the 'odd' harmonic series). Fourier analysis of the pulse shows the fundamental ac component as having the same frequency as the pulse prf, and the amplitude of successive harmonics decreases according to a sinusoidal function.

The frequency spectrum of a carrier wave of 9400 MHz modulated by a rectangular pulse shape is shown in Fig. 14.1.

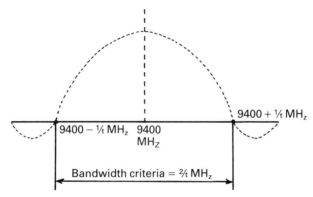

Fig. 14.1   Modulation of rf with square pulses

The spectrum of the pulse train has its first zero amplitude point at a frequency $1/t$ MHz, in which t is the pulse duration (δ). Marine radars usually have a bandwidth to accommodate all the harmonics up to the first zero amplitude point. It can be shown that the spectrum of the transmitted pulse comprises the carrier frequency plus the video spectrum and the carrier frequency minus the video spectrum. As a consequence, the bandwidth is given by $2/\delta$ MHz, centred on the carrier frequency. An increase in the bandwidth in an attempt to preserve the pulse shape results in a lower gain and an increase in noise. In a single stage amplifier, the gain bandwidth product remains constant for that amplifier. Therefore, doubling the bandwidth will half the gain. If, for example, an amplifier had a gain bandwidth product of 100 000. Then, with a gain of 50, the bandwidth would be 2 kHz; and conversely if the gain was reduced to 10, the bandwidth would increase to 10 kHz. A compromise is reached where the IF bandwidth is set at $1.2/\delta$ Hz, where δ is the narrowest pulse length used in an attempt to give a reasonable representation of the pulse whilst at the same time minimising the effects of noise. A pulse duration δ of 0.08μ seconds given an IF bandwidth of 15 MHz.

The IF bandwidth being set at, as in the example, 15 MHz to allow for the worst possible case, the bandwidth of the video amplifier stages is usually made switchable with pulse duration. When short pulse duration is selected the video amplifier bandwidth is made as wide as possible: typically 8 MHz. The reasoning behind this is that short pulse transmission will be employed on short ranges where the need for good range discrimination and high definition are paramount. If the bandwidth was any less than this, not all of the harmonics would be received, and the pulse leading and trailing edges would become less steep, and the echoes on an analogue display would be less sharp on the ranges where this factor is critical. The very wide bandwidth on the shortest ranges will naturally result in a reduction of amplifier gain, but this is insignificant as the target echo returns from close-by targets will be at their strongest.

On long ranges, long pulse lengths are transmitted, for example $\delta = 1\mu$ second, to give maximum energy to the pulse ($Pt \times \delta$ J). The use of long pulses means that the video amplifier bandwidth can be reduced accordingly to typically, 500 kHz, thereby reducing the noise level and increasing the gain in readiness to receive weak echo returns from long range targets.

14.3 Logarithmic amplifier

Targets at close range will return echoes which are very strong, while those from distant, long-range targets will be very weak. The two extremes of signal strength describe the dynamic range to which a radar receiver IF amplifier will be subjected during normal operation. Because the dynamic range is so large it would cause a problem if a conventional linear amplifier were to be employed for signal processing. Such a linear amplifier would be saturated by close-by echo returns and clutter, and it would be more than likely that the sea clutter (swept gain) control would have to be adjusted regularly to prevent this occurring. In the hands of an expert radar engineer the combination of a linear receiver and swept gain would provide the best results of all. However, the radar is usually in the hands of a navigator who does not have the time to devote to such mundane tasks.

Logarithmic amplifiers have a large dynamic range, typically 95 dB with a transfer characteristic of 20 dB/volt, and so can handle the full range of very weak, through to very strong, signals without the risk of saturation. The amount of gain, or amplification a signal receives depends on its strength, with very weak signals receiving the full receiver gain while strong signals do not receive as much. In other words, the receiver has a logarithmic response, with the gain decreasing automatically as saturation is approached.

A logarithmic amplifier usually consists of several cascaded stages, each having a logarithmic gain characteristic so that the output follows approximately; $V_0 \times \log V_{in}$. A video detector is provided at the output of each stage, the outputs from each stage being summed together.

Figure 14.3 shows a schematic diagram representing a logarithmic receiver. A weak signal, one coming from a long range target, would be amplified by each of the four stages in succession, each stage providing a video output level which contributes to the total video output. As the signal strength increases, the last stage of the amplifier chain would saturate first, leaving only three stages of amplification. A further increase could result in stages three and four being saturated, allowing only stages one and two to provide amplification, etc.

If it is assumed that each of the four amplifier stages had a saturated output of 1 volt, and a gain of 10, then the amplifier response to a range of signal level from $100\mu V$ up to 100 mV would be as shown in Table 14.1.

In a modern radar the logarithmic amplifier is in integrated circuit form, the bandwidth switched filters being placed midway along the chain.

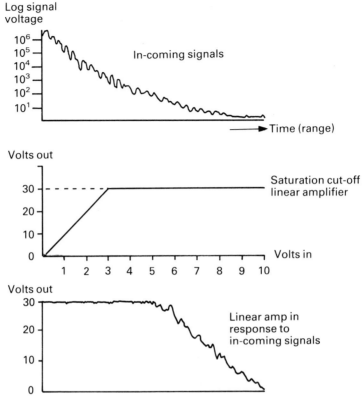

Fig. 14.2A   Linear receiver amplifier response to incoming signals

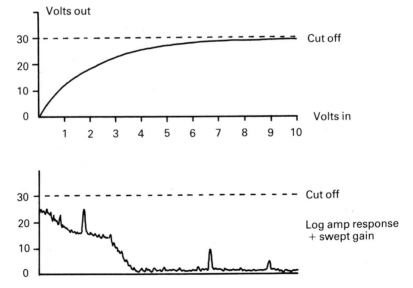

Fig. 14.2B   Logarithmic receiver amplifier response

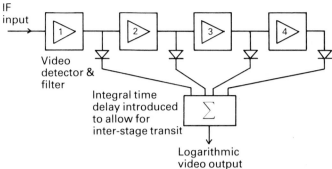

Fig. 14.3 Logarithmic receiver

Table 14.1

IF *i/p*	*O/P* 1	*O/P* 2	*O/P* 3	*O/P* 4	Σ total
100μV	1 mV	10 mV	100 mV	1 V (sat)	≈ 1 volt
1 mV	10 mV	100 mV	1 V (sat)	1 V (sat)	≈ 2 volt
10 mV	100 mV	1 V (sat)	1 V (sat)	1 V (sat)	≈ 3 volt
100 mV	1 V (sat)	1 V (sat)	1 V (sat)	1 V (sat)	4 volt

14.4 Video

The video detector, sometimes referred to as the 'second detector' (the first detector being the mixer stage) is, in modern radar equipment, an integral part of a dedicated integrated circuit which also performs the function of the logarithmic amplifier. In older equipment, the video detector takes the form of a conventional 'envelope detector' of the style used in a.m. radio receivers. The purpose of the video detector is to convert the pulses of 60 MHz IF which represent target echo returns into pulses of negative-going dc voltage, which are called 'video'. The time duration of each detected video pulse corresponds exactly to the 60 MHz IF pulses, and their amplitude to that of the returned echo, with short range targets returning strong echoes, and long range targets returning weak ones. The amplitude of the dc pulses has to be controlled in the video amplifier which follows the receiver, by means of a video limiter to prevent overloading of the picture tube. The echo returns can cover a range of between 40–60 dBs (power gain of 10 000–1 000 000). As the picture tube can only handle brilliance changes within a range of approximately 12 dB (power gain of approximately 16) the signal amplitude has to be compressed to within this limit. The most obvious way of doing this is to cut off all signals above a predefined amplitude; this is known as video limiting. Maladjustment of this control will result if strong targets defocused on the display whilst weaker signals appear normal; this is due to the overloading of the video amplifier. It is at this point in the signal processing chain that the video is subjected to a fast time constant 'rain clutter' control. A pictorial representation of this circuit action is shown in Section 2.13.

14.5 Automatic frequency control

A linear amplifier connected in parallel with the logarithmic amplifier input may be used to provide a sample of the IF to a discriminator where it is compared with a reference frequency for use in an automatic frequency control circuit. The automatic frequency control circuit, as well as providing a tuning voltage to the local oscillator to ᴋᴄᴇp it below the incoming signal frequency by an amount equal to the IF, may also be used to provide a front panel visual tuning indicator. Such an indicator may take the form of an analogue meter, a 'magic eye', or a light emitting diode, the brilliance of which increases when on-tune.

14.6 Swept gain

A trigger pulse, produced by taking a sample of the modulator pulse fed to the magnetron, is applied to the receiver to either gate-off the amplifier chain during transmission, or to apply reverse bias conditions to the first stages on the chain —which prevents receiver paralysis resulting from leakage of the transmitted pulse through the T-R cell. In some equipment the swept gain (sea clutter) facility is provided at this point. The swept gain facility may be of a manual type as already described in Section 2.10, or it may be of an automatic 'dynamic' type, where the gain of the amplifier is adjusted automatically to confine the control only to areas where sea clutter exists. As the degree of sea clutter may not be uniform around the ship the circuit will adjust the gain according to the averaged signal strength—rather like an a.m. receiver's automatic gain control which compensates for general signal fading. An example of this operation is illustrated in Fig. 14.4.

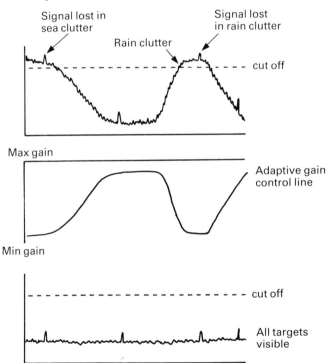

Fig. 14.4 Adaptive gain control

The detected video signal from the receiver is today referred to as 'raw video'. It is at this point in the story that the major split between analogue and digital radar systems becomes apparent. In an analogue system the raw video signal is mixed with all the calibration, heading marker and power monitor signals, to produce a 'composite video' (not to be confused with the same terminology used in television and video engineering, where it refers to a video signal mixed with sync pulses) and applied as a negative-going signal to the cathode of a crt to intensity modulate the electron beam. By making the crt cathode negative with respect to the grid a greater number of electrons in the beam pass through the grid aperture to increase the brilliance of the light spot on the crt screen. Chapter 15 refers.

An analogue radar employing a ppi display with a conventional timebase deflection system will drive the spot of light across the radius of the tube face at a speed relating to the displayed range. If, for example a 406 mm (16 in) diameter picture tube is used, the radius being 203 mm (8 in), when the 0.5 mile range is selected the 203 mm represent 0.5 miles, and the timebase will deflect the spot across the screen in 6.1μ seconds ($0.5 \times 12.2\mu$ seconds). When the same picture tube is used to represent the 48 mile range, the 203 mm now has to be scanned by the light spot in 585.6μ seconds ($48 \times 12.2\mu$ seconds) which is 96 times slower. This, together with the fact that the 'paint' length of the same target will decrease as progressively higher ranges are selected (a target paint may measure, for example 4 mm on a short range, but only 0.25 mm on a long range—assuming the target can still be discerned at the longer range). It will also combine to produce a display the brilliance and contrast of which change from range to range. Such a display is best observed in shaded conditions, either by the use of a daylight viewing hood placed over the tube, or using a darkened room or curtained-off section of the bridge. Whichever method has been chosen in the past, none of them provide for what is termed 'Daylight viewing'. Daylight viewing enables more than one person to view the same screen simultaneously under normal light conditions, with the exception of direct sun. A modern radar employing digital signal processing overcomes these problems and provides 'daylight viewing' as just one of the many advantages offered over an analogue system.

14.7 Digital video

The problems inherent in an analogue system, where the picture brilliance changes from range to range due to the crt spot speed, and the associated timebase velocity required for each range alters the 'step' to 'ramp' ratio (Chapter 16) which in turn creates problems in timebase alignment, can be overcome by the use of 'retimed video'. Retimed video uses a constant timebase sweep for all radar ranges, and relies on feeding the video information to the crt at a rate different to that at which it is received. To achieve this, the in-coming video is 'stored' (written) into memory at the correct rate during the 'real time' that it is being received. The stored video data is then read out from the memory during the time period of the timebase scan.

The concept of retimed video

The 'raw' video signal is fed to a comparator, where its amplitude is compared to a reference 'threshold potential'. If the raw video amplitude exceeds the threshold potential the video is recognised as a target, and the comparator output goes to logic level '1'. The logic level '1' is then held in a latch. The contents of the latch will subsequently be written into memory by a clock pulse. As the comparator is receiving a constant stream of video information which has to be compared against the threshold potential—and the clock pulse operates on a cycle—there is a need to latch the comparator output to ensure that no video is lost between consecutive clock pulses. If a target has been recognised (by the comparator) a logic '1' will be written into RAM from the latch by the clock pulse. Where no signal has been recognised the comparator output will be logic '0', consequently logic '0' will be written into memory by the clock pulse.

At the instant that a pulse is transmitted a 'range gate' pulse is initiated, the duration of which, determined by the range in use, is the normal ranging period (12.2μ second per mile × selected radar range in miles). The 'range gate' provides the 'write enable' for the RAM and also enables the 'write' clock pulse. The clock pulse frequency is a function of the range in use, often being derived by a divider circuit linked to the radar selector switch. It is set so, that by the end of the write gate the whole of the 1 K RAM has been addressed. Each clock pulse increments the address counter by one, so that the in-coming video is written into an address which corresponds to its time of arrival, and therefore, its range. As each piece of target information is separately addressed in a time/range sequence, it is said to be stored in a range cell.

At the end of the 'range gate' period, the fixed timebase scan is started, and at the same time the 'read gate' pulse is initiated. The read gate pulse has a fixed time duration (the same as the timebase scan) during which the read clock pulse has to read the whole of the RAM contents. The address counter increments are the same as during the write cycle so that the data is read out in the same sequence in which it was written, i.e. in correct range sequence.

In practice, the 'raw' analogue signal is converted into a digital signal by applying it to two (three or even four) comparators. The in-coming 'raw' video signal amplitude is compared against a threshold potential, with each of the comparators having progressively higher thresholds.

A signal the amplitude of which exceeds the threshold potential is passed as a logic level '1', to be latched and stored in a random access memory (RAM). If only one comparator was used to digitise the video all echoes would be displayed with the same intensity regardless of their origin, be it yacht, rain drop or ocean liner. By using two, three or four comparators it is possible to display targets with a brilliance which reflects the true size of the target. Where three comparators are used, the binary digits '00' are used for no video, '01' for video exceeding threshold 1, '10' for video exceeding threshold 2, and '11' for video exceeding threshold 3. The two bits are stored in two RAMs as already described. The threshold potentials are variable in accordance with the setting of the video gain and sea-clutter control circuit. As the 'raw' video output from the receiver will contain both echoes (returned from targets) and noise, both of which appear as signals when viewed on an oscilloscope, randomly varying in amplitude with time, it will only be signals whose amplitude rises above the detection threshold level which will be processed. Thus processing noise (grass) can be removed from the signal.

It is possible, under certain conditions, for noise to be mistaken as a true echo, possibly because the detection threshold has been set too low. When this occurs, the mistake is known as a 'False alarm' for obvious reasons, and the use of a receiver employing adaptive gain as illustrated in Figure 14.1 will eradicate the problem. Failure to do this will result in a 'constant false alarm rate' occurring which, for computer controlled tracking of targets (as in an ARPA system), could render the processor paralysed and unable to process the vast range of apparent 'targets' from, for example, sea clutter returns.

The digitised video is stored by 'writing' it into RAM in real time (real time being the interval corresponding to the radar range in use, and not to the fixed timebase period), and 'reading' the stored data out from memory during the fixed timebase scan period. To achieve this, the clock frequency used for the read and write cycles must differ as in the example:

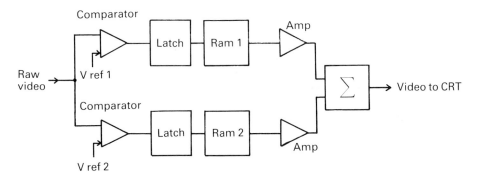

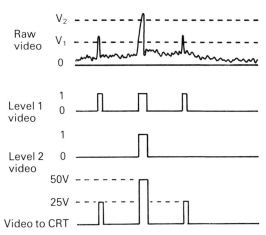

Fig. 14.5 Multiple level video

RAM size: 1 K Bit
Display range: 6 miles
Fixed timebase scan: 150μ seconds.

6 miles at 12.2μ seconds per mile = 73.2μ seconds
A 1 K Bit RAM capacity is 1024 bits.
Therefore, in a time interval of 73.2μ seconds, 1024 bits of information have to be stored in the memory.
The 'write' clock frequency must therefore equal

$$\frac{1024}{73.2\mu s} = 14 \, \text{MHz}$$

The time interval during which this same amount of data can be read out is fixed at 150μ seconds, therefore the 'read' clock frequency must equal,

$$\frac{1024}{150\mu s} = 6.82 \, \text{MHz}$$

As the display range is decreased the 'write' period is increased pro-rata, but the 'read' period remains the same. As a consequence video signals are contracted on ranges greater than the selected timebase scan period, and expanded on ranges below this. They can only be normalised when the equipment is operating on the range of the timebase scan period being used.

The RAMs are typically 1 K Bit capacity, with two being used for each of the comparator video outputs. Each memory can, therefore, be operated at half of the read/write frequency. By multiplexing the video on the write cycle prior to latching, and demultiplexing the memory output on the read cycle it is possible to achieve a 4-phase mode. This not only has the effect of substantially enhancing the short range resolution of the display, but also has appears to increase the memory size. Because, on short ranges, the timebase scan period is much slower than would normally have been the case of an analogue display, the targets can be painted much brighter than previously possible. On long ranges the pulse length is artificially lengthened (pulse stretching) again to provide a bright display; although this function does not apply to targets which are near ownship, in order to maintain definition and so as not to enhance the sea clutter in the immediate vicinity. The display can be further brightened by rereading the stored video two or even three times, repainting the same screen phosphor with the same information during the 'dead time' interval before the next transmission pulse. The phosphor material integrates the brilliance of the repainted targets, producing a very bright display which can be viewed under normal daylight conditions.

The technique of storing two successive scans of video in separate memories, and using a correlation technique at the memory outputs during the 'read' cycle, makes it possible to detect and remove anything other than legitimate radar targets. This enables interference signals to be removed from the display. Only the echoes returned from 'real' targets would be present at precisely the same range on two successive scans, whereas interference signals, which are random in nature would appear at different ranges on each of the scans.

Both the interference and wanted echoes, having both been converted into logic levels '1' and '0' can, during the 'read' cycle, be checked against one another. If the two RAMs' output levels are simultaneously at '1' or '0' the signals correlate to reflect a legitimate target, whereas if one RAM output was at '1' when the other is at '0' (or vice-versa) the signals do not correlate, and are subsequently suppressed and not displayed.

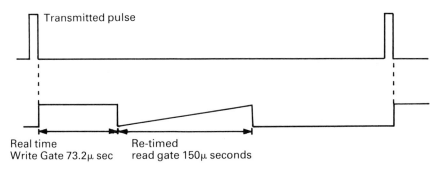

Real time
Write Gate 73.2μ sec

Re-timed
read gate 150μ seconds

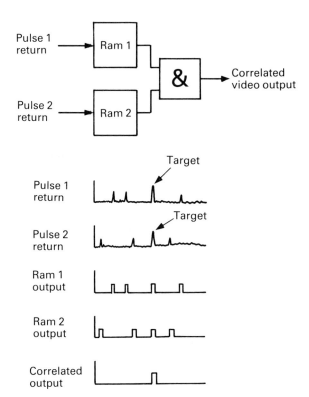

Fig. 14.6 Re-timed video and correlation

15
Cathode Ray Tube (ppi display)

At the time of writing, the lion's share of the marine radar market uses the cathode ray tube (crt) as the display screen, either in the form of a conventional ppi (plan position indicator—Chapter 1), or in newer equipment as a rasterscan display. A minority use liquid crystal displays, these being mainly in the small craft market. The tubes used for ppi and raster scan displays (together with their deflection requirements) differ in several ways and will, therefore, be discussed in separate chapters. Chapter 19 refers to raster scan displays (Fig. 15.1).

The cathode ray tube can be thought of as being in three sections:

1 an electron gun assembly;
2 a beam deflection system;
3 a fluorescent screen.

The electron gun assembly is enclosed under high vacuum conditions inside a glass envelope. Thermionic emission is used to produce the electrons which are used to form the beam. A non-inductively wound heater (which prevents the magnetic field normally associated with a conventional heater element disturbing the electrons) is placed inside, and used to raise the temperature of a nickel cylinder called the cathode. The end of the cathode nearest to the screen is closed, and coated with a material which will readily emit electrons when heated. Strontium or barium oxide are two popular coatings used for this purpose.

The indirectly heated cathode will emit electrons at approximately 1000° K. The electrons will be drawn by electrostatic attraction down the length of the envelope towards the screen in a beam by the application of a very high positive potential. A second closed cylinder is placed concentrically over the cathode cylinder to control the number of electrons in the beam. Known as the 'grid' the closed cylinder has a small hole drilled into the end through which all the electrons have to pass. The number of electrons which are allowed to pass through the grid aperture is controlled by the relative potentials of both the grid and the cathode. Both grid and cathode are kept at negative potentials, the grid potential being variable between, typically, -15 to -100 volts. When the grid is made more negative with respect to the cathode fewer electrons are able to pass through the aperture, and conversely when the grid is made less negative with respect to the cathode a greater number of electrons can pass through.

The number of electrons in the beam determines the brilliance of the spot of light, with the brightest spot being obtained when the greatest number of electrons pass through the grid, and the dimmest when only a few pass through. By feeding negative-going video signals to the cathode with respect to the grid, the effect is the same as making the grid less negative, thus allowing more electrons through the grid to create a brighter spot. In this way, the video signal intensity modulates the electron beam to produce bright spots of light which are coincident with target echoes. The control which varies the grid voltage is, therefore, called the 'brilliance' control.

A positive-going rectangular voltage, the 'bright-up' pulse is superimposed on the grid voltage to brighten the display during the timebase scan period. The display is blanked in between scans.

The electron beam leaving the grid aperture is on a converging path for a short distance, after which the electrons start to diverge once more after passing a cross-over point. The diverging electrons are focused into a beam by means of either a magnetic field applied from an external coil assembly, or an electrostatic field produced internally by potentials applied to cylindrical anodes placed axially along the beam path. Electrostatic focusing is the more common of the two methods, and relies on the potential difference between the first (that nearest to the electron gun assembly) and the second anode (the anode nearest to the screen). The second anode potential must be more positive (with respect to the cathode) than the first anode, with typical potentials being for anode one +150 volts and for anode two +15 to 20 kV. The final anode voltage is determined by the size of the tube, larger tubes employing higher voltages. The relative potentials set up an electrostatic field inside the space between the two anode cylinders, which both accelerates the electron beam and at the same time drives the electrons back into a converging beam which is brought to a focal point on the tube face (screen). The focal point may be adjusted by alteration of the first anode potential, the second anode being internally linked to the eht connector the applied potential of which is a fixed value.

The inner surface of the tube face is coated with two layers or coatings of chemicals. The focused electron beam strikes the first coating of a phosphor material which becomes luminous under bombardment and is said to be fluorescent. The luminescence is prolonged by the phosphorescence of the second coating, an effect known as the 'afterglow'.

Because of the very high positive potential which attracts the electrons the length of the tube, the electrons strike the screen with an appreciable velocity (20–30 thousand miles/second) and force. Their impact dislodges other electrons from the screen by way of secondary emission, and a static charge builds up on the screen face. If left to

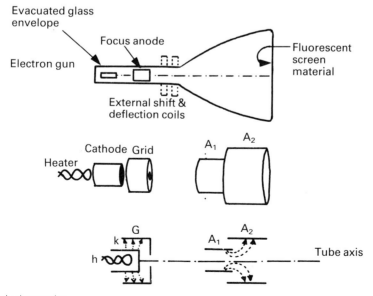

Fig. 15.1 Cathode ray tube

build up the static charge would reach a point where it would repel any further electrons and the beam would be cutoff. To prevent this happening an aquadag coat is applied around the bowl of the tube. Being a graphite material it provides a return path for the electrons back to the power supply unit.

The high vacuum conditions inside the tube present an implosion risk should the envelope be damaged. When handling picture tubes a face visor and leather gloves/apron is considered sensible attire. The point where the crt neck joins the bowl is particularly vulnerable, and under no circumstances should a crt be picked up or moved by holding only the neck. Care should also be taken when removing a crt, a task which ideally should only be done in port when the vessel presents a stable platform on which to work, to avoid knocking or exerting undue force on the tube neck. The glass at the tube face is relatively thick, but can be substantially weakened if scratched by, for example, a diamond ring. Should the tube implode, try to avoid breathing in the dust which may contain beryllium.

A defective tube should be disposed of by repacking it in its original carton and sending it ashore to a responsible disposal authority.

16
Shift and deflection

16.1 Shift

The light spot produced must be positioned exactly in the centre of the screen (this is of particular importance when using a relative motion, ship's head-up display presentation, and reliance is being placed on a mechanical bearing cursor). Despite the precision and care taken in the manufacturing process it is possible that the beam may not be exactly centralised, and in addition when the tube is placed in the equipment it is possible that external magnetic fields—including those of the earth itself—could pull the beam off-centre. Protection against the effects of any external magnetic field is provided by placing the tube inside a magnetic screen in the display unit.

To centralise the light spot, two pairs of coils are positioned at right angles relative to one another around the neck of the tube. Through each pair of coils flows a steady direct current the flow of which can be varied in magnitude. The coils are wound so that each pair provides a magnetic field across the inside of the tube neck acting at right angles to each other. By definition, a moving stream of electrons forms an electric current. When viewed from above, an electron leaving the cathode and heading upwards towards the screen (or out of this page) will be surrounded by a magnetic field turning in an anticlockwise direction. If one of the pair of coils produces an external magnetic field running down the page with North at the top and South at the bottom, the interaction between the two magnetic fields will drive the spot across to the right; and conversely, if the magnetic field ran up the page, North being at the bottom and South being at the top, the electron would be deflected to the left.

Extending this reasoning further, one pair of coils will move the spot vertically, the other will move the spot horizontally. The pairs of coils are known as the 'shift coils', and by varying the polarity of the supply between, typically +10 and −10 volts, the current flowing in the coils can be changed both in direction and magnitude. The controls which effect this are known as the 'Y' (or North–South) shift for vertical movement, and the 'X' (or East–West) shift for horizontal movement. Manipulation of the two controls will enable the spot origin to be positioned centrally on the screen (See Fig. 16.1).

16.2 Deflection

The principles established for the positioning of the spot by the use of a magnetic field can be extended to that of spot deflection by a timebase. To achieve this a further set of coils are placed around the tube neck above those used for shift.

It has already been established that one of the requirements of the timebase is that it will deflect the spot linearly across the whole radius of the tube. It follows, that in order to produce a linear deflection, the current flow in the deflection coil must also change in a linear manner—the sawtooth current ramp which rises up, from zero when the spot is at the tube centre, to the maximum value required to create a magnetic

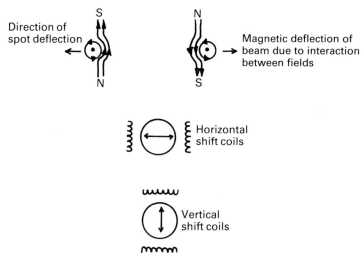

Fig. 16.1 Magnetic deflection and shift

field of sufficient strength to drive the spot to the outer limits of the screen radius. However, although the current waveform applied to the coil is a linear sawtooth, the voltage which produces the current has to be of a different shape. If the deflection coils were purely inductive, it would be possible to apply a rectangular (step) voltage waveform to obtain a sawtooth current change. The deflection coil can, however, be shown to be of a more complex nature, with a value of series resistance in addition to the inductance (if all the effects of capacitance are ignored).

When a step voltage is applied to a coil the current in the coil will begin to rise from zero. As the current increases an increasing proportion of the applied voltage is developed across the series resistance, leaving less voltage appearing across the inductance. Because of this the rate of current increase falls off producing an almost exponential current rise rather than a sawtooth (Fig. 16.2).

To produce a linear sawtooth the applied voltage waveform must comprise a rectangular (step) voltage to start the rate of increase of current in the coil, but in addition a rising sawtooth of voltage has to be superimposed on to the step voltage to overcome the voltage drop across the resistance. The combination of the rectangular (step) voltage and the sawtooth voltage is referred to as either a trapezoidal or a pedestal voltage waveform. This can be illustrated by simple calculation:

A coil consisting of inductance $L = 50$ mH with a series resistance of 400Ω requires a maximum current of 100 mA to deflect the spot to the edge of the screen. The 3 mile range is being used.

For the voltage step:

$$VL = \frac{\mathrm{d}I}{\mathrm{d}t} \times L = \frac{0.1}{36.6\mu} \times 0.05$$

$$= 136 \text{ volts.}$$

For the ramp:

$$VR = I \times R = 0.1 \times 400$$
$$= 40 \text{ volts.}$$

The voltage waveform is shown in Fig. 16.2.

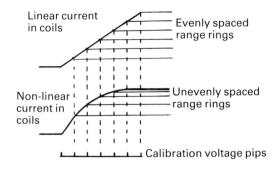

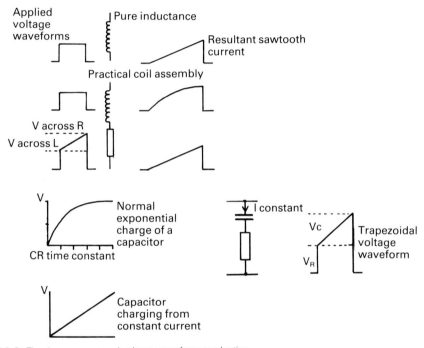

Fig. 16.2 Timebase current and voltage waveform production

The amplitude of the voltage waveform is high (176 volts maximum) in order to be able to deflect the spot across the screen in the time available. If a longer range is selected, the spot will be deflected more slowly, and the maximum voltage required will fall accordingly as in the next example. Here the same coil assembly is used, the current required to deflect the spot to the edge of the screen remains the same (same tube, same coil, same magnetic field, therefore same current for all ranges).

12 mile range:

For the step:

$$\frac{0.1}{146.4\mu} \times 0.05$$

$$= 34 \text{ volts.}$$

For the ramp:

$$= 40 \text{ volts}$$

On the 12 mile range, the maximum amplitude of the voltage waveform is only 74 volts.

As the voltage ramp remains constant for all ranges, it can be seen that it is the voltage step which established the rate of increase of current in the coil. The step voltage amplitude could range from 410 volts on the 1 mile range, down to 4.27 volts on the 96 mile range (the ramp remaining a constant maximum value of 40 volts throughout). To enable this, the supply voltage to the timebase output amplifier is switched as ranges are increased and decreased.

The traditional technique of producing a trapezoidal waveform is by the charging of a capacitor from a constant current source; the capacitor being in series with a resistor across which the voltage step is developed, and the linear rise in capacitor voltage providing the ramp. The step is set for each range by selecting a separate resistor/capacitor pair for each range, the voltage developed across the resistor being proportional to the constant current supplied. The slope of the voltage waveform will depend on the value of the capacitor, with the smallest values of capacitance producing the steepest slopes.

The amplitude of the step voltage is adjusted by the timebase 'linearity' control, while the amplitude is adjusted using the timebase 'velocity' control, this regulates the value of the constant current provided.

The trapezoidal voltage waveform is fed to a power amplifier which in turn supplies the deflection coils, either directly via silver coated slip rings and brushes when rotating deflection coils are employed, or indirectly via the rotor and stator windings of a sine/cosine resolver when stationary deflection coils are used. Any non-linearity of the timebase will be most noticeable when the range rings are displayed. Their appearance should be of evenly spaced concentric circles, non-linearity will show as uneven spacing between the rings.

If an analogue radar is to display target range accurately, it is essential that the timebase scan starts at the instant an echo from a zero range target arrives at the crt cathode. To achieve this, the synchronisation (trigger) pulse (obtained by sampling the modulator pulse) is delayed by the use of an artificial line (Chapter 5). The delay line is tapped to allow for adjustment at installation depending on the propagation delay experienced in the waveguide (which is a function of the length of the run) on both transmission and reception, plus the delay inherent within the receiver. It is possible on installations where particularly long delays are experienced that the timebase delay is insufficient, in which case the signal can be delayed on the video board so that it arrives at the crt cathode at precisely the correct time.

17
Display presentation

Up to this point the impression has been given that only one style of display presentation is possible, where ownship position is dead-centre on the screen, and the heading line points permanently to 000°. This, however, is just one style of presentation, known as 'Ship's head up'.

A ship's head up display has several distinguishing features when viewed from the deck of a moving vessel:

1 All targets which are known to be stationary, i.e. buoys, land masses etc will appear to move on the display, on a reciprocal course to own vessel, and at own vessels speed. The effect may be compared to that experienced when seated on a moving bus and looking out of the side window. Shops and houses appear to move past you in the opposite direction to which you are heading at the same speed as your bus (you are going forward, the shops and houses appear to be heading to your rear). The faster the bus travels the faster the shops and houses race past. As the movement of stationary targets is relative to your own direction and speed, this display is known as a 'relative motion' display.

2 All moving targets will move 'over the ground' with their correct relative velocity components which are usually resolved into vertical and horizontal vectors. (Here it is assumed that, although a vessel will move through the water at some finite speed, it is, never the less, moving over the 'ground', the sea bed under the water. As a vessel utilises water as the medium to enable it to transit from one place to another it moves 'over the ground'.) Ownship moves over the ground with its correct course and speed, therefore all moving targets appear to be following a course and speed which is the vector sum of ownship's course and speed and not that of the moving targets. Because of this, a navigator must continually plot the predicated position of all moving targets relative to his ship. When several targets are involved simultaneously this can be both tedious and dangerous.

3 The advantage of using this style of presentation is that the navigator 'sees' targets as he or she would from the ship's bridge, with target positions being correct relative to ownship. However, the disadvantage is that the compass bearing must be added to or subtracted from the bearing information of the target if the navigator has to place the position on to a chart. Furthermore, if ownship changes course, the whole display will swing through the reciprocal bearing change which, due to the after glow of the ppi screen phosphors, will result in a blurring of all targets for several trace rotations, leaving the vessel blind. No vessel can ever hope to steer or maintain an exactly straight course. The ship's bow will swing from side to side, no matter how slight, an effect known as 'yawing'. The visible effect on the radar is to blur all target echoes while leaving the heading line clear, and pointing to 000°.

The reason for the shortcomings outlined in (3) above, are due to the display being operated independently from a compass which would orientate the display to a permanent reference point, North (other than the ship's bow). Because of this detachment, a ship's head up display is known as an 'unstabilised' display.

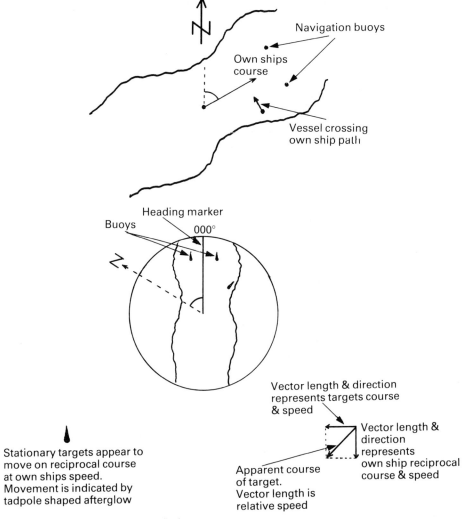

Fig. 17.1 Ship's head up relative motion display

To overcome these problems an input from a compass is introduced into the bearing transmission system to 'stabilise' the display. The compass input can either be from a transmitting magnetic compass which uses flux gates to pass direction information to remote locations, or from a gyro compass (the more usual alternative). Because both of these compasses themselves reference to North the display is known as a 'North up' display, a 'stabilised' display, or occasionally as a 'chart plan' display.

To incorporate a compass input to the bearing transmission system a differential transformer is used in analogue systems. Digitally encoded bearing information from an optical encoder, which is normally referenced to the heading marker pulse at 000°, will have a binary representation of the compass bearing either added to or subtracted from the count as appropriate. An example of the use of a differential transformer is shown in Fig. 17.2.

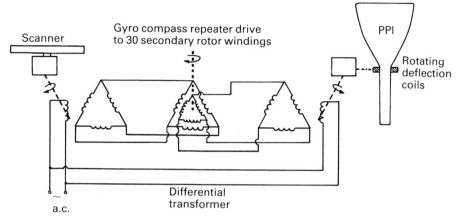

Fig. 17.2 Gyro stabilisation for North-up relative motion display

A differential transformer is basically a three-phase transformer in which the primary windings can be turned through 360°—the rotor, while the secondary windings remain stationary—the stator. A stepper motor drive from a gyro compass repeater turns the rotor as the vessel's course changes to keep the top of the display oriented at 000°, 'true North'. Turning the rotor causes a displacement of the emfs induced in the three secondary windings by a phase angle equal to the difference between North and the course steered. Only when the vessel is directed towards true North will the displacement angle between the rotor and the stator windings be zero—in which case the bearing transmission system will function as described in Chapter 11. Any displacement introduced to the bearing transmission system will either advance or retard the bearing information at the receiver and cause the displayed information to be advanced or retarded accordingly. Because of this aspect, the heading line on a stabilised display will point to the steered course at all times and not to 000°.

A stabilised, relative motion display can be recognised by the following:

1 All fixed targets move at ownship speed, on a reciprocal course.
2 All moving targets move with speeds, scaled to the display vector calculation necessary, relative to ownship's heading line.

The advantages are:

1 The top of the display is 000° (true North).
2 The heading line indicates ownships course.
3 Bearings taken of targets can be transferred directly to navigation charts (which are oriented with North at the top of the chart)—hence the name chart plan display.
4 If the ship changes course the heading line swings to the new heading, leaving the echoes unblurred.
5 If the vessel is yawing the heading line will blur, not the targets.

The one problem which remains is that of blurred fixed targets due to the relative motion aspect of the presentation. When the problem is addressed and overcome, the display presentation produces movement which is returned back to normality, where land masses remain stationary, and moving targets move with their own 'true' course and speed. In addition to receiving directional information from a compass input the radar will also require information pertaining to the vessel's speed. Incorporating speed and direction information will produce a 'true motion' presentation.

18
True Motion

True motion is achieved by moving the whole of the displayed picture, including ownship, across the screen at a speed, and in a direction corresponding to ownship's true speed and course. The movement of the picture is achieved by applying to the 'X' and 'Y' shift coils a slow-rising voltage ramp, the associated current creating a magnetic flux, slowly increasing in strength and moving the centre spot (scan origin) across the tube face. The speed at which the voltage ramp rises will naturally determine the speed at which the spot moves across the screen. This, in turn, has to represent accurately the true speed of the vessel over the ground (and not through the water); the direction in which the spot moves must similarly represent the vessel's steered course.

The vessel's course information is derived by use of a differential transformer driven by a gyro, or transmitting magnetic compass input as already described. The speed information can be obtained automatically from the ship's log, or manually from an 'artificial log' in the true motion unit. Several alternative types of speed log may be used with any one radar, with provision usually being made to accommodate inputs from a dual axis doppler log—this being the most accurate of all—and less accurately from tachometer logs, pitot logs, engine (propeller) revolutions etc.

On a type approved radar, provision has to be made to incorporate an artificial log in addition to the speed log. In general, the speed logs will provide a dedicated output for the radar, usually taking the form of pulses (or a switch contact opening and closing) at the rate of 100 or 200 pulses for each mile travelled through still water. The pulses are converted by a speed amplifier into a dc voltage, the amplitude of which is directly proportional to the pulse rate, with higher pulse rates providing the higher voltage output. A common value quoted is 10 volts, equating to 30 knots. Modern radars have provision to accept much higher speed inputs than used to be the case, to allow their use on surface skimming or semi submerged plane vessels.

18.1 Scaling amplifier

Most radars only offer true motion facilities on ranges limited to those covering navigation at close quarters with other vessels and coast lines. This facility is, therefore, precluded from the very shortest and very longest range scales. A radar will typically offer true motion facilities on the 24, 12, 6, 3 and 1.5 mile ranges. It is evident that the same display tube is used for all the radar ranges, and that its radius has to represent the maximum range. If, for example, a 406 mm (16 in) tube is employed on the 3 mile range, using relative motion presentation; the 203 mm (8 in) representing the 3 miles could be covered by a target moving relative to ownship on a converging course in 15 minutes, representing a speed of 12 knots (12 nautical miles per hour). If the set was now switched to the 12 mile range, the same target would take one hour to move across the 203 mm radius, while on the 24 mile range it would take 2 hours to cover the same 203 mm. This example serves two purposes: firstly, it illustrates how slowly the current in the shift coils rises, taking up to several hours to reach its maximum value, and secondly it illustrates the need for 'range scaling' in order that the scan origin is moved in accordance with both the ship's speed and the displayed range.

When the true motion facility is used, it is normal practice to start the scan origin at any point the screen radius away from the tube centre, the start point usually (but not necessarily) being in the reciprocal direction to that which the vessel is heading, thereby giving the greatest 'look ahead' facility. If, for example, a vessel was steering course 315° true (north west), the reset point would be at 135° (south east) on $\frac{2}{3}$ tube radius. To extend the range in this way necessitates extending the length of the timebase scan period by approximately 1.7 times in order not to leave a bald edge on the screen, and to allow all of the screen to be filled with picture. A radar using the 6 mile range will, therefore, have a maximum 'look ahead' facility of 10 miles ($\frac{2}{3}$ of 6 miles = 4 miles {which takes the spot to the centre of the screen from the reset point} + 6 miles radius to the extreme edge of the screen).

In an analogue radar true motion unit, range scaling can be effected by the use of a conventional operational amplifier in the inverting mode, having a series chain of high tolerance feedback resistors, with values with in multiples of 2 (the same scale factor

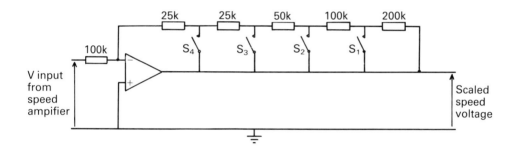

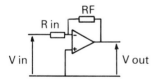

Fig. 18.1 Scaling amplifier

that exists between ranges), and capable of being switched in and out of circuit as required. An illustration of this is shown in Fig. 18.1.

The voltage gain of the amplifier in Fig. 18.1 is given by:

$$Av = \frac{-Rf}{Ri}$$

where Rf = value of feedback resistor
Ri = value of input resistor
(the minus sign indicates a change of polarity between the input and output voltage since the inverting mode is used).

Each of the switches, S1–S4 islinked to the range change switch, and only one of the switches may be closed at any one time. Therefore, with all the switches open, the gain will be

$$Av = \frac{-400 \text{ k}}{100 \text{ k}}$$

$$Av = -4.$$

Closing the switches in ascending order will cause a successive reduction of the amplifier gain by a factor of 2, so that with S4 closed the gain will be -0.25.

As the requirement is for the scan origin to move across the tube face at the slowest rate on the longest (true motion) range, and to move the fastest on the shortest range, it follows that

when S4 is closed the radar must be on the 24 mile range,

S3	do.	12	do.
S2	do.	6	do.
S1	do.	3	do.

and when all the switches are open the radar must be on the 1.5 mile range.

The scaled speed voltage has to be resolved into two velocity components (N–S and E–W) to represent the speed in the steered direction. The most commonly used device for resolving the ship's speed and course is the sine-cosine potentiometer.

18.2 Resolver

The sine-cosine potentiometer is a single-turn, 360° pot, made by winding resistance wire on to a card which has been contoured, so that the track provides a sine wave voltage variation output. External connections are made at four points on the circular track, one each at the top and bottom (180° displaced), and one at each side, midway between top and bottom (also 180° displaced.

Two wipers, 90° apart from each other, and electrically isolated, are mounted on the same shaft and rest on the potentiometer track. A positive voltage supply is connected to the top (000°) connection, and a negative supply, of equal magnitude to the positive, is connected to the bottom connection (180°). The centre tapped points of 090° and 270° are both connected to zero volts. Thus, when the shaft is at 000° or 180° one wiper—the cosine wiper—is at the maximum positive or negative point on the track, while the other—the sine wiper—is at a zero volt point. This bears out the sine-cosine law:

$$\cos 000° = 1, \cos 180° = -1, \sin 000° = 0, \sin 180° = 0.$$

The voltage output from the cosine wiper is used to provide the north–south speed component, while the sine wiper provides the east–west speed component.

To supply the sine-cosine potentiometer with scaled speed voltage of both positive and negative polarity a second operational amplifier is employed as a unity gain inverter. The value of the input and the feedback resistors being equal, the gain of the amplifier is set at one (unity), while the use of the inverting terminal provides a positive-going output voltage for a negative-going input voltage, and vice versa. Therefore, if the polarity of the speed amplifier output was negative, the output polarity of the scaling amplifier would be positive and could be directly connected to the top 000° terminal of the sine-cosine potentiometer; while a unit gain inverter placed between the output of the scaling amplifier and the bottom 180° terminal of the sine-cosine potentiometer would provide a negative scaled voltage equal to that applied to the positive terminal.

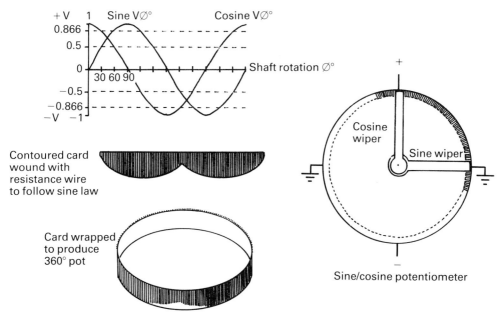

Fig. 18.2 Sine-cosine potentiometer

For any given course and speed, the outputs from the sine-cosine potentiometer will be:

$$V \text{ speed} \times \cos \Theta \text{ volts, and}$$
$$V \text{ speed} \times \sin \Theta \text{ volts.}$$

To transfer this output into a voltage ramp, to provide vertical deflection from the cosine output and horizontal deflection from the sine output, an integrator is used (See Fig. 18.3).

18.3 Integrator

An operational amplifier in the inverting mode can be used as an integrator by using a capacitor in the feedback path, together with an input resistor. The output voltage ramp from the integrator is given by:

$$Vo = \int Vi \times dt$$

$$Vo = \frac{-1}{CR} \times Vi \text{ volts/second}$$

The value of the capacitor-resistor combination determine the time constant '*t*', therefore the output voltage is changing at a rate determined by the magnitude of *Vi*, and the values of *C* and *R*.

For example, if:

$$Vi = 3 \text{ volts, } C = 100\mu\text{F, } R = 2M\Omega$$

$$Vo = -3/0.0001 \times 2\,000\,000 \text{ volts/second}$$

$$Vo = -3/200 \text{ volts/second}$$

$$Vo = -0.015 \text{ volts/second}$$

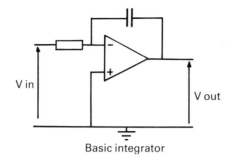

Basic integrator

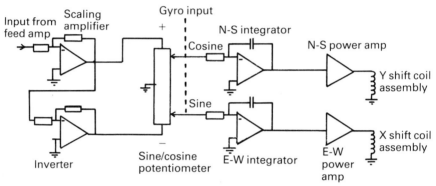

Fig. 18.3 Integrator in true motion unit

Identical integrator circuits are used to provide the linear vertical and horizontal voltage ramps which supply identical N–S and E–W power amplifiers, the output current of which is applied to the static shift coils to drive the scan origin across the screen.

It should be noted that when the 'true motion' facility is selected, the switching action automatically disconnects the shift coils from their previous connection to a potential divider dc supply voltage.

18.4 In-line tidal correction

The vessel's speed over the ground and the vessel's speed through the water are not necessarily the same, as tides and current, and to some extent, wind will contribute to either increase or decrease the speed indicated by the ship's log. A ship at anchor in the mouth of a fast-flowing river could have a speed log indication of several knots due to the relative movement of the water past the log transducer, although the actual speed of the vessel over the ground is zero. Conversely, a ship assisted by a strong current would find its speed over the ground being the sum of the speed through the water plus the speed of the current. If the tide, current or wind forces are acting in-line with the ship, either dead-ahead or dead-astern the correction for speed is relatively straightforward. One possible solution is outlined (Fig. 18.4).

A stabilised voltage is supplied to a potentiometer from which a voltage representing the tide (current or wind) speed is picked off. This voltage can be applied directly to a summing junction at the input to the scaling amplifier. A summing junction involves the connection of a second, identical-value input resistor in parallel with that connected to the speed amplifier. For tide (current or wind) which is acting in the same direction as the vessel's course (a following tide increases speed over ground), the voltage from the in-line tide correction potentiometer will be of the same polarity as that already obtained from the speed amplifier, so that their algebraic sum produces the correct speed voltage to the scaling amplifier. When the tidal force is contrary (a contrary tide slows down speed over the ground although the speed through the water may be higher) the voltage picked off from the potentiometer is first fed through a unity gain invertor and then applied to the summing junction. The opposing polarity of the in-line tide correction voltage subtracts from the speed amplifier voltage so that the scaling amplifier input voltage, being the algebraic sum of the two, is reduced accordingly.

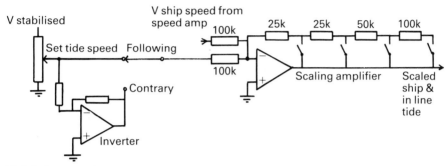

Fig. 18.4 In-line correction

The setting of the tide speed potentiometer is almost guesswork and based on the navigator's experience, however, the visible indication of an incorrectly set (or not even applied) tide speed is that stationary targets (land masses etc) will move on the screen. When the tide speed setting is correct stationary targets remain stationary.

It would be naive to imagine that tides and current forces can only act in-line with the vessel's course. Indeed, for the majority of the time these forces come from other directions, and so some method has to be devised to counteract them. The circuit employed for this purpose is the Resolved tide circuit.

18.5 Resolved tide

The provision of both positive and negative potentials from the tide speed potentiometer for in-line tide correction enables a second sine–cosine potentiometer to be employed to resolve the direction effects, as well as the speed, of tides and current to be off-set (see Fig. 18.5).

The resolved tide sine–cosine potentiometer shaft is brought out as a front panel operator control, calibrated in cardinal points of a compass. By setting the tide speed potentiometer correctly, a voltage can be resolved by applying both the positive and negative potentials to the terminals of the resolved tide sine–cosine potentiometer, turning the shaft to the direction to correct the effect, and producing from the resolver two voltages: the Tide speed voltage $\times \cos \Theta$ tide direction and Tide speed voltage $\times \sin \Theta$ tide direction.

As with the ship's course resolver, the cosine component is used for north–south tidal correction while the sine is used for the east–west correction. Both the sine and the cosine voltages are applied to summing resistors at the input of both the north–south integrator and the east–west integrator to resolve the directional tide effects.

The effect of a true motion display presented to an observer is similar to that which

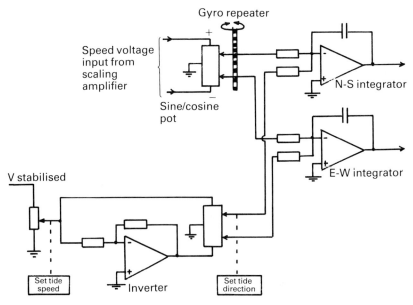

Fig. 18.5 Resolved tide correction

would be obtained if the same scene was viewed from above the observing ship from a helicopter. The reason why true motion gives the effect of land remaining stationary is that as a vessel approaches a stationary target, at say 20 knots, it not only moves towards the target at this speed, but also shortens the range accordingly at the same rate of 0.33 miles per minute. Thus as the scan origin moves across the screen towards a stationary target its own forward movement is offset by the corresponding reduction in range between target and ship, as a result, the target remains stationary while the ship moves—exactly what happens in reality.

When the scan origin has progressed across the screen to the ⅔ radius 'barrier', an automatic reset operation takes place. The navigator will, in general, set the controls to produce a reset point which affords the greatest look ahead facility as well as maximum vision to port and starboard. At previous discussed, a vessel steering towards 315° would be reset diametrically opposite to 135°. The reset process can be an automatic operation, brought about anywhere within the screen radius as set by the navigator. The control 'reset radius' sets a reference voltage to which the integrator voltage ramp will be aiming. When the two voltages are the same amplitude a reset operation will take place. Alternatively, by pushing a 'reset' button, this operation can be advanced to any time during the tracking cycle. The 'reset direction' can also be set by the navigator using a third sine-cosine potentiometer, with a front panel control of the same name. The 'reset radius' voltage is applied both directly and via an invertor to the 'reset direction' sine-cosine potentiometer to reset the north–south and east–west integrator voltages according to the desired direction before the tracking cycle recommences.

As previously noted, the timebase scan duration will have to be extended to approximately 1.7 times its normal value to accommodate true motion presentation, and similarly, the range ring generator will produce sufficient rings to cover the whole of the timebase sweep, likewise the heading line, electronic bearing indicator and variable range marker all have their normal range extended to cover the whole of the off-set display.

18.6   Digitally controlled true motion

An analogue true motion unit of the type described is prone to many problems. Ageing of components causing change of value, thermal effects and even humidity affecting the integrator capacitors are all factors which contribute to the accretion of errors and the loss of accuracy. A digitally controlled true motion unit is superior in so far as simpler circuitry can be employed, and the reliability factor is increased together with accuracy.

The true motion unit is usually placed under the control of a microprocessor, although simpler devices such as PLAs (programmable logic arrays) may well be employed to carry out the same functions.

As with an analogue system a digitally controlled true motion unit requires information supplied pertaining to both the speed of the vessel and its steered course relative to North. The speed information obtained from the ship's log can be converted from log pulses to an analogue voltage as previously described, and for the analogue voltage to be converted into a digital representation by a conventional *A–D* converter.

'Artificial log' speed information can either be keyed in from a key pad or, by keeping a button pressed, the speed value can be incremented by means of a clock into a register where the processor can access the data. It is usual for this information to be display 'on-screen' by means of computer generated graphics running in conjunction with the processor.

Bearing information can be obtained from an optically encoded disc providing binary course information. The disc is rotated by a drive from a gyro compass repeater output, and the light pulses converted into binary representation of the steered course. As with an analogue true motion unit, a digitally controlled true motion unit will be presented with the following inputs from peripheral devices. All the inputs are in digital format, having either been encoded originally or converted from an analogue source.

- speed log (vessel's speed),
- tide speed,
- gyro compass (vessel's course),
- tide direction,
- display range selected (for processor scaling function),
- reset radius,
- reset direction,
- manual reset facility.

The inputs are interfaced to the processor through suitable logic interface devices, with buffers used as and when necessary. The microprocessor runs a sequence program which is stored in an 'on-chip' area of RAM in the microprocessor during normal operation. Unfortunately, this is a volatile memory, and when powered-down the program sequence information is lost. However, a ROM which holds the arithmetic integration and scaling programs also holds the sequence program firmware in its non-volatile memory. When powered-up the ROM loads the microprocessor RAM area with the sequence program during reboot. During the reboot procedure the program counter address is set to zero in readiness to fetch the first instruction and data.

Each of the peripheral inputs has a unique address which allows the microprocessor to address each input device in turn, by a technique known as 'polling'. An address decoder generates a 'chip select' control, addressed to one particular input device only, all other input devices being effectively isolated from the data bus during this time. The selected chip feeds data from the input device on a data bus to the microprocessor during the 'read' cycle. The processor stores the data in RAM and polls the next input in the sequence as it cycles through the input devices at a rate determined by the microprocessor clock. The data subsequently processed by the microprocessor and appear in digital form at the output, addressed to the appropriate device, during the 'write' cycle. They are then converted from digital into analogue voltage levels representing the integrated, scaled calculation of the input data, and applied to north–south and east–west power amplifiers to cause spot movement as described for analogue systems. The time taken to carry out the mathematical calculations is extremely short, and can therefore be repeated many thousands of times per second. If the results of all the calculations are averaged, it can be seen that the accuracy of the digital system far outweighs that of the analogue integration method.

It should be appreciated that the data from the peripheral input devices do not change radically for the majority of the time, with speed and course remaining relatively unchanged when the vessel is at sea. The process of continually polling all of the inputs is wasteful, and a more efficient system of interrupt could be used to advantage. In an interrupt system the peripheral device generates an interrupt request whenever it requires to communicate a change of input to the microprocessor. When not engaged in servicing the input devices the microprocessor engages in other tasks, which include general system management and target timer updating in addition to up-dating the true motion plot. When operating in the interrupt mode, the processor also regularly polls the operator keyboard controls to provide service to the operator as and when required. When a device requests an interrupt the microprocessor leaves the task in which it is engaged, serves the input device, it then returns to the original task.

19
Raster scan display

The 1980s saw the introduction of raster scan display in the marine radar market as a modern replacement for the traditional ppi display. The raster scan display incorporates digital scan conversion (DSC), which is an amalgamation of the techniques already discussed, namely, multiple level video, auto correlation on a two-out-of-two and scan-to-scan basis, noise minimisation, and retimed video. The raster scan display introduces 'memory mapping', 'synthetic video' and colour to the display. In addition, the display presents the viewer with a picture devoid of the rotating trace which typified a ppi screen.

19.1 Raster

The word 'Raster', which gives its name to the display, is a complete set of lines as displayed on a television receiver.

As is well known, a television picture is produced by scanning the face of a cathode ray tube with a spot of light produced by an electron beam. The scanning sequence when viewed directly from the front, is from left to right, top to bottom, with each line being scanned at a shallow angle away from horizontal, rather like a very shallow zigzag. The light spot is only visible when scanning from left to right. When it arrives at the extreme right hand edge of the screen it is blanked-off before 'flying back' (invisibly) to the left hand side—known as 'flyback'.

19.2 Interlaced scanning

Although a television picture is said to have 625 lines (UK PAL system) they are not produced in a numerical sequence 1, 2, 3, 4, etc but, due to transmission bandwidth restrictions, the lines are scanned using an 'interlaced' technique. An interlace system scans all of the odd numbered lines (lines 1, 3, 5, 7, etc) from screen top to bottom, producing half of the total number of lines before the spot is blanked-off and returned back to the screen top left hand corner, positioned such that it can then scan down the screen placing the even numbered lines (lines 2, 4, 6, etc) between the already scanned odd lines. The time taken to scan one line is 64μ seconds and, due to the persistence of the screen phosphors (and that inherent in the human eye) the screen appears as a tightly packed series of fine lines. In the absence of a modulated video input the screen appears blank (only showing white lines on a monochrome system); the complete set of lines being known as a 'raster'. Each picture (or frame) is composed of two, interlaced fields each of approximately 312.5 lines. A total of 25 frames are 'shown' each second on a 50 Hz system, (30 fps on 60 Hz) producing flicker-free viewing.

The adoption of a television style monitor is the first stage in the raster scan system.

19.3   Raster scan crt

The crt used for a raster scan display uses the same principles to produce a spot of light on the screen, in so far as an electron gun assembly produces a controllable beam of electrons which can be focused by an electrostatic field on to a screen phosphor, and deflected by an externally applied magnetic field running across the neck of the tube. The most obvious difference is that of tube shape. The glass envelope of a raster scan display being identical to that of a commercial television tube, having a short neck and large, rectangular face allowing for wide angle beam deflection. The screen phosphor material of a commercial television tube is of only a low persistency (the picture fades very quickly after it has been painted) to permit fast moving picture information to be displayed without any unnecessary afterglow of previous frames remaining. Economic constraints and common sense have dictated that conventional tubes be adopted for use in marine radar raster scan displays. However, because of the low persistency it is necessary to up-date the picture information more frequently than before. This is achieved by using a very high line frequency.

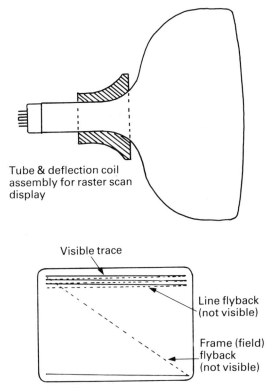

Tube & deflection coil
assembly for raster scan
display

Visible trace

Line flyback
(not visible)

Frame (field)
flyback
(not visible)

Fig. 19.1   Raster scan picture tube and line scanning

19.4   Colour displays

The use of colour for the display enhances the viewing properties of the radar, although the picture is 'coloured' rather than in colour as in a television system. Targets are displayed using one colour against a background of another with calibration details using a third; the colours can be reversed to provide suitable backgrounds for day and night viewing conditions at the flick of a switch. The colours used for the depiction of targets, calibration markers etc are based on IMO/IHO 1990 recommendations thereby providing a standard for manufacturers to adopt.

For daylight viewing conditions a light blue background is used with bearing scale, range rings, heading marker, vrm electronic bearing indicator etc showing as white, uncorrelated targets show initially in brown, then yellow when correlated. A black afterglow provides track history. At night, the background is switched to black, the bearing scale etc to green, and the track history goes to blue.

19.5 Shadow mask tube principles

The majority of colour raster scan displays use the shadow mask technique in which the tube has three separate electron gun assemblies, each positioned 120° apart around the central axis of the tube. Each electron gun is supplied with one only, of the red, green or blue (RGB) video inputs. The three, undeflected electron beams (one from each gun assembly), converge at a common point just in front of the screen after which they begin to diverge once more. At the point at which the three electron beams converge a thin metal sheet, perforated with over 500 000 pin-prick size holes, is suspended, parallel to the screen. The metal sheet is known as the shadow mask, and the holes as shadow mask apertures.

The three beams are aligned so that each can pass through all of the apertures at any point on the screen. Beyond the shadow mask, where the beams start to diverge are the colour phosphor dots, one each for red, green and blue, and arranged as a triad. The dimensions of the phosphor dots and their pattern enable the whole of the screen to be evenly covered with an equal number of each phosphor colour. The tube geometry and alignment will permit, for example, the red electron gun beam to pass through any shadow mask aperture and impinge only on to the red phosphor dot associated with that particular aperture, exciting it to produce a red dot on the screen—the other phosphors are masked from the beam, and lie in a shadow, and do not light up.

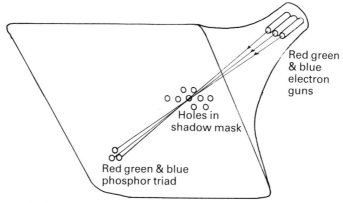

Red green & blue electron guns

Holes in shadow mask

Red green & blue phosphor triad

Fig. 19.2 Shadow mask tube

The human eye is unique in that it is capable of performing an averaging operation on coloured light. If the red, green and blue guns all emit electron beams of the same intensity then all three colour phosphor dots will glow with the same intensity—the human eye averaging this as a white light. By controlling the intensity of any of the three electron beams the phosphors can be made to glow with differing intensities, and the human eye will detect a wide colour spectrum depending on the relative beam current.

19.6   Deflection systems

The deflection requirements of a raster scan display differ from those of a ppi. Both types of display require a timebase to deflect the spot linearly across the screen, but whereas the ppi timebase has to deflect the spot only laterally (with trace rotation achieved by either rotating the deflection coils or the current in them), a raster scan requires simultaneous lateral and vertical deflection systems. In addition, whereas the ppi trace is visible during its transit from the centre of the tube to its outer edge (assuming a centred display) before blanking (due to end of bright-up pulse) and flyback (due to the end of the gate pulse), a raster scan has more complex requirements. The raster scan requires blanking at the end of each line and also at the end of each field, together with associated flyback periods. In a television system, the line sync and field sync pulses are mixed with the video, and transmitted as a composite waveform to provide the necessary references for the deflection system. In a radar system only the video signal, referenced to the transmission pulse, is available initially. Therefore a microprocessor raster controller is used to generate the necessary sync pulses for the display. Two timebase generators operate under the control of a display processor; the frame (vertical) timebase scan being derived from an oscillator which is synchronised to the incoming signal, while the line (horizontal) timebase scan is derived from a free-running oscillator. Both the frame and the line timebase generators produce sawtooth current waveforms which are fed to the frame scan coils and the line scan coils respectively.

19.7   Video

The video signal is produced by a conventional logarithmic receiver as for an analogue system, in which 'rain clutter' control can be applied if required. The incoming 'raw' video signals are digitised into multilevel video using comparators referenced to threshold levels as previously discussed. The threshold levels are determined by the manual 'gain' and 'sea clutter' controls. The use of an adaptive gain circuit which continuously monitors the incoming signal level provides sea clutter rejection. By integrating the clutter signal suitable attack and decay parameters are set, which allow for a light speckling from clutter returns while at the same time maintaining the ability to detect weak targets by keeping the first threshold level relatively low. The digitised multilevel video is latched before being written into RAM during a microprocessor generated 'write gate'. The contents of the RAM are read out during the fixed time 'read gate' as retimed video. The digitised signals arrive in polar form (polar coordinates of range and bearing) and are converted by the digital scan conversion process into cartesian form ('X' amount horizontally and 'Y' amount vertically to suit a monitor screen display) before being stored in a dynamic RAM which forms part of a multiplane memory.

19.8   Memory Mapping

Whereas a domestic (UK PAL system) television provides high quality pictures using a 625 line system, (not all of which are used for picture information, nor are all of the

625 lines displayed), a raster scan display provides high resolution pictures using almost twice as many lines.

The width of the lines 'drawn' on a television screen is determined by the diameter of the spot of light, the two being the same. It follows that a spot of greater diameter would produce a wider line, and that fewer wide lines could be fitted into the same size screen as was originally used; and, conversely, a spot of smaller diameter would produce thinner lines, and more lines could be accommodated on the same screen. The size of the light spot, therefore, is an essential factor in determining the minimum size of a picture element—a pixel. A shadow mask television screen, when viewed at almost point-blank range, shows a myriad of coloured mosaic dots. Each coloured mosaic is a pixel. By dividing the screen into a number of pixels, vertically as well as horizontally, it becomes possible to identify any pixel location on the screen by quoting the number of horizontal pixels and the number of vertical pixels, in the same way as cartesian map coordinates can be quoted using a reference grid.

The number of pixels chosen is the same as the number of bits held in a 1 K RAM, (1024) and the number of lines. Thus the screen is divided into a 1024 × 1024 mosaic of pixels, and each pixel is given a unique address in a static RAM.

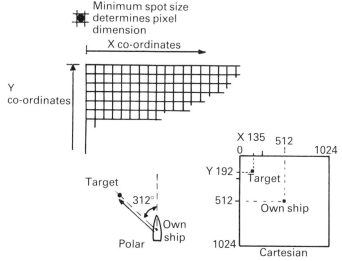

Fig. 19.3 Memory mapping

Digitised video information is presented to the processor as targets referenced against a timing pulse from the start of transmission, with nearby targets returning the first echoes which are given the first addresses in RAM, and the long range targets arriving later in the cycle which are given progressively later addresses. At the same time, the processor is receiving bearing information, supplied in binary form from the bearing transmission system. Pulses, from an optically encoded disc are fed to a phase locked loop the output of which provides, typically, ten pulses per degree of scanner rotation. The bearing information is reference to the heading marker at 000°, and can have an offset applied from the gyro compass as previously discussed. The first task for the processor at start-up is to find the heading marker zero reference pulse. Acting on an interrupt cycle from the bearing transmission system the processor outputs from ROM, stored sine-cosine look-up tables to a maths coprocessor to calculate the cartesian 'X' and 'Y' pixel references for the polar (range-bearing) video input.

Thereby every in-coming video target is allocated a location in the pixel mosaic—hence the term 'memory mapping'. As the scan progresses the bearing information system continues to pass rotational information to the arithmetic unit, which in turn produces a rotating trace on the raster display as with a conventional ppi.

A static RAM is used to store 'synthetic video' information which includes calibration markers (range rings, variable range marker, electronic bearing indicator) and heading line. Also included is an alpha-numeric display of information pertaining to range in use, spacing between range rings, the settings of gain and clutter controls etc which are displayed simultaneously with the radar information. The outputs from the static RAM, together with the video information from the dynamic RAM, combine to produce a composite picture on the monitor screen. It is usual practice to display the static RAM contents on the periphery of the screen so as to leave the centre clear for the 'radar' screen as with a ppi display.

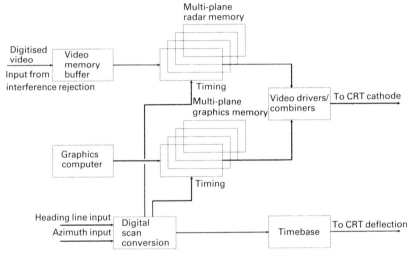

Fig. 19.4 Typical raster scan radar

By scrolling the dynamic RAM contents 'true motion' can readily be incorporated into the system. The scroll rate being under the control of the processor, operating either a polling or interrupt request system from a vessel's speed log.

The processor addresses every pixel on the radar screen as the raster is scanned, with a view to updating the pixel status and to provide scan-to-scan correlation of information. The pixel status is first examined to determine its current status before a decision is made whether to change the status or not. For example, a pixel may initially be illuminated using the pale blue daylight background colour (as no target information is coincident with that particular pixel location).

The first (uncorrelated) 'hit' from a target, with range and bearing (polar) the same as the pixel's own (cartesian) position, will cause the colour of the pixel to be changed to brown. The decision making is based on an algorithm which, as well as providing correlation between scans, helps eliminate false target information being displayed. When the target has been correlated as a true target, the decision is made to change the pixel colour from brown to yellow. Later, when the relative motion between ownship and the target has changed, the position of the target on the screen the pixel will be changed to black, representing the target trail, or afterglow. On a conventional ppi display the duration of the afterglow of a target is a function of the screen phosphor material, possibly lasting several minutes before completely fading out. The raster scan tube, however, is of a short persistency, and therefore the afterglow of targets has to be represented synthetically—in some radars by the use of one plane of a multiplane memory.

The time for which a target afterglow remains visible on the screen is under the control of the operator, with the dynamic RAM contents being recycled for this period. To produce a visible decay, a pseudo-random algorithm may be employed to randomly break up the trail (rather than attach fixed length/duration afterglow to all targets), which makes the afterglow look more like that of a ppi. After the predetermined afterglow time, the pixel colour will gradually appear to fade from afterglow black to daylight background blue once more.

The raster scan display enables the navigator, at a glance, to assimilate easily not only the position of targets, but also the setting of all controls and equipment status. As the 'one man bridge' concept becomes reality the raster scan principle, extended into an ARPA will become essential. The incorporation of an on-screen menu of peripheral device and radar statuses, with parameters being changed using the minimum of buttons (techniques which are similar to a 'mouse' on a computer system) will make operation much simpler for the navigator. The replacement of circuit boards by single, dedicated electronic devices (DEDs) will increase reliability, simplify maintenance and keep repair time down to an absolute minimum.

Portable radar displays which sever the conventional link between transceiver and display are now available for use by harbour and river pilots. The display, which is sufficiently compact to fit into a briefcase, rather like a lap-top computer, receives its data from either a vhf radio link or a commercial quality telephone circuit. Raw analogue video in 'A' scan form (Fig. 1.3) from a remote transceiver IF output is digitised and data compressed prior to committing to radio or line. The display presents the user with real time images with the possibility of switching between transceivers at more than one location.

20
Inter-switched radar systems

On almost any radar, it is possible to extract raw video and sync pulses and connect them into a second display unit. The advantage of doing this is to provide an alternative location from which to view radar display. This has been done in the past, sometimes as a gimmick with a display located in a passenger observation lounge or, more ominously, in the Captain's cabin. Such a connection cannot offer anything more than a duplicate copy of the bridge radar screen.

A more beneficial installation would be a duplicate of all the radar hardware: two scanners, two waveguide runs, two transceivers and two displays. On rare occasions, the radars will require separate, dedicated power supply units, one for each radar, in which case these would also be duplicated. In addition to having two independent radars mounted almost side-by-side the flexibility and availability of the radar can be extended by the incorporation of an inter-switch unit.

An inter-switch unit can best be described by referring to the two installations as 'A' and 'B'. With an inter-switch facility interconnecting two transceivers, waveguide and scanners operating in the same band ('X' or 'S'), it would be possible to:

- run displays 'A' and 'B' from either their own transceiver, or both from transceiver 'A', or both from transceiver 'B'.
- connect transceiver 'A' to either waveguide 'A' or waveguide 'B'
- connect transceiver 'B' to either waveguide 'B' or waveguide 'A'
- connect scanner 'A' to either waveguide 'A' or waveguide 'B'
- connect scanner 'B' to either waveguide 'B' or waveguide 'A'.

It is not possible to connect both transceivers to the same waveguide run simultaneously, nor is it possible to connect the two waveguide runs into one scanner.

Connection between waveguide and transceiver is not usually effected electronically (although there is nothing other than expense which precludes this from being done), but is more usually connected manually (with flexible waveguide section if the distance between transceivers is not great). In cases where a dual horizontally and circularly polarised scanner are mounted back-to-back, the change-over between scanners can be effected using waveguide switches, otherwise inter-scanner connection would be effected as for the transceiver end of the run.

The electronic inter-switching unit has inputs of sync pulse, video and bearing information fed from the above-decks units of installations 'A' and 'B', and is capable of providing a 'Master/slave' output configuration. If installation 'A' in its entirety (scanner, waveguide, transceiver and display) is designated 'master' then display unit 'B' becomes a 'slave' of 'A'. As a result, scanner, waveguide and transceiver 'B' become temporarily redundant, which may be by design or default, allowing opportunity for essential maintenance whilst preserving continuity of (almost) full service; or because of damage to, or failure of scanner/waveguide/transceiver 'B'.

The master display differs from the slave in so far as it is only at the master display that the transceiver can be controlled:

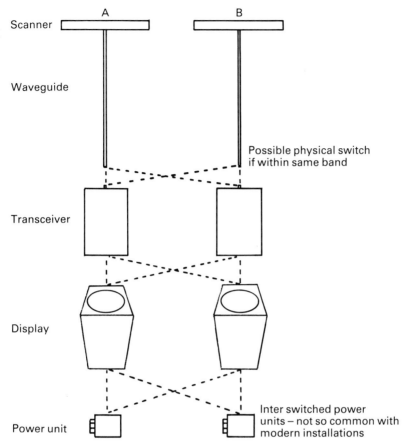

Fig. 20.1 Inter-switching between dual installations

- from standby to run or off,
- from long pulse to short pulse,
- for receiver tuning of the local oscillator,
- for checking the performance monitor.

The slave is unable to carry out these operations, but be used independently on ranges other than those in use at the master, turn on/off and adjust calibration markers, tube brilliance, contrast etc.

The relative advantages of 3 cm and 10 cm radar systems has led to the installation of both, side by side, on large merchant vessels since about 1975. The 3 cm system provides the navigator with fairly high resolution display suitable for use when navigating in confined or congested waters, but which suffers significantly from both sea and precipitation clutter effects. Although the effects can be minimised by electronic manipulation, the presence of clutter can still be discerned even on the very latest digital systems. The 10 cm system, operating on a much lower frequency (with a correspondingly longer wavelength) is not affected by either form of clutter and therefore, overcomes the shortcomings of the 3 cm system. However, the resolution obtained with a 10 cm system is very much less than that of the 3 cm system. Targets which show as pin-head size on a 3 cm radar appear more like house bricks when the two systems are viewed side by side.

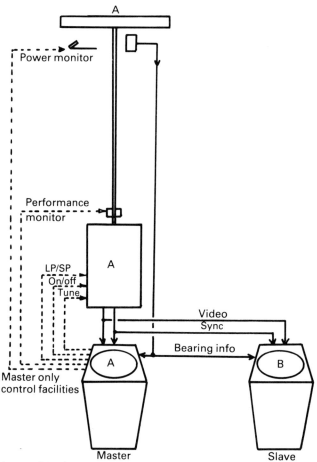

Fig. 20.2 Master/slave configuration

When inter-switching is considered for a dual installation of 'X' and 'S' Band radars, it is only the displays (and possibly the external power supply units) which can be interchanged. Because of the respective frequency bands and wavelengths, an 'X' Band transceiver cannot be connected to an 'S' Band waveguide (or coaxial cable) run, nor to an 'S' Band scanner. Similarly the 'S' Band transceiver can only be connected to 'S' Band waveguide and scanners. Both transceivers can, however, output video and syncs which have been derived from their system, and output these to any display, enabling, at the very least, two 'X' Band displays, or two 'S' Band displays, and when not inter-connected one each of 'X' and 'S' Band. As before, a master/slave configuration will result, together with the constraints imposed on operational controls at the slave.

In making a comparison between 'S' (10 cm) and 'X' (3 cm) Band systems, a target picked up by an 'S' Band system at a range of 16 000 yards (8 miles) would be picked up by an 'X' Band system at 29 000 yards (14.5 miles) under identical conditions. An 'S' Band system does not perform as well as an 'X' Band system when detecting low coastlines and mud banks, while to 'X' Band offers better long range performance after the turn-over range, when the range equation changes from fourth root to eighth root power, see Chapter 4.

21
Radar Reflectors

Although there is a military requirement to make objects 'invisible' to radar systems, there also exists a non-military requirement to enhance the reflecting capability and detection ranges of targets. As can be appreciated from the basic principles on which primary pulse radar is built, a target will return a detectable echo back to the receiver providing:

- The target is of an adequate size to return an echo which is above receiver detection threshold.
- The target presents a sufficiently large cross-sectional area to the transmitted energy.
- The target shape is such that energy is 'reflected' and not scattered by the target.
- The target is of a material capable of having voltage induced into it, allowing current to flow for energy to be reradiated.

These conditions assume that the target is within the normal radar horizon of a fully operating radar.

The aspects of a target are beyond the control of the radar designer, but never-the-less, there are times when a marine radar has to detect what are in effect 'poor targets'. Small wooden or fibreglass vessels (which includes the majority of ships' lifeboats), navigation markers and buoys all have to present acceptable targets, and each could have serious consequences if undetected.

Objects similar to those listed can be made to return stronger radar echoes by fitting 'radar reflectors'. The simplest of all radar reflectors take the form of flat sheets of metal held at right angles to the direction from which the radar energy originates emanates. Metal, having a high coefficient of reflection is capable of having emfs induced into it, and reradiating a large portion of the incident energy. However, should the plate not be exactly at right angles to the direction of propagation, the majority of incident energy would be deflected in some other direction to that required. Should the plate be mounted, say on a small vessel which is at sea, there would perhaps be times when the metal plate was correctly aligned so as to reflect energy efficiently, but moments later, due to the movement of the vessel only a small portion of the energy would be reflected. The effect is similar to that which would be observed if the metal plate was polished to act as a heliograph. When the alignment is correct the sun would be able to 'glint' on the polished surface. The terminology 'glint' is used in this context in radar engineering.

An improvement on the flat metal sheet would be to mount a second flat metal sheet at right angles to the first, to make a corner. With the corner suspended vertically a horizontal radar beam can enter the corner, bounce from one sheet to another and exit on a reciprocal path to entry. However, if the reflector is tilted, or the beam directed either upward or downward into the corner it will not be reflected back on a reciprocal path.

If a third metal plate is mounted at right angles to the existing two, a corner reflector results. Its shape being that which would be obtained if a corner was cut diagonally from a hollow cube.

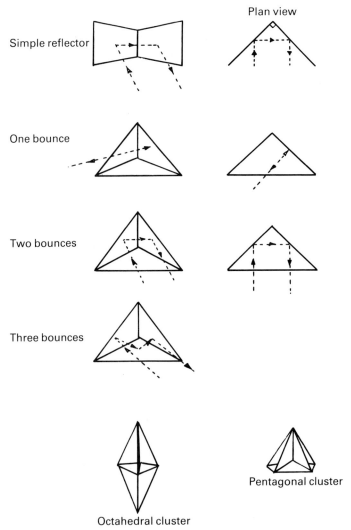

Fig. 21.1 Radar reflectors

Energy entering the corner from any direction will not be scattered, but the major portion will be reflected once, twice, or even three times before leaving on a reciprocal path. Corner reflectors are usually mounted in clusters which produce octahedral, tetrahedral and pentahedral shapes. The shape combinations ensure that radar signals picked up from any direction can be returned to origin despite the fact that the reflector may be mounted on a wildly pitching vessel. The addition of a passive radar reflector to a target will considerably increase its detection range, and may have additional benefits including the ability to pick out one particular navigation buoy from others in the same area. Alternatively, as is the case in the entrance to the port of Southampton, the port-hand buoys are fitted with reflectors but not the starboard. The port-hand buoys therefore produce a stronger echo than those to starboard enabling each side of the channel to be identified.

Radar reflectors of the type described find application for navigation buoys, fishing vessels and, in a collapsible form, for ships' lifeboats. Yachts very often employ a reflector which takes the form of a long, slim plastic cylinder which can be suspended easily in the rigging without unnecessary difficulty. Inside the cylinder, long strands of metal film are arranged in a manner similar to chaff. The echoing area of such a device is considerable, giving a much enhanced echo return from the yacht. (A yacht with sails wet with sea-water will provide a better target than one with dry sails).

22
Secondary radar

Secondary radar is the name given to a system in which a device can be interrogated by radar to obtain a response which gives both the position and the identification of the device. Secondary radar is used extensively in both the military and aeronautical fields under different system names, as an example for friend/foe identification, or as an aid to traffic routing and ground control of aircraft. In the maritime field, secondary radar is employed as an enhanced navigation aid, serving to provide identifiable markers wherever they may be needed. Very often, their exists a need to make an unaided, poor target, into one which is 'radar conspicuous'. The acronym which follows from this expression is Racon.

22.1 Racon

A Racon is a beacon, capable of transmitting and receiving in the radar band, powered by batteries, possibly aided by solar rechargeable power supplies, and only radiating low power transmissions. The size and weight size of the Racon is correspondingly small, making it suitable for installation on buoys, where unattended operation and long intervals between servicing are normal features of working life. Its transportability features extend its applications to over a much wider spectrum.

The Racon beacon is a transponder, which responds to the receipt of a ship's normal primary radar transmission, usually in the 'X' (3 cm) Band, and, to a limited extent, in the 'S' Band (10 cm) also. On detecting the transmission the beacon will 'reply' using a pulsed transmission, coded in international morse. A ship within range of the beacon's transmission will receive and display the code on the radar screen. The beacon identification is by the morse character(s) painted on the screen (- - · for the letter G for example), the relative bearing of the beacon being given by the direction in which the morse symbols are painted on the screen. The range of the beacon will be approximately the distance from ownship out to the start of the first morse symbol. The measured range will be in error due to the internal delay of approximately 0.5μ seconds in the beacon between its reception and subsequent retransmission. When navigating at a distance, the start of the Racon response will be behind its true position by approximately 75 metres (246 feet), but as the range closes the structure on which the racon is mounted can be detected and true range (within the accuracy of ship's radar) can be measured.

The receiver section of the beacon is fed by an omnidirectional wide-band antenna. The omnidirectional characteristics enable a vessel approaching from any direction to obtain a response from the beacon, both on reception and transmission. The wide bandwidth covers each individual radar transmission frequency within the band on reception, while on transmission the beacon frequency is swept over the whole band allowing for individual ship's receiver tuning positions.

The antenna is connected to a three-port strip-line circulator which directs in-coming echoes into the receiver section, while on transmission it connects the

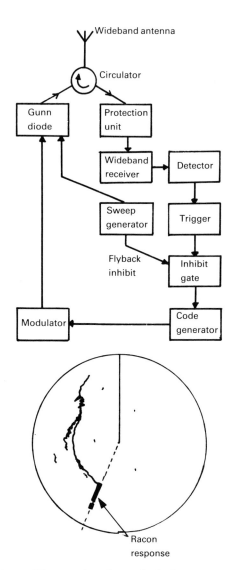

Fig. 22.1 Racon

antenna to the transmitter. The receiver input includes a protection varactor diode to safeguard the receiver crystals. A sensitivity of typically −72 dBW (0.000 000 08 W) and a signal to noise ration of 17 dB provide for a good response from the beacon while at the same time ensuring that the beacon is not excessively prone to false triggering. The possibility of the beacon being triggered by side lobes radiated from a ship's scanner is acceptably remote because at longer ranges, when the beacon would be within the side lobes, their relative power levels would be insufficient to trigger the beacon, whereas at closer range when their power level would be higher the side lobes would invariably pass over the top of the beacon. Sea trials on beacons have confirmed this fact to be so. The detected video is amplified before being passed to a trigger unit which initiates the beacon's response.

The triggering of a pulse code generator to set the morse identification code is the first stage in the response sequence. A code, comprising of up to four digits in total can be set on installation. To ensure that no range-reading ambiguity is introduced, it is recommended that only characters which start with a 'dash' (as opposed to a dot) are used: i.e. B, C, D, G, K, M, N, O, Q, T, X, Y, Z. The longest characters require four digits, i.e. 'X' - · · -, while the shortest character 'T' requires just a single dash. The overall duration of a single letter code is approximately 15μ seconds (which corresponds to a paint equating to 1.22 miles) and is set to be a compromise between unnecessarily congesting the screen and the possibility of misreading the code.

On beacons capable of radiating two-letter identifications the response could be as long as approximately 43μ seconds (about 3.5 miles length). The reply code causes a Gunn diode transmitter to produce a pulsed rf output of approximately 300 mW mid-band, falling to 120 mW at the band edges, which is fed via the circulator to the antenna. To ensure that all ships' radars are able to detect the beacons' responses regardless of their individual tuning, the radiated output frequency of the beacon is swept across the whole of the radar band. The tuning is effected by a frequency sweep generator producing a voltage ramp which is applied to a varactor diode. The varactor diode and the Gunn diode combination operate inside a cavity in the same manner as when a local oscillator assembly is used in a primary radar system, with tuning being effected in the same manner.

The sweep period can be varied to between 48–120μ seconds, a rate which is fast enough to refresh radar displays, and at the same time sufficiently slow to ensure the response is not missed by the scanner. In general, the sweep time is sufficient to allow the paint from the beacon to fade completely before being refreshed. This ensures that targets which might lie under the beacon code are not masked.

False triggering of the beacon due to reradiation of its own emission, due to close range targets or sea clutter returns is prohibited by the incorporation of a 200μ second delay before the beacon can be retriggered.

22.2   Search and rescue radar transponder (SART)

The Global Maritime Distress and Safety System (GMDSS), which has taken over from the traditional distress alerting and search and rescue system, uses SARTs as part of the system. The transponder takes the form of a beacon of similar size and weight to an Emergency Position Indicating Radio Beacon (EPIRB), and may be used by a vessel in distress to indicate its position by radar. The activated beacon transmits signals in the 'X' Band which can be detected and displayed in a manner similar to a Racon beacon. As the beacon height above the water may be only a few feet (zero in the case of a beacon floating in the sea), its radar horizon and corresponding range will not be great—a fact which should be borne in mind.

As with the Racon, the SART rapidly sweeps the 9.2–9.5 MHz band, taking 7.5μ seconds for each sweep; each forward sweep being followed by a 0.4μ second return period, with 12 sweeps completing the response. An omnidirectional antenna with a ±12.5° vertical beamwidth is used for both transmission and reception; horizontally polarised signals being emitted. The receiver detects the presence of 'X' Band search craft radar, and responds to signals in excess of 50 dBm within 0.5μ seconds after receipt. A visual indication on the beacon displays the operational status, and periods during which the beacon is responding to interrogation. The transmitted power is typically 400 mW effective isotropic radiated power (EIRP) for a minimum period of 8 hours from its battery supply. The battery has a shelf life of approximately 5 years and can be replaced by the ship's staff as part of a routine maintenance programme.

Part Two

AUTOMATIC AIDS

23
Introduction to ARPA

The use of radar allows the observer to determine the effect of the movement of his own ship relative to targets shown on the radar screen. Targets could be fixed land masses or other ships which could be moving. Radar as a navigational aid has been, and is still, used to provide auxiliary data on a clear day and/or in heavy traffic conditions, its use being invaluable in adverse weather conditions or at night.

Many aids are available to assist the observer in the task of extracting data from the radar screen to provide tracking information. Only those aids which conform to the IMO ARPA (Automatic Radar Plotting Aids) specification (see Appendix 1) qualify as ARPA installations.

Radar gives the range and bearing of a target and, with time, the movement of the target, i.e. the 'history' of the target. An approved ARPA should be able to display at least four equally time-spaced past positions of targets being tracked over a period of at least eight minutes. Such history tracks may be in true or relative mode. When the ARPA is used in true mode, providing the log is giving ownship speed through the water, the tracks would be sea-stabilised. Tidal effects can be allowed for by using an autodrift facility which locks the display to some fixed target and provides a ground-stabilised display. An ARPA uses radar data, stored in a database, to provide the relevant target information needed by an observer. Such data can relate to many targets and can be updated to provide tracking information in vector or graphic form to indicate the targets' predicted motion. Vectors can be used for display purposes which show the course of any target relative to ownship's course. Speed can be obtained by calculation and comparison of vector lengths for the target and ownship.

Data may be collected automatically to allow targets to be selected and tracked without the active participation of the observer in the process. Alternatively, the observer may select targets manually which once acquired will be automatically tracked. Automatic acquisition may result in several vectors being displayed, not all of which are actually necessary, possibly causing confusion to the observer. Manual acquisition would give the observer only targets of immediate interest.

An automatic tracker circuit will store the range and bearing of a certain number of targets, the data being continuously updated. For manual tracking, the selected target data is stored and since range and bearing can be selected directly by the observer, the amount of memory required for storage of the data is reduced. Automatic acquisition has its difficulties because of the need to select targets and to continuously update the data on them in order to produce an apparent motion track. It is usual to convert data into cartesian coordinate form and to establish the rate of change of these values to provide the tracking information. When a target is manually acquired, using a joystick, and placed within the tracking gate, the gate automatically centres itself on the target and the computer tracks the gate. Data are updated with each radar scan. If a scan detects no target response, the gate does not move and if the target response, when it comes, is outside the gate, the target is 'lost'. One of the ARPA requirements is that any 'lost' target should be indicated in some way, together with the last tracked position of such a target. The computer having identified the movement of a target, however, could predict its next position with every scan and move the gate to the position predicted by the tracker circuit. This could have a disadvantage since, if two targets are close together and only one is being tracked, for example, the computer may move the tracker gate towards the target's predicted position which could cause the unwanted target to be acquired (especially if the wanted tracked target had altered course). The newly acquired unwanted target would then be tracked automatically. This is known as target swop.

Information available from ARPA, in alpha-numeric form, should include predicted target range at closest point of approach (CPA) and the predicted time to CPA (TCPA). The observer should be able to set limits for CPA and TCPA and if these are violated by a tracked target, whether its vector actually reaches the warning area or not, an alarm should automatically be activated. The offending target should also be highlighted in some way for ease of identification.

Additionally guard rings and zones may be set and if a target closes to a range, or transits a zone, chosen by the observer, an alarm should sound and the target should be highlighted in some way.

An ARPA should also provide a simulation of the effect on all tracked targets of an own ship manoeuvre, using a trial condition, without affecting the updating of target information. A trial manoeuvre is one carried out before any action is implemented, in order to assess the result of the proposed action.

Most ARPAs allow navigation lines to be produced on the display. The Nav lines, which are adjustable for position and length, may be used to indicate navigation limits and danger areas and are useful for pilotage. Extra features such as way points, traffic separation zones etc, are also possible. Maps may be formed and a certain number of these may be stored and recalled as required.

Since ARPA manufacturers must meet the IMO specifications, the systems produced by various manufacturers will differ only in detail. For the purposes of this text a particular system is used to illustrate the ARPA concept; the principles involved are likely to be similar to those used in other systems.

In the chapters that follow, a technical description of a particular ARPA system together with its operating conditions will be described. At the end of the book will be found four appendices; these are all relevant to the ARPA Part and include a glossary of terms. The appendices are referred to in the text wherever necessary, while the glossary is meant to identify any terms used in the text that may need defining in more detail. The reader is recommended to check the appendices and glossary when in doubt about any aspect of the text.

24
An ARPA system

24.1 Introduction

The system to be described is part of the Kelvin Hughes HR series with a 'Concept' display using digital scanning conversion (DSC) techniques, which gives a high resolution raster radar picture. The keyboard for the ARPA model is the 3000A which, although similar to the 3000T (True motion) keyboard in layout, has extra keyboard facilities as required for an ARPA. A processor unit, standard fitting for all variants of the HR series radars, can provide a RELATIVE motion display, TRUE motion, interfacing and ARPA facilities.

The ARPA display includes target acquisition and automatic tracking facilities. The HR ARPA plotting aid is claimed to exceed the requirements of the IMO specification and includes the provision of the following parameters:

- Manual/automatic acquisition of up to 20 targets ranging from 0.5 to 24 nautical miles (nm).
- Single or double guard zones acquisition, with 0.5 or 1 nm zone width and variable bearing limits.
- Tracking of targets with relative speeds of 150 knots ranging from 0.1 to 40 nm.
- Operation on all range scales from 0.25 to 24 nm.
- Vectors adjustable in length from 1 to 60 minutes. Up to 4 fixed targets for generating, autodrift, drift reference and anchor watch.
- Numeric target labelling on request.
- True vectors in true motion, relative vectors in relative motion.
- Vector mode facility to reverse vector presentation.
  CPA/TCPA alarm limits of 0.1 to 12 nm/ 1 to 60 minutes.
- Bow crossing range and time.
- History:
  Four × 2 minutes past positions of all targets.
- Alarms:
  Collision, new target, lost target, tracking overload, system failure and anchor watch.
- Simulation mode:
  Four synthetic targets that move either to a known or random solution. Test facilities, on and off line.
  Full target data of all tracked targets or designated targets, via a serial interface including:
  Ownship data, target CPA/TCPA, target course, speed, range and bearing.
- Trial manoeuvre:
  Simulation of change in course, speed and delay with auto cancel.

The basic display uses processors to control all the radar functions, while the ARPA version uses more processors within the ARPA computer and yet another processor to handle data transfer between the radar and ARPA systems. The block diagram is shown in Fig. 24.1.

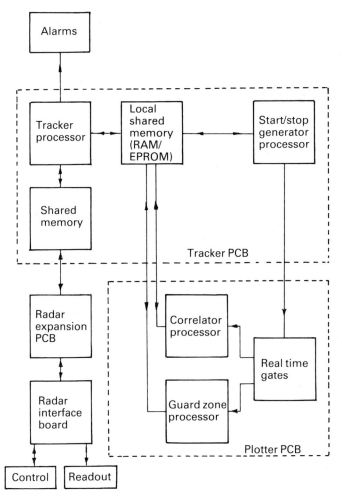

Fig. 24.1 ARPA system block diagram

PPI information may be passed to or from the TRACKER processor via the RADAR EXPANSION circuit, which uses a Z80 processor, through shared memory. The tracker forms the main part of the processing circuitry, using positions of targets from the correlator to predict the next position. Additionally it performs ARPA calculations such as CPA and TRIAL MANOEUVRE.

The other processors (start/stop, correlator and guard ring) also communicate with the tracker, and to each other, via shared memory. The tracker passes information to the start/stop generator estimating a target position in terms of range and bearing; an azimuth count is used to determine whether a 'gate' should be opened on the bearing and then, in real time, whether a range counter should open the gate in the correct part of the return. The opening and closing of a gate is signified by a control line being active in real time for each of the gates as necessary. Gate control lines enable discrete logic, which stores the range of the front edge of any target found during the enable period. At the end of the gate period the start/stop generator stores the azimuth at which that return occurred. On completion of a gate cycle the start/stop generator interrupts the correlator which moves all the information from the gate to allow reuse of the real time data acquisition hardware. The correlator then analyses the data, returning the results to the tracker for the next filter prediction.

The guard ring processor works in an identical fashion to the correlator but since it operates over larger zones, the length of the range and azimuth numbers is greater, requiring different real time gate circuitry from the correlator gates.

24.2 Tracker

The processor is an Intel 8086 with an 8087 arranged as a coprocessor with maximum mode signals (MN/MX pin grounded). With MN/MX low, a bus controller, the 8288, is used. The bus controller decodes three processor outputs, S0, S1 and S2 (pins 26, 27 and 28 of the processor respectively), and generates control signals INTA, ALE, DEN, DT/R, IO/M, WR, HLDA and HOLD (for a definition of these signal functions and brief details of the processors and associated circuitry, see Appendix 3). This arrangement allows many signal functions to be available, due to the encoding, while only utilising three pins of the 8086. The 8086 is a 40 pin device using 16 data lines and 20 address lines; the 8086 multiplexes the 16 data lines with the 16 low address lines. The address-latch enable (ALE) line indicates whether the address/data lines carry an address or data. The main processor has been arranged to be functionally identical to an Intel single board computer (SBC) which permits a standard arrangement of RMX88. Memory decoding is thus simplified since full decoding is not necessary; the I/O ports will respond to the correct addresses for RMX and to other addresses which are not required. Provided these other addresses are not enabled there is no contention. The basic block diagram of the processor/memory connections is shown in Fig. 24.2.

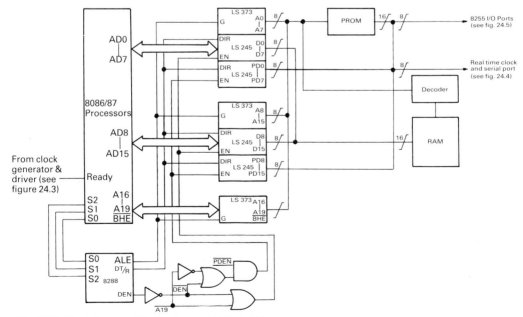

Fig. 24.2 Block diagram of the Tracker processor and Memory

The address bus is produced using the ALE output as an enable input to D-type transparent latches (LS373). Two data busses exist: one for the PROMs and I/O while the second is for the various RAM devices. Separation into two busses is required because the PROM or I/O devices would not be able to drive all the bipolar buffers on the bus. Decoding of the RAM data bus is via inputs A19 and DEN while the second data bus is enabled via A19, DEN and PDEN.

The arrangement for the PROM allows up to 64k words to be allocated if memory devices type 2764 are used. Other devices may be fitted using a header in a dil socket. 64k words of dynamic RAM are available, controlled by an 8203 decoder device.

The 8086 uses a system which requires an input to be applied to the READY pin; unless this input is HIGH the processor is in the wait mode and can be held there until the peripheral device raises the READY line. Devices like the PROMs and I/O do not need the processor to be held in a wait state and for these devices the input AEN1 on the Clock generator and Driver (8284) chip is used to provide an immediate READY signal to the processor. This is achieved by gating S2 and A19 into the 8284 device. AEN2 is used for devices requiring wait states; in this case it is the three RAM areas each of which provides an active low acknowledge signal which is used, via gates, to provide an input into the AEN2 pin of the 8284 device. Figure 24.3 shows the arrangement.

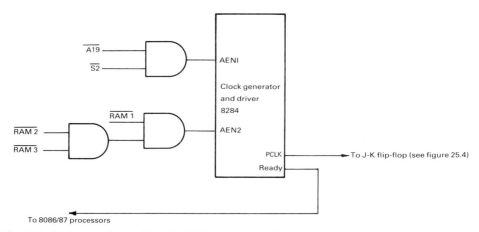

Fig. 24.3 Arrangement for providing the READY signal to the Tracker processor

An Interrupt controller (8259) is used with some inputs configured; interrupts required by the RMX88 are hard-wired to IR0, IR6 and IR7 (real-time clock, RxR and TxR respectively). The remainder can be configured in priority using a header in a dil socket; the socket has been wired such that, provided there are no software alterations, the links will go directly across the socket.

A real-time clock and serial port is provided as required for the operation of RMX88. An 8251 USART (Universal Synchronous Asynchronous Receiver Transmitter) device provides the serial port linking via the data bus to the processor; port decoding is via a 1 of 8 decoder device LS138 which also provides decoding for the I/O ports (8255 devices), the Interrupt controller (8259) and the Programmable interval timer (8253–5). The transmit clock frequency (TxC) and receive clock frequency (RxC) inputs are common and have a frequency determined by the output of pin 17 of the 8253–5 device. The clock input on pin 20 of the USART must have a frequency at least 30 times greater than the transmit/receive clock. The clock input to pin 20 is taken from a JK flip-flop connected in toggle mode with its input clock coming from the Clock generator and driver (8284) (see Fig. 24.3). The serial data that is output/input to the USART is TTL compatible and an interface to RS 232 levels is made via the 1488 transmitter device and/or the 1489 receiver device. The basic arrangement is shown in Fig. 24.4.

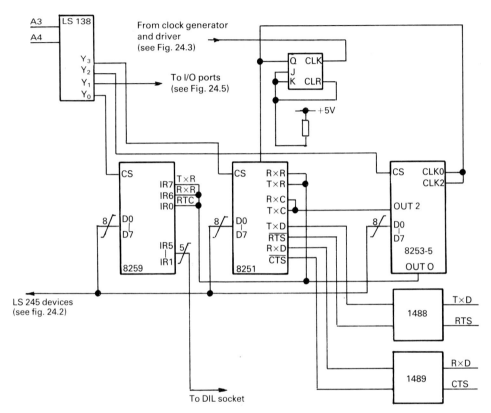

Fig. 24.4 Serial port link to the Tracker processor

The I/O ports on the Tracker pcb are obtained using two 8255 devices. The 8255 is a Programmable peripheral interface (PPI) and has three individual ports A, B and C. The processor may, by virtue of a control input, configure the 8255 to operate in an input, output or bi-directional mode. The 8255 is selected when the signal level on its CS input goes active low. Inputs A0 and A1 are logical lines which determine which part of the device is in communication with the processor. RD and WR pins, when receiving an active low input signal, would determine the type of electrical communication that will occur on the data bus. The inputs to the RD and WR pins in this case will come from the IOR and IOW pins of the 8288 Bus controller which are active low. The RESET input to the 8255 is active high and is applied to the device for power on reset. It may also be applied to the device at any time as a reset pulse in order to set the internal configuration of the device to a known state.

In this arrangement the two 8255s are wired as word ports with connections arranged as follows:

- Lower port

PA0-4	Latched A0–A4 Z80 lines	Used for control
PB0-7	Latched D0–D7 Z80 lines	switch reading
PC0	Mode interrupt	
PC1	Alarm reset	
PC5	Gate video control	
PC6	Short range guard ring video enable	
PC7	Long range guard ring video enable	

- Upper port.

The significence of the switch (S1) settings is:

Switch 1
settings
'1' '0'

		7.5	15	30	45	60	75	90	120	Deg./min
MSB	1	0	0	0	0	1	1	1	1	Rate of
	2	0	0	1	1	0	0	1	1	change of
	3	0	1	0	1	0	1	0	1	course

4	0 = 0.5 miles 1 = 1.0 mile	zone width
5	0 = 1.0 mile 1 = 3.0 miles	inner limit

		0.5	1.0	2.5	5.0	7.5	10	15	20	knots/min.
MSB	6	0	0	0	0	1	1	1	1	Rate of
	7	0	0	1	1	0	0	1	1	change of
	8	0	1	0	1	0	1	0	1	speed

PB0–7   Warning indicators to ARPA display with following significence:

0   System failure
1   Track overload
2   Collision warning
3   Anchor
4   Lost target
5   New target
6
7

PC0	Correlator reset/Range clock inhibit
PC1	Guard reset
PC2	Start/Stop generator reset
PC4–7	Read dil switch (S2) with following significance:

4
5   Baud rate high
6   Diagnostics (i.e. terminal attached)
7   Scenario on/off.

The circuit arrangement of the 8255 I/O ports is shown in Fig. 24.5

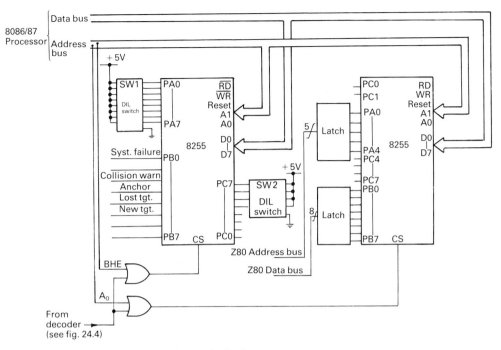

Fig. 24.5 Input/Output port connections to the Tracker processor

24.3 Start/Stop generator

The start/stop generator is an Intel 8088 processor run in minimum mode and with 8 k of ROM and 2 k of RAM. The configuration is in a normally ready state with only the common memory requiring wait states. Minimum mode means that no bus controller is required and pins 25, 26 and 27 (ALE, DEN and DTR respectively) are used to determine address and data busses. The main function of the processor is to generate the gate control signals by monitoring the azimuth and checking when to open the gate.

There are two data busses: one for the PROM, I/O and RAM and the other for the common RAM and start/stop RAM. The processor/memory and decoding layout is broadly similar to that shown for the tracker processor in Fig. 24.2.

A range counter is compared against a number stored in the start/stop RAM, and when the numbers are equal the address of the RAM is incremented giving a new gate control bit pattern and a new range number for the next beginning or end of a gate. Access by the processor to the start/stop RAM is via one of the outputs (PA1) of the I/O port. The I/O device is memory mapped to speed response to a non-maskable interrupt (NMI). The NMI request will invoke an interrupt handling program by the processor which extensively uses the control signals provided by the A port of the I/O device so that the commands are provided as a block move. This is achieved by having the command register and port addresses 2000H apart so that block moves repeatedly address the same location.

The arrangement of the I/O lines of the 8255 I/O port is as follows:

PB0–7   Range azimuth bus R4–R11
PC4–7   Range azimuth bus R0–R3

PC0–1   Range filter control
PC2   Guard filter—Auto tracking reject (active high)
PC3   Auto/Manual video select
PA0   Stop/Start memory—Real-time access (active low)
PA1   Stop/Start memory—Processor access (active low)
PA2   Comparator flip-flop reset/video mono clear
PA3   Comparator inhibit
PA4   Azimuth counter latch/output enable
PA5   Preset target flip-flop
PA6   Enable range counter output/azimuth indicators for gates
PA7   Reset target flip-flops

The generation of gate control lines, which signify whether a gate is open in range, is achieved by the use of a 12-bit counter clocked at 8 MHz and comparing the output with the contents of the start/stop RAM.

Radar returns occur approximately every millisecond but the ARPA only operates up to 40 nautical miles, approximately equal to half a millisecond. Hence when the range counter reaches its maximum value it generates an NMI (non-maskable interrupt) to the processor which allows the processor about half a millisecond to store the appropriate bit pattern in the start/stop memory.

The data stored in the stop/start memory has the format:

1 bit	12 bits	6 bits
S	Range	Gate control
1	Stop range 2	0 0 0 0 1 0
1	Start range 2	0 0 0 0 0 0
1	Stop range 1	0 0 0 0 0 1
1	Start range 1	0 0 0 0 0 0
		G5 G0

This information is stored by the processor in the non 'real-time' period of the return; access control for the RAM is handed over to a 4-bit counter which generates the address by activating PA1 (low) and PA0 (high). A simplified circuit arrangement is shown in Fig. 24.6 from which it can be seen that PA1 going high will remove the 'clear counter' input to the LS691 counter associated with the address generation for the start/stop memory. Also PA0 going low will remove the enable input from the latch that provides address inputs to the start/stop memory via the address bus, while at the same time providing the enable signal to the LS691 counter. At this time the address lines will be provided by the counter and all of them will be at zero.

While the range counter is counting, but not yet at its maximum count value, the RCO output will be low; thus FF1 of Fig. 24.6 is in inhibit mode with Q low and $\overline{Q}$ high. The $\overline{Q}$ output of FF1 is used as an input to the CLR terminal of FF2 and the CCLR terminal of the range counter; thus FF2 and the range counter will operate 'normally' with the Q output of FF2 acting as clock input to the range counter. When the range counter reaches its maximum value RCO goes high and this sets the Q output of FF1 which generates the NMI input to the 8088 processor. At the same time $\overline{Q}$ of FF1 goes low which clears the output of FF2 inhibiting the clock to, and resetting, the range counter. RCO falls low again but since $J = K = 0$ at FF1 the flip-flop is inhibited and the outputs remain at their previous level, Q high and $\overline{Q}$ low.

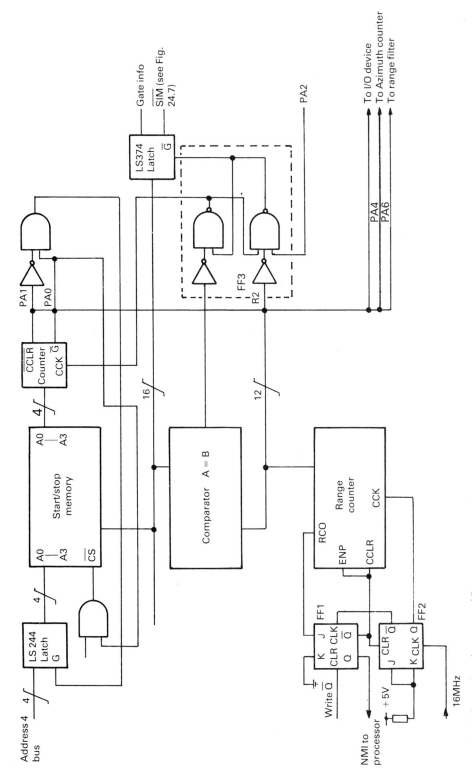

Fig. 24.6 Generation of gate control lines

The 'real-time' period starts when the CLR input of FF1 goes low via the write $\overline{Q}$ input; this sets Q low, $\overline{Q}$ high. Thus FF2 is again enabled as is the range counter which counts from zero. When the count reaches start range 1, the comparator will give an output which will set FF3. Prior to this the outputs of FF3 gave a low on the CCK input to the LS691 counter and high on the CK input of the LS374 octal latch; as the flip-flop is set the clock input to the LS691 goes high which increments the counter and hence increments the memory location accessed, taking the data to stop range 1. Also the clock input to the LS374 goes low. The input R2 from the range counter is used to reset FF3 since this gives time for the data from the RAM to settle before the reset action puts a high on the clock input to the LS374 which allows the gate control bits to be latched.

Thus at start range 1 the gate control pattern stored will be 000001 while at stop range 1 the pattern stored will be 000000. This in effect opens gate zero. In a similar fashion, gate one is opened between start range 2 and stop range 2.

The effect of the NMI input to the 8088 processor is to initiate the NMI routine which in turn produces a sequence using PA lines as follows:

PA0/1   Takes control of the start/stop memory to store a new table of ranges and control lines.

PA2   Resets comparison flip-flop FF3, causing the gates to latch azimuth count.

PA3   Inhibits the comparator to prevent spurious comparisons while the start/stop memory is being loaded.

PA4   Latches the azimuth counter and enables its output buffer (active low), allows azimuth to be interrogated by the start/stop generator via ports B and C, and the storage of azimuth in the gates.

PA5/7   Controls the target outputs. Used to stimulate the gates into storing azimuth signals.

PA6   Inhibits the range filter (a shift register consisting of 74S74s).

24.4   Video generation

Video control signals are required to be provided to the RADAR EXPANSION circuit for three purposes:

1   Guard ring video
2   Gate bright-up (for test purposes)
3   Simulation video.

Two video lines are available, WVID1 and WVID2. The signal WVID2 causes the writing of the video while WVID1 controls the level as a two-step grey scale. Fig. 24.7 shows the arrangement for producing these signals.

Guard ring video is required at the beginning and end of each gate being used for target extraction in the guard zone (gates 4 and 5). Thus the control lines G4 and G5 are fed via an OR gate to edge detectors and then to monostables. The monostables are required to give pulses of two different durations, which can be selected by the tracker to give a ring thickness appropriate for the range in use.

The resulting video pulse is ORed with the simulation video (the circuit of Fig. 24.7 actually uses two NAND gates to achieve the OR function, since inverted inputs to a NAND gate give an output that is equivalent to the output from an OR gate using non-inverted inputs). As shown in Fig. 24.6, simulation video is controlled by the start/stop generator and is one of the signals latched into the LS374 device. This signal, like guard ring, needs to be bright and is thus fed to both WVID1 and WVID2.

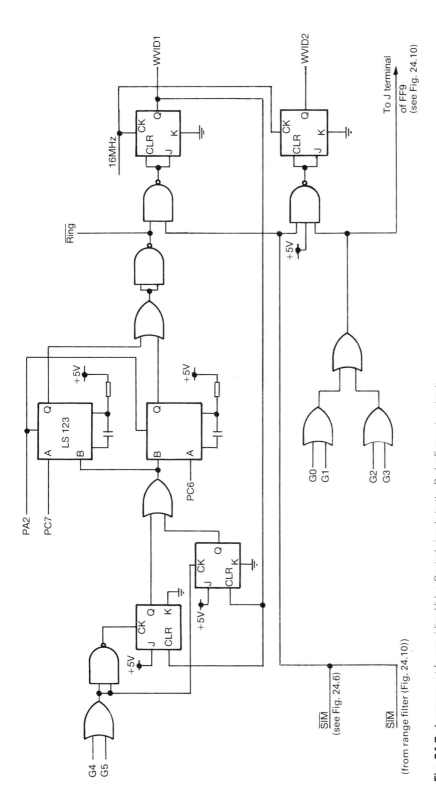

Fig. 24.7 Arrangement for providing Video Control signals to the Radar Expansion circuit

The D-type flip-flop in the final stage of the production of WVID1 and WVID2 is required to synchronise the signals with the radar video memory.

Gate video is required for testing purposes and is produced by ORing all gate control lines together as shown in Fig. 24.7. To ensure that targets (real and simulated) can be seen against the background of the gate video, the brightness of the gate video is required to be low level by requesting WVID2 only. The production of gate ring video is controlled by PC5 from the tracker, which operates this line in response to the dil switch (S1) configuration.

24.5   Correlator/Guard ring processors

The correlator is an 8088 processor run in minimum mode with 8 kbytes of ROM and 64kbytes of ROM. As the block diagram of Fig. 24.1 shows, the processor takes lists of ranges and azimuths from the real time storage and produces the range and azimuth of the target within the gate most likely to be the one being tracked.

The guard ring processor circuitry is identical to the correlator except that it requires 12 bit range and azimuth information compared to the 7 bit data required for the correlator, since it has no knowledge of the approximate position of the target.

The correlator receives this data from the tracker as the predicted position after the previous run of the filter. The correlator and its access to gate 0 will be described, but the description applies equally for gates 1, 2 and 3 and also for the guard ring processor and its access to gates 4 and 5.

The processor circuitry is similar to that described in Fig. 24.2 except that, once again, with the processor in minimum mode configuration, no bus controller is used and the outputs Address latch enable (ALE), Data transmit/Receive (DT/R) and Data enable (DEN) are used to determine address and data busses. The processor operates in normally ready mode, with READY only being switched off when DRAM or common RAM is accessed, and turned on again when the appropriate acknowledge signal is received.

Parallel I/O Ports

The I/O port for both the correlator and guard ring processors is selected whenever the processor output pin IO/M is high. Hence any I/O instruction at any address will cause the port to operate. The use of the I/O lines for each processor is as follows:

Correlator
PA0	Gate 0 overflow
PA1	Gate 1 overflow
PA2	Gate 2 overflow
PA3	Gate 3 overflow
PB7	Correlator interrupt (to tracker). Used when new target R0 is available
PC0	Gate 0 Write enable
PC1	Gate 0 Range azimuth latch output enable
PC2	Gate 1 Write enable
PC3	Gate 1 Range azimuth latch output enable
PC4	Gate 2 Write enable
PC5	Gate 2 Range azimuth latch output enable
PC6	Gate 3 Write enable
PC7	Gate 3 Range azimuth latch output enable

Guard ring
PA0	Gate 5 overflow

PA1   Gate 4 overflow
PB7   Guard ring interrupt (to tracker)
PC0   Gate 5 Data bus upper half write enable
PC1   Gate 5 Data bus lower half write enable
PC2   Gate 4 Data bus upper half write enable
PC3   Gate 4 Data bus lower half write enable
PC4   Gate 5 Range—azimuth latch output enable
PC5   Gate 4 Range—azimuth latch output enable

Addresses for the gate memory are generated by a counter during real-time acquisition. Parallel loading on the counters is used to generate the address in processor access periods. The arrangement is shown in Fig. 24.8 for gate 0.

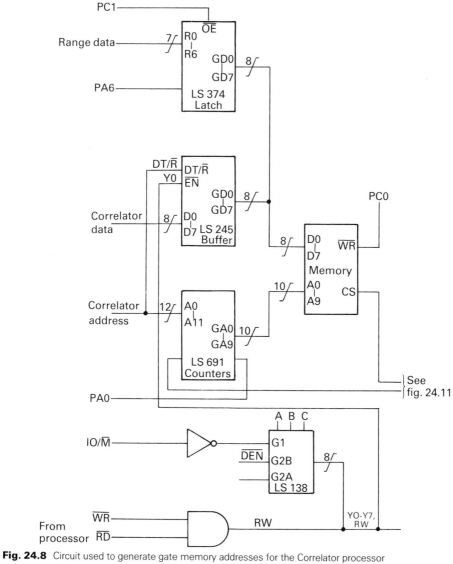

Fig. 24.8 Circuit used to generate gate memory addresses for the Correlator processor

The write enable line for the memory is active during writing operations by virtue of control line PC0. The range azimuth latch and the correlator data buffer share a common data line to the memory; during the period that the processor is writing, the range azimuth latch is turned off by control line PC1. During real-time operation the write line remains active but with the range azimuth latch turned on. The processor sets up the access as a Read or Write (RW) before performing its access. The gate memory chip select line is used for this purpose with its input determined by a combination of RW and Y0, the latter signal also being used to enable the data buffer as Fig. 24.8 shows.

For guard ring access to the gates the process is similar to that described above and much of the circuitry is the same as that of Fig. 24.8 for gate 0. However, the guard ring processor requires full information on target position and uses twelve bits of range and azimuth data, whereas the correlator, by only updating position, can only use the least significant part of the data. The difference in processor access is in the 16 bit to 8 bit accessing involving gate to processor. In this case two chip selects are generated and, considering gate 5, one is for the lower half of the data bus (Y0) and one for the upper half (Y1). These directly control the appropriate data bus buffer. Additionally Y0 and Y1 are combined so that access to either half will generate the address in the same way as described earlier for gate 0. Separate write control lines are required for each half of the bus and these are provided, for gate 5, by PC0 and PC1. Figure 24.9 shows the arrangement.

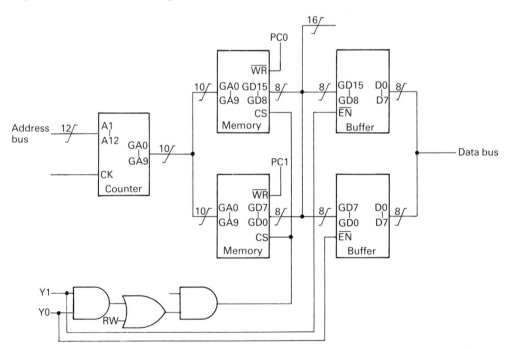

Fig. 24.9 Circuit used to generate gate memory addresses for the Guard Ring processor

24.6 Range Filter

The range filter is a shift register and bipolar PROM that generates 'target' pulses which are used to store range data in the gate memories. The gate memories have two signals that control the storage of data. Gate control lines generated by the start/stop generator enable the gate memory, which then stores range whenever a 'target' is received. These signals can be generated in the non real-time period to allow storage of azimuth in the gate memory at the end of each radar return when the gate is on. The arrangement is shown in Fig. 24.10.

The start/stop generator control line PC3 together with manual or auto video input will determine the radar video input to the filter. The filter itself consists of flip-flops FF1 to FF6 which are connected as a shift register with FF1 wired to detect very small targets. The shift register outputs, together with start/stop generator control lines PC0 and PC1, form the input to the PROM. The PROM detects patterns that should be recognised as a target, e.g. 001100, and the patterns are such that detection of two or three 'ones' will produce a target pulse in a particular position in range. The bit patterns that form the logic of target detection can be selected from a choice of four using PC0 and PC1. Flip-flops FF7 and FF8 in the output circuit help to remove any glitches from the PROM output. With the start/stop generator control line PC2, input to FF9, at 'zero', the output for both gate targets is the same. However, with PC2 at 'one', FF9 can clock through the output of the OR gates that represents any tracking gate being active. This stops the filter PROM from detecting targets for the guard ring gates and prevents multiple tracking.

24.7   Gate sequencer operation

The gate memory has its address generated by a counter and is enabled for writing by the correlator processor. The gate sequencer circuit used for detecting a target is shown in Fig. 24.11.

The flip-flops FF1 to FF4 are initially reset with all Q outputs low. This means that $\overline{Q}$ of FF4 is high which enables FF1 and FF3; $\overline{Q}$ of FF3 is high enabling FF2 while FF4 has a low on its CLR input.

Considering only gate 0, when the gate line G0 goes high at the J input of FF1 it only requires a negative edge to the clock input to make Q of FF1 go high. The clock input for FF1 is the target pulse and the leading edge will latch the target range. The clock input for the remaining flip-flops is provided by the 16 MHz clock line and after Q of FF1 has gone high the next 16 MHz clock pulse trailing edge will make Q of FF2 high also; this generates the write pulse via $\overline{Q}$ of FF2. The trailing edge of the next pulse will make Q of FF3 high which resets FF2 via its CLR input and ends the write pulse. Also the $\overline{Q}$ output of FF3, together with the next clock pulse going high, will clock the address generating counter ready for storage of the next reading. The trailing edge of the clock pulse will set $\overline{Q}$ of FF4 to zero and reset FF1 and FF2 via their CLR inputs. FF4 is then itself reset by Q of FF1 as it goes low.

The sequence has been described for range storage. The process for azimuth storage is similar, using artificial stimulation of the gate control and target pulses by the start/stop generator. The correlating processor determines whether the information in each memory location is range or azimuth by checking the most significant bit, which is the stored value of PA6 ('1' means azimuth is stored, '0' is range).

24.8   Common memories

The common memories between the tracker and raster controller Z80, and between all the ARPA processors, are controlled by ROM based synchronous sequencers. In all cases when a processor requires access it goes into a 'wait' or 'not-ready' state until

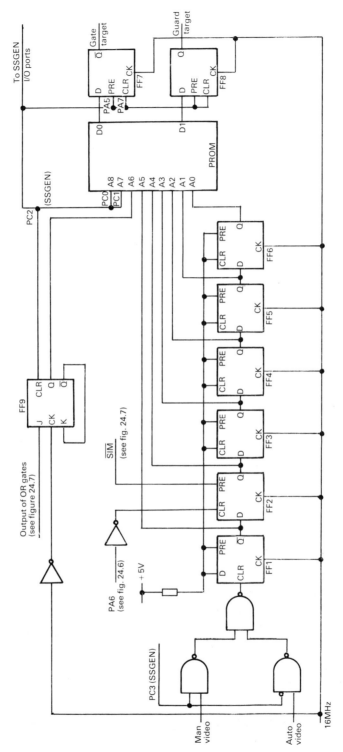

Fig. 24.10 Arrangement for generating 'target' pulses used to store range data in the gate memories

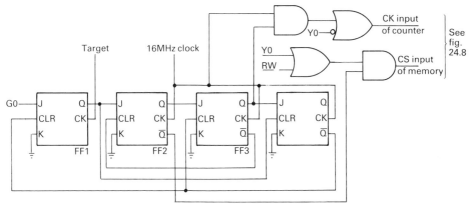

Fig. 24.11 Gate sequencer circuit

the buffers giving access have been turned on, and acknowledgement of this has been sent.

The shared memory of the 8086 and Z80 processors consists of 4 k of CMOS RAM arranged as a 16 bit word, with address and data buffers that can be connected to the address/data busses for access by either the Z80 or the 8086 device. The memory is accessed via a chip select input to a ROM based synchronous sequencer clocked at 16MHz. The output from the ROM is connected to logic gates via D-type flip-flops. The inputs and outputs are clocked into and out of the ROM in phases with feedback to prevent glitches. Figure 24.12 shows the arrangement.

The normal, unaccessed, output of the ROM is logic 1 given by the ROM location values of FF. Thus the enable inputs of the LS244/245 buffers are high ensuring that all buffers are off and neither processor has access to the RAM.

If for example the Z80 requires access, the Z80 CS input goes low which causes the WAIT input to the Z80 processor to go low. As the outputs of the ROM go low the Z80 acknowledge line goes high, taking the WAIT input to the Z80 high again. The buffers are enabled since the Q outputs of the D-type flip-flops go low and this reaches the buffers via the combinational logic. The direction of data movement can be controlled by the WR and RD inputs from the Z80.

For the 8086 processor, when it selects the common memory, it is in a not-ready state and waits for an acknowledgement which provides the ready signal. This is via the 8284 device and pin AEN2 as discussed earlier for the 8086 and shown in Fig. 24.3.

Whichever processor requests access, the particular logic circuit enables the particular buffers which give address and data access to the shared memory. The acknowledge signal for both circuits is a delayed version of the input request, and this allows time for the address and data lines to settle before the data is used. In addition the write signal is controlled by the acknowledge signals so that during a write cycle the data has settled before the write action is implemented.

Buffering and arbitration between the four processors works on the same principles as the shared memory described above. The sequencer hardware is similar but with additional signals, and all the design requirements regarding access requests buffering and its control and delaying of write pulse apply. The logic inside the sequencer ROM is more complex as a result of arbitrating between four processors.

24.9 Radar expansion board

The radar expansion board is the link between the ARPA system and the radar

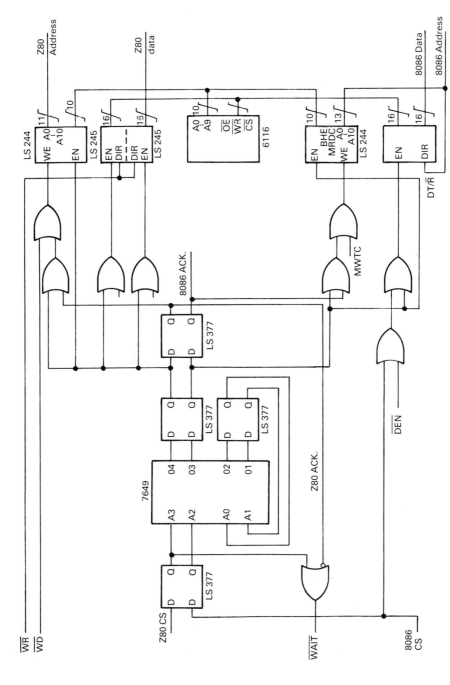

Fig. 24.12　Shared memory for the Tracker and Raster Controller processors

interface board (see Fig. 24.1). The main features of the HR Concept radar are dealt with elsewhere and this chapter, although only concerned with the HR ARPA version, will examine the radar expansion board simply because it does provide an interface with the ARPA computer. Additionally the board permits a serial communications link to any peripheral that can be interfaced with the HR series (an RS 422/3 interface providing an NMEA 0183 input for a position fixing system, printer etc). Information can be sent as an output from the ARPA system, giving ownship's and target data on all tracked or selected targets.

The radar expansion board also provides battery backed up clock calendar information.

The processor used on the board is a Z80 with associated RAM (8 k × 8 bits) and ROM (16 k × 8 bits) as shown in Fig. 24.13.

Data movement between the Z80 processor and the 8088 on the radar interface board is achieved using address and data buffers and a shared RAM (8 k × 8 bits). Either the Z80 or the 8088 may access the shared RAM to store or extract data. Messages and data are sent between the processors using a software 'handshake' via the shared RAM. A bus arbitration state machine combination of a 1 k PROM, D-type flip-flops and combinational logic is used to control the enable inputs of the address and data buffers to prevent bus contention. A state machine is a system that can be defined in terms of a set of states that may exist in the system. Once in a particular state, the states should remain stable for a period of time even if the inputs that caused the states are changed. The outputs from the system will depend on the states that exist in the system and the inputs that caused them. The system may progress from one state to the next and the next state will depend on the previous state and the new inputs. Figure 24.14 shows the arrangement for the bus arbitration state machine. The D-type flip-flops of the HC 374 device form a memory element that is reinforced by the outputs of the 82S129 PROM. Inputs to D-type flip-flops 3, 4, 5 and 6 of the HC 374 are from the outputs of the 82S129, and these values are available at the Q outputs of the flip-flops when the next clock pulse goes positive. In turn the memory accessed on the 82S129 at any instant depends on the Q outputs of flip-flops 1, 2, 3 and 4 which form the memory address lines. The input to flip-flop 1 is from the decoder output Z80 SRE, while the input to flip-flop 2 is the 8088 input from the radar interface board. The combinational logic will send control signals to the relevant processor, depending on which has requested shared memory access, and will also send the enabling signal to the required set of address and data buffers allowing access to be completed. The WAIT (Z80) or READY (8088) signal will be sent to the correct processor as soon as the memory access request has been made; the WAIT, or READY, signal will change state some time afterwards according to the change in the output state of flip-flop 7, or 8 as the case may be.

A further set of address and data buffers is used to enable messages to be sent to and from the shared RAM on the ARPA computer. Figure 24.13 shows the details.

The radar expansion board also generates and transfers radar signals required by the ARPA computer. A 16 MHz clock reference frequency is also provided.

Serial communications between the radar expansion board and peripherals consists of a switchable RS422/3 link provided by the Z80 DUART. The DUART, which interfaces with the Z80, is accessed by 2 address lines which select channels A or B and control or data input; chip enable is achieved via a decoder. The DUART can receive or transmit serial data via 3691 and 88LS120 devices. Hardware handshaking is provided.

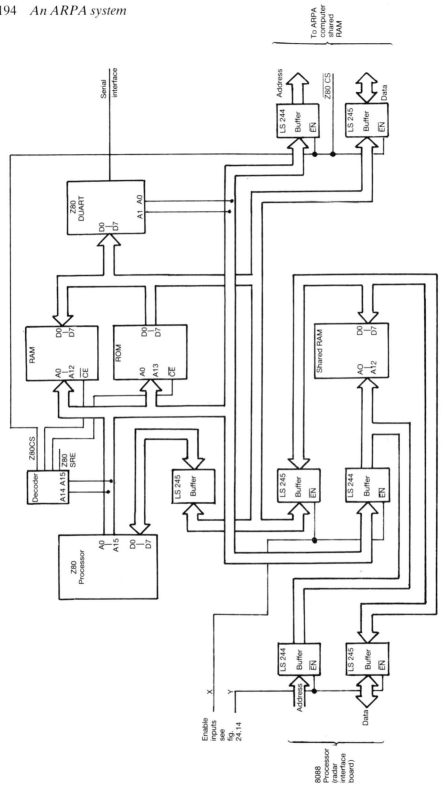

Fig. 24.13 Block diagram of the Radar Expansion board

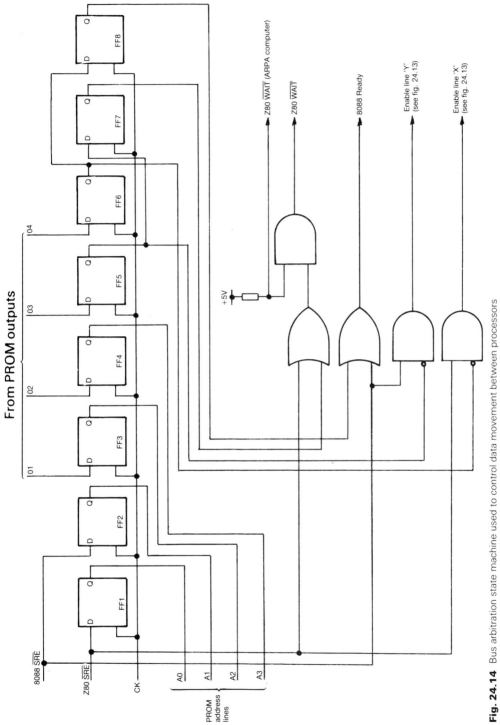

Fig. 24.14 Bus arbitration state machine used to control data movement between processors

25
Operating Information for Kelvin Hughes HR ARPA

25.1 Introduction

The HR series displays and keyboards may be used in several system configurations:

- Master (Radar 1)
- Master (Radar 1): Slave (Radar 2)
- Slave (Radar 1): Slave (Radar 2)

The display and keyboard only control the transceiver functions when they are designated as 'Master'. The ARPA version could be fitted as a Master or a Slave.

The HR3000A combined radar and ARPA system with a colour monitor is shown in Fig. 25.1. Monochrome monitors are also available.

Fig. 25.1 HR3000A console with colour monitor (courtesy Kelvin Hughes)

The system is flexible in that the monitor and keyboard could be separated from the processor unit by up to 15 metres. Also the monitor and keyboard could be separated from each other to allow for different fitting configurations, e.g. console mounted display and bench mounted keyboard. Further flexibility results in the possible fitting of remote monitors.

The layout for the HR 3000A ARPA keyboard is shown in Fig. 25.2. The keyboard controls are colour coded to assist identification and operation. Main controls are orange, secondary controls are yellow while alarms are red. An arrow graphic to one side of a control indicates that the control function is used with the joystick. Related groups of controls are outlined or linked with white lines.

It must be stressed that in the sections that follow, the description is that of a particular ARPA system with its own terminology and symbols. These may not be the same as used by other ARPA manufacturers. Moves are afoot to standardise ARPA symbols and control names, and the International Electrotechnical Commission (IEC) has published a document which attempts to address this issue. This proposal, reproduced as Appendix 2, is at the time of publication still only a discussion document and must not be regarded as a final draft.

The Kelvin Hughes ARPA facility provides:

- *Target acquisition*   A target with relative speeds of up to at least 120 knots can be acquired out to a range of 24 miles. Up to 20 targets can be acquired either manually using the joystick or automatically using single or dual guard zones.

- *Guard zones*   Two guard zones are available, one fixed, the other variable. When a target, which has not previously been acquired, enters a guard zone, an alarm is given and the ARPA automatically acquires the target.

- *Tracking*   Acquired targets are automatically tracked to a range of 40 miles and vectors are generated which show the course and are proportional to the speed of the target. All acquired targets can be labelled, and data on target course, speed, range, bearing, CPA and TCPA can be displayed. For the ARPA tracking is done in True motion.

- *Vector mode*   This gives the option of true vectors when the display is in the RELATIVE motion mode, and relative vectors when the display is in the TRUE motion mode.

- *Target history*   This displays a target track history, showing four past positions for each target, each separated by three minutes.

- *Fixed targets*   Tracked targets can be designated as Fixed targets.

- *Autodrift*   Drift is automatically calculated using the average movement of designated Fixed targets.

- *Anchor watch*   All designated Fixed targets are monitored for movement, relative to ownship, and if any one target moves in excess of the Anchor watch limit, the ANCHOR WATCH alarm will be triggered. The limit is defined in the fault parameters with possible values of 100, 200 or 500 yards. Default value is 100 yards.

- *TCPA/CPA limit*   The limits define the time and range of target that will trigger the COLLISION WARNING alarm. TCPA limit can be varied between 1 and 60 minute increments, CPA limit can be varied between 0.1 and 6.0 nautical miles in increments of 0.1 nautical miles. The default values are 15 minutes and 1 nautical mile.

Fig. 25.2 HR3000A ARPA keyboard (courtesy Kelvin Hughes)

- *BCR/BCT*   Once data is available on a target the bow crossing range and time can be requested. The information is only available while the control is operated and replaces TCPA/CPA in the data field.

- *Trial manoeuvre*   Allows the effects of an intended change of course or speed to be assessed in advance or avoiding action to be planned when a potential collision situation exists.

- *Simulation*   Provides both a training and test facility, the simulation can be based on a known solution or, if required, a random solution. The known solution is the basis for testing the integrity of the ARPA computer.

- *Lost target*   When a previously tracked target is lost, its last known parameters are tested to see if it is likely to be of interest to the operator. The target is assumed to be of no interest if its range is greater than 12 nautical miles and it has a negative TCPA. If the target is designated of interest, then the alarm sounds and the Lost target alarm flashes. Acknowledgement of the alarm places a Lost target symbol (L) on the display at the last known position of the target. If the Lost target was previously designated as a TCPA/CPA violation then both the Lost target and Collision warning alarms operate.

- *Tracking overload*   An alarm indicates attempted acquisition of the twenty-first target and requires that one or more targets should be released from tracking.

- *System failure*   This is indicated by an audible alarm and the display reverts to Radar only until the fault is cleared.

25.2   Using the ARPA system

ARPA Controls

The full layout of the ARPA keyboard is shown in Fig. 25.3. A description of the use of these controls for the purpose of ARPA plotting is contained in the sections that follow.

- *Acquire target*   To acquire a target manually, the joystick marker should be positioned over the target and the ACQUIRE TARGET control pressed. The target will be labelled, within one rotation of the trace, with an 'X' symbol. Releasing the ACQUIRE TARGET control will allow the use of the joystick for other operations. A target vector will be generated within 1 minute and the vector will be stable within 3 minutes.
    If in TRUE motion, and the true speed is less than 2 knots, then for zero speed targets a 'Z' is displayed.

- *Select*   To select a target the joystick marker should be positioned over the target and the SELECT control pressed and released. The target plot symbol and vector will flash to acknowledge selection. Once a target is selected, full target information is available in the target data field (see Fig. 25.4).

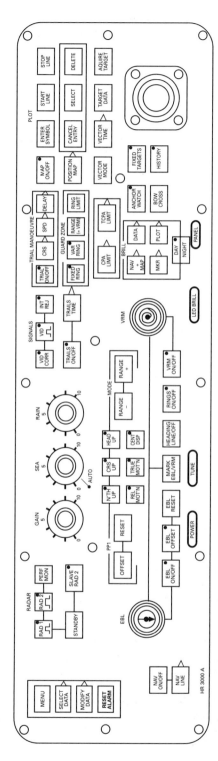

Fig. 25.3 Layout of the HR3000A ARPA keyboard (courtesy Kelvin Hughes)

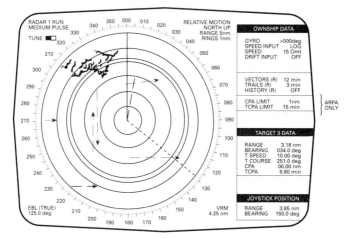

Fig. 25.4 Example of screen data fields (courtesy Kelvin Hughes)

When the SELECT control is pressed, the target vector, map or navigational line or symbol nearest to the joystick marker will flash. An incorrect selection can be cancelled by pressing the CANCEL ENTRY control.

- *Cancel entry* Pressing and releasing the CANCEL ENTRY control will cancel the current control operation and return the display to its previous status. Thus if a target had been selected in error, or target data is no longer required, CANCEL ENTRY control will return the display to its previous status.

- *Delete* To cease tracking a single target the joystick marker should be positioned on the target and the SELECT control pressed. The target symbol and vector will flash. Pressing the DELETE control will cause tracking/plotting on the target to stop; targets causing a collision warning cannot be deleted.

- *Cancel entry/Delete* Pressing the CANCEL ENTRY and DELETE controls simultaneously will delete all tracked targets, plots and vectors. This does not apply to targets with collision warnings displayed.

- *Vector mode* The vector presentation mode can be reversed by pressing and holding the VECTOR MODE control. This displays relative vectors while in TRUE motion or CENTRED DISPLAY (CD). This does not apply in the TRIAL MANOEUVRE mode.

- *Vector time* By pressing and holding the VECTOR TIME control the vector time may be changed between 3 and 60 minutes. The change, in increments of 3 minutes, occurs when the joystick is operated in the vertical plane to increase or decrease the time shown next to VECTORS in the OWNSHIP DATA field.
  The default or initial value of vectors is 15 minutes divided into 3 minute intervals. The length of the vector is proportional to the speed of the target (e.g. if target speed is 12 knots then vector length is 3 nm, which is the distance the target will travel in 15 minutes). See Fig. 25.5.

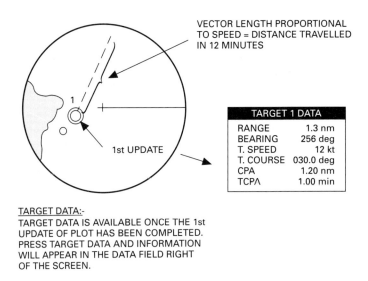

Fig. 25.5 Display of target data (courtesy Kelvin Hughes)

- *Target data*   To display target data the joystick marker should be positioned on the required target/vector and the TARGET DATA control pressed. The target plot symbols and vector will flash and all targets will be labelled with identification numbers while the TARGET DATA control is pressed. Target data on the selected target will be displayed in the target data field. see Fig. 25.4.

  Between acquiring a target and the ARPA generating a vector the TARGET DATA is not available.

  Target data on the selected target will be transmitted via the serial interface each time the TARGET DATA control is pressed. Data includes:

  —Target range and bearing.
  —Target course and speed.
  —Closest point of approach (CPA).
  —Time to closest point of approach (TCPA).
  —Ownship course and speed.

- *CPA limit/TCPA limit*   The CPA limit or the TCPA limit may be varied by pressing and holding the CPA limit control or the TCPA limit control. At the same time the joystick should be operated in the vertical plane to increase or decrease the limit value. Releasing the CPA or TCPA limit control will enter the new values in the data line.

  Alternatively, the CPA and TCPA limits may be changed by pressing and holding the SELECT control and using the joystick to position the menu cursor at the required data line then releasing the SELECT control. Pressing and holding the MODIFY DATA control and using the joystick in the vertical plane will increase or decrease the limit values. TCPA has a range of 1 to 60 minutes, in increments of 1 minute; CPA has a range of 0.1 nm to 6 nm in increments of 0.1 nm.

  The default values are 15 minutes (TCPA) and 1 nm (CPA).

- *Bow cross: (BCR/BCT)* Bow crossing range (BCR) and Bow crossing time (BCT) can be obtained on any target which has previously been acquired and is being tracked. The target may be selected by placing the joystick marker on or near the target/vector and pressing the TARGET DATA control. The target/vector will flash and target data will be displayed in the target data field. If the BOW CROSS control is pressed and held the ARPA acquisition gates will be displayed and BCR and BCT data will replace the CPA and TCPA data in the TARGET DATA field. This new data will continue to be displayed during the time the BOW CROSS control is held pressed. An example of BCR/BCT is shown in Fig. 25.6.

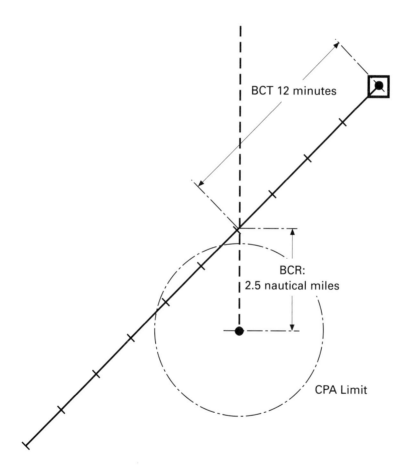

BCT 12 minutes

BCR: 2.5 nautical miles

CPA Limit

Relative Motion
Relative Vector
Vector length: 30 minutes
Calculated BCR: 2.5 nautical miles
Calculated BCT: 12 minutes

Fig. 25.6 Example of BCR/BCT (courtesy Kelvin Hughes)

- *Fixed target*   A target may be designated as a FIXED target provided it has previously been acquired, is being tracked and is travelling at less than 10 knots.

  To designate a Fixed target the joystick should be positioned on or near the required target and the SELECT control pressed. The target/label will flash and if the FIXED TARGET control is pressed the status LED will illuminate and the target label will change to 'F'. The target/label will continue flashing until another target, map line etc is selected, or CANCEL ENTRY is pressed.

  Up to four targets can be designated as Fixed targets. The average movement of all Fixed targets is used to calculate AUTODRIFT.

  To deselect a Fixed target position the joystick marker should be positioned on or near the target/label and the SELECT control pressed. The 'F' label will flash and if the FIXED TARGET control is pressed the target label will revert to 'Z' (provided the target speed is less than 2 knots).

  An example of the use of Fixed targets is shown in Fig. 25.7.

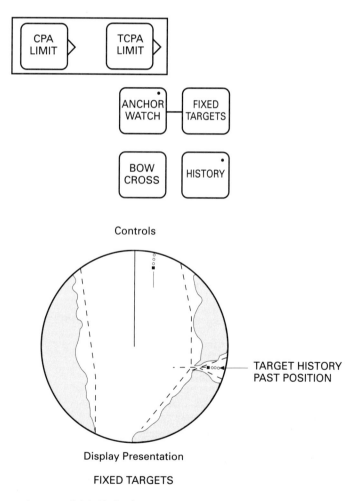

Fig. 25.7 Fixed targets (courtesy Kelvin Hughes)

- *Anchor watch*   This can only be selected when one or more targets have been designated as Fixed targets and are labelled 'F'.
    To select Anchor watch the ANCHOR WATCH control is pressed which will illuminate the status LED and the label 'F' on all Fixed targets will change to '⚓'.
    Subsequent operation of the ANCHOR WATCH control will cause the Anchor watch function to be turned off, the status LED to extinguish and target labels to revert to 'F' as Fixed targets.
    All targets designated as Anchor watch '⚓' targets are monitored for relative movement exceeding the ANCHOR WATCH limit. The default value of this distance is set at 200 yards.

- *History*   Target history can be displayed by pressing the HISTORY control. The status LED will light and four past positions, separated by a period of three minutes, will be displayed for every target being tracked.
    History information is true in True motion and CD modes.
    Subsequent operation of the HISTORY control will turn the History function off and extinguish the status LED.

Guard Zones

There are two Guard zone rings, one a Fixed ring and the other a Variable ring, with each ring 0.5 nm wide.
    The Fixed ring can be activated alone, while the Variable ring cannot be activated unless the Fixed ring is activated. If the Variable ring is activated without first activating the Fixed ring then the Fixed ring will automatically be activated.

- *Fixed ring*   The Fixed ring guard zone is preset between 4.0 nm and 4.5 nm (see Fig. 25.8).
    To activate the Fixed ring guard zone the FIXED RING control should be pressed; the status LED will light and the Fixed ring guard zone will appear on the screen at 4.0 nm to 4.5 nm, scaled to the range in use.
    Subsequent operation of the FIXED RING control will turn the Fixed ring guard control off; the status LED will be extinguished and the guard zone ring will disappear from the screen.
    Targets acquired and tracked when the Guard zone was activated will continue to be tracked when the Guard zone is switched off.

- *VAR ring*   The Variable ring guard zone can be positioned to any range from 5 nm out to 24 nm.
    The Variable ring guard zone may be activated by pressing the VAR RING control. This causes the status LED to light and the Variable ring guard zone will appear on the screen at the default initialisation range of 6 nm to 6.5 nm, scaled to the range in use, see Fig. 25.8.
    If the Fixed ring guard zone has not already been activated, the status LED on the FIXED RING control will illuminate and the Fixed ring guard zone will appear on the screen at 4.0 nm to 4.5 nm range.

- *Range (= VRM)*   To change the range of the Variable ring guard zone, set the VRM control to ON; the status LED will illuminate and the VRM ring will appear on the screen. Using the VRM rotary control the VRM ring may be set to the required range, see Fig. 25.9.

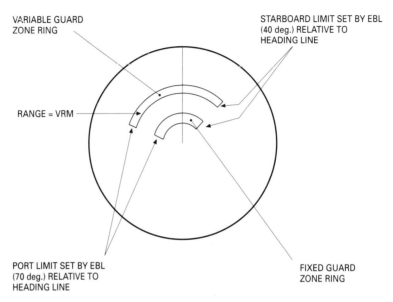

Fig. 25.8 Guard zones (courtesy Kelvin Hughes)

If the Range (= VRM) control is pressed, and the Variable ring guard zone is activated, the Variable ring guard zone will move to the limit set by the VRM.

● *Ring limits*   The port and starboard bearing limits of both the Fixed and Variable ring guard zones default to ∓180° relative to ownship's heading line, see Fig. 25.8.
   To change the bearing limits, the EBL control should be set to ON when the status LED will light and the EBL line will appear on the screen. Using the EBL rotary control the EBL line should be set to the required bearing limit Port and, pressing the RING LIMITS control, the EBL line should be set to the required bearing limit starboard and the RING LIMITS control again pressed.
   The port and starboard limits will change to the new limits set by the EBL control.

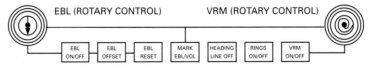

Fig. 25.9 Marker controls (courtesy Kelvin Hughes)

25.3 ARPA alarms

ARPA alarms are displayed in the data field to the right hand side of the screen, see Fig. 25.10. An audio alarm also sounds.

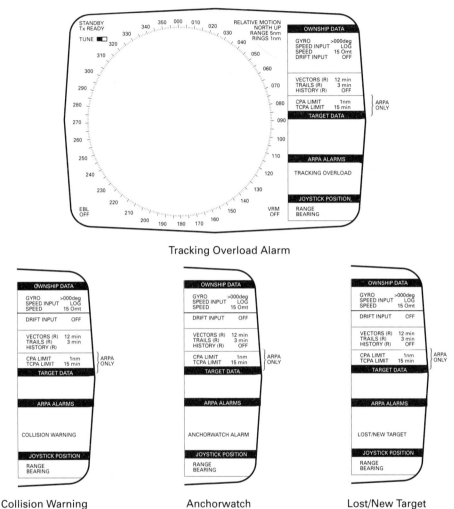

Tracking Overload Alarm

Collision Warning
Alarm

Anchorwatch
Alarm

Lost/New Target
Alarm

Fig. 25.10 ARPA alarms (courtesy Kelvin Hughes)

The alarms are as follows:

- *New target* This alarm is activated if an unacquired target enters the acquisition zone. The alarm flashes until the target is acknowledged by pressing the ALARM RESET.

- *Tracking overload* This alarm indicates the attempted acquisition of the twenty-first target. One or more targets should be released. This can be achieved by placing the joystick marker over target/vector for the selected target and pressing

the SELECT control; the target/vector will flash. Pressing the DELETE control
will stop the tracking of the selected target.

- *Collision warning* Violation of both the CPA and TCPA limits by a tracked target
  will result in the data field and audio alarm being started. A square symbol will be
  generated on the encroaching target. The audio alarm may be cleared by operating
  the ALARM RESET button. The target now ranks as 'selected' and its data will be
  displayed and continually updated on the readout panel.
    The target vector and square symbol will continue to flash until the parameter
  violation ceases. Any other target may be selected while a collision alarm exists,
  and the data field will indicate the selected target data for 10 seconds before
  reverting to the previously displayed collision target.

- *Lost target* When a previously tracked target is lost, an audio alarm will sound and
  the LOST TARGET symbol (L) will be generated over the last known position of
  the target. This situation persists until the operator presses the ALARM RESET
  button.
    If the range of the lost target is greater than 12 nm and has a negative TCPA then
  it will be considered to be no longer of interest.

- *Anchor watch* This indicates a movement of more than the ANCHOR WATCH
  limit (set in the default menu) relative to a target designated FIXED while in the
  ANCHOR WATCH mode.

- *System failure* This may originate in one of two ways:
    1 By a hardware watchdog on the ARPA tracker PCB; this flag is received by the
      ARPA adaptor PCB and indicates that data passed through the shared system
      memory should be disregarded. The alarm remains active while a fault persists
      and an audio alarm will sound until acknowledged by the operator. The PPI
      display reverts to Radar-only operation until the watchdog flag clears.
    2 By faulty handshaking through the shared system memory. This will indicate, in
      software, that shared data travelling in either direction may be corrupted. All
      data in the memory is disregarded until the handshaking is successful. ARPA
      symbology is suppressed until the fault clears.

25.4 Trial manoeuvre

These controls and an example of their use is shown in Fig. 25.11.

- *Trial ON/OFF* This control activates the trial mode. The annotation TRIAL will
  be displayed at the bottom of the screen. Status is indicated by an LED.
    A trial menu will appear in the menu area, indicating: COURSE; SPEED;
  DELAY.
    The course and speed will default to ownship's present course and speed (i.e.
  values at the instant that 'trial' is activated). The delay (time before the manoeuvre
  is started) will default to 10 minutes.

- *Delay* The delay may be set to any value, in one minute increments, from 1 to 30
  minutes. The delay will count down to zero from the selected delay period. The

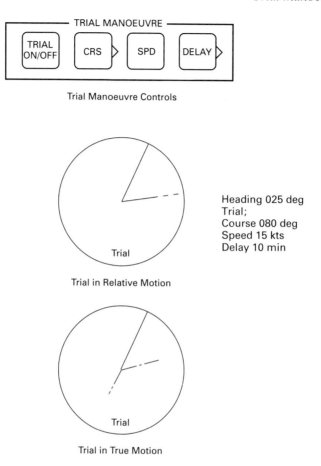

Fig. 25.11   Trial manoeuvre (courtesy Kelvin Hughes)

DELAY may be adjusted by using the joystick in the vertical plane while pressing the DELAY button.

At delay time 'zero', the trial will be cancelled, the menu area cleared, the 'TRIAL' legend cancelled and the display will revert to normal operation.

● *Trial course/Speed*   TRIAL COURSE will operate in five degree steps while the TRIAL SPEED will operate in 1 knot increments (0 to 99 knots). For example, if default ownship course is 126 degrees true, starboard trial course adjustments will select 131, 136, 141 etc.

The trial course and speed are varied using the joystick in the vertical plane while pressing the COURSE or SPEED button, as appropriate.

The trial manoeuvre will function in true and CD mode. In true motion, ownship's vector is displayed along the heading line, then turns on to the TRIAL COURSE. The DELAY TIME is defined as the time from the initiation of the delay period to the time that ownship has completed the manoeuvre.

There are eight rates of change for course and speed, defined by preset switches on the ARPA computer PCB.

25.5 Simulation mode

A simulation mode is provided and this gives both a training and a test facility. The simulation can be based on a known situation or, if required, a random situation.

Four targets are generated by the simulation program and these move within a 15 mile radius of the radar origin.

The simulation program is initiated by:

1 Selecting STANDBY, indicated by a status LED.
2 Selecting MENU, MAIN MENU appears in the data field to the right hand side of the screen.
3 The joystick may be used, with SELECT DATA control, to select the SIMULA-TION MODE and the MODIFY DATA control pressed.
4 Wait until the ARPA NOT READY message disappears from the ARPA alarms area.
5 For the known situation, the ACQUIRE TARGET control should be pressed to initiate the scenario.
6 To generate a random solution, the joystick should be operated, in any direction, and the ACQUIRE TARGET control pressed to initiate the scenario.
7 The scenario can run for about 60 minutes. To terminate the simulation mode, the STANDBY control should be pressed.

The known situation is shown in Fig. 25.12 and is a basis for testing the integrity of the ARPA computer.

Ownship parameters for rate of turn and rate of change in speed are preset on the ARPA computer tracker board. The parameters are normally set on installation and affect the trial manoeuvre simulation accuracy.

25.6 Mapping facilities

The Kelvin Hughes HR ARPA system has the facility for superimposing maps on the radar picture. Up to 16 maps, each of 64 lines or 128 symbols, or a combination of both four types of line and eight types of symbols can be drawn, see Fig. 25.13. Different types of common symbol include anchor, way points and turning points. Once drawn, maps can be stored in a non-volatile battery-backed memory for future use. Recalled true motion maps are annotated (T) and can be positioned by means of the control panel joystick to match up with reference points. Graphics in true motion mode are SEA stabilised, or are LAND stabilised if a drift input is used. AUTO-DRIFT can also be generated in order to stabilise the maps.

Map Construction for True Motion and ARPA systems is as follows:

- *Map Menu* With the equipment in the RUN mode (RAD 1 ⌐, RAD 1 ⌐ or SLAVE RAD 2), the MAP ON/OFF control should be pressed; the status LED will light and the MAP MENU will appear in the data field to the right of the screen, see Fig. 25.14.
  The MAP MENU will not be displayed if the ARPA TRIAL MANOEUVRE is ON, or if a radar system failure is indicated.

- *Map selection* The map selection (MAP NO. XX) in the MAP MENU will default to the last MAP NO. used or, when no maps have been stored, it will default to MAP NO. 1. It will also default to a full line (——) and diamond symbol (◇).
  The SELECT DATA control should be pressed and held while the joystick is

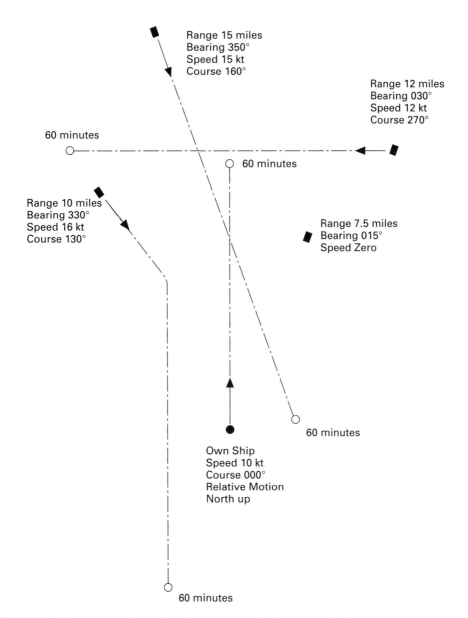

Range 15 miles
Bearing 350°
Speed 15 kt
Course 160°

Range 12 miles
Bearing 030°
Speed 12 kt
Course 270°

60 minutes

60 minutes

Range 10 miles
Bearing 330°
Speed 16 kt
Course 130°

Range 7.5 miles
Bearing 015°
Speed Zero

60 minutes

Own Ship
Speed 10 kt
Course 000°
Relative Motion
North up

60 minutes

Fig. 25.12 Simulation mode starting position for 'known situation' (courtesy Kelvin Hughes)

used to position the menu cursor next to MAP NO.   . The SELECT DATA control should then be released.

If maps have already been saved, it will be necessary to select a free map number. This will be indicated by MAP NO. XX 99% FREE. Pressing and holding the MODIFY DATA control while using the joystick in the vertical plane enables map numbers to be selected until a 99% FREE map appears in the MAP MENU. The MODIFY DATA control can then be released.

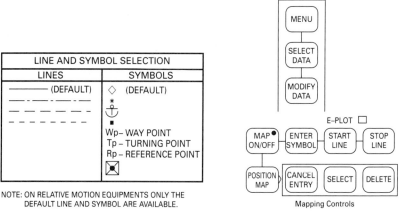

Fig. 25.13 Mapping symbols and controls (courtesy Kelvin Hughes)

- *Start line* The joystick marker should be moved to the required 'map start' position and the START LINE control pressed. The joystick marker should then be moved to the first 'turnpoint' position, a map line will appear on the screen with one end fixed at the 'map start' position and the other end following the joystick marker.

  The START LINE control should be pressed to fix the first 'map line' in position with respect to land or other stationary targets. If the joystick is moved to the second 'turnpoint', a second line will appear on the screen with its origin at the first turnpoint and its other end following the joystick marker.

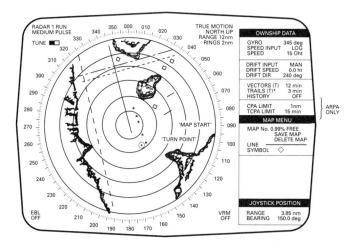

Fig. 25.14 True motion equipment in 'Run' mode 'Map on Selected (courtesy Kelvin Hughes)

Map lines can be positioned and fixed at other 'turnpoint' positions using the joystick marker and 'START LINE' control. Additionally, a facility exists for modifying (rubber banding) existing lines. By placing the joystick marker near the end of a line, or a turnpoint, and pressing SELECT the joystick marker can be automatically locked to the line end, or the turnpoint. Moving the joystick marker allows the line end, or the turnpoint, to follow the joystick marker. The map lines are fixed by pressing STOP LINE and this also frees the joystick marker for other purposes.

- *Stop line*   A map line may be terminated by pressing the STOP LINE control, freeing the joystick marker for other uses.

- *Enter symbol*   Single map symbols may be positioned by placing the joystick marker in the required position and pressing the ENTER SYMBOL control.

- *Line and symbol options*   Other types of line or symbol may be selected by pressing, and holding, the SELECT DATA control and using the joystick to position the menu cursor next to LINE, or SYMBOL, data lines in the MAP MENU.
  Pressing the MODIFY DATA control will cause the next line or map symbol to appear in the menu, see Fig. 25.13. The lines or map symbols can be used in map construction as described earlier.

- *Save map*   A map may be saved by pressing, and holding, the SELECT DATA control and, by means of the joystick, positioning the menu cursor next to SAVE MAP in the MAP MENU. The SELECT DATA control should then be released and the MODIFY DATA control pressed.
  The map orientation (R) or (T) is stored at the same time as the map is saved. Correct gyro alignment is therefore necessary for map registration. Maps saved in True motion, CENT. DISP are defined as Relative (R).

- *Delete map*   To delete a complete map from memory the SELECT DATA control should be pressed and held while the joystick is used to position the menu cursor next to DELETE MAP in the MAP MENU. Releasing the SELECT DATA control and pressing the MODIFY DATA control completes the process.
  To delete single map lines and symbols the joystick marker should be positioned near the centre of the line, or on the symbol, and the SELECT control pressed. The line or symbol will flash until the DELETE control is pressed when the line or symbol will disappear.

- *Cancel entry*   Operation of the CANCEL ENTRY control cancels the present operation.

- *Map on/off*   Pressing the MAP ON/OFF control will cause the status LED to go off and the map and map menu to disappear from the screen.

- *Relative and true maps*   Depending on which mode a map is drawn, and saved, stored maps may be defined as RELATIVE or TRUE.
  Maps drawn in true motion mode are defined as TRUE while maps drawn in relative motion or centred display modes are defined as RELATIVE.
  The type of map stored is displayed in the map menu to the left of the map

number. (R) is for RELATIVE maps, (T) for TRUE maps and a blank space for an empty map.

The type of maps that can be displayed depends on the type of map stored and the display mode:

> For Relative motion or Centred display modes, only RELATIVE stored maps can be displayed
> For True motion mode, only TRUE maps can be displayed. The 'scratchpad' map is always displayed.

Maps cannot be positioned using the POSITION MAP function in Relative motion or Centred display modes.

In True motion mode the 'scratchpad' map and TRUE stored maps can be positioned by the POSITION MAP function.

If maps are ON and true motion is selected with the current stored map RELATIVE (and hence not displayed), the POSITION MAP function is disabled. The maps will have to be turned OFF or a TRUE, or empty, map will have to be selected before the POSITION MAP will operate.

- *Map retrieval (true motion and ARPA)*   With the equipment in the RUN mode (RAD 1⌐⌐, RAD 2⌐⌐or SLAVE RAD 2), the MAP ON/OFF control should be pressed. The status LED will light and the MAP MENU will appear in the data field to the right of the screen, see Fig. 25.14.

The MAP MENU will default to the last MAP NO. used (e.g. MAP NO. 6. 65% FREE)

The SELECT DATA control should be pressed and held while the joystick is used to position the menu cursor next to the MAP NO. data line. The SELECT DATA control should then be released.

The MODIFY DATA control should be pressed and held while the joystick is moved in the vertical plane to select the required MAP NO. in the data line.

The MODIFY DATA control should then be released and the SELECT DATA control pressed which causes the selected map to be displayed on the screen.

If the NAV PLOT mode is being used then retrieving a map will cause the NAV PLOT to be superimposed on the map, providing the line symbol count is within the total allowed for a single map; (64 lines or 128 symbols or any combination where 1 line = 2 symbols). The NAV PLOT data may be added to the map by using the SAVE MAP procedure before the map is switched off. If the line or symbol count exceed the allowed total a warning will be indicated in the data field showing the excess value. The map will not be displayed until the NAV PLOT is reduced in symbol/line count by the deletion of individual lines or symbols.

- *Position map*   In order to position the map correctly, with respect to any fixed target, the POSITION MAP control should be pressed and held using the joystick in the *X* and *Y* axes to move the map. Releasing the POSITION MAP control will fix the position of the map.

It should be noted that any map stored in Relative motion cannot be positioned and an OPERATOR WARNING will be displayed in the data field, see Fig. 25.15.

External position fixing inputs can be used to position maps automatically as the following section will show.

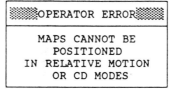

Fig. 25.15 Operator error warning in the data field (courtesy Kelvin Hughes)

25.7 Interfacing options

As discussed in Section 24.9, the ARPA has the facility to output data to a peripheral or to input data from a source. Applications include the reception of data from a Navigational positioning fixing system (e.g. SATNAV) which could be displayed within the screen area. This option could be selected from the main MENU.

Also ownship and any target data could be sent to an external printer. The data is transmitted via an RS422/423 interface within the main processor and can give ownship coordinance, speed, bearing and drift. Additionally data on selected targets can be sent as specified by the ARPA computer. Data includes Range, Bearing, Speed, Course, TCPA and CPA of targets within the radar area dependent on range selected, i.e. data from only those targets actually displayed on the screen.

The two options are selected from the main MENU with the equipment in the STANDBY mode. On selection of INTERFACE OPTION they are designated as follows:

CHANNEL A : NAV. SYS (or NOT USED).
CHANNEL B : PRINTER (or NOT USED).

Setting up the display for NAV.SYS

The procedure for setting up the initial installation is as follows:

The display power switch should be set to ON and the MENU control depressed. The SELECT DATA control should then be pressed and, using the joystick, the cursor positioned next to INTERFACE OPTIONS. Releasing SELECT DATA control, the MODIFY DATA control should then be pressed. The INTERFACE OPTION menu should appear with the joystick cursor adjacent to the CHANNEL indication (see Fig. 25.16).

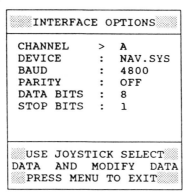

Fig. 25.16 Setting up the display for Nav. Sys. (courtesy Kelvin Hughes)

CHANNEL A should be selected using the MODIFY DATA control. Pressing SELECT DATA, and using the joystick, the cursor should be moved to the DEVICE annotation. MODIFY DATA should then be pressed until the NAV.SYS. selection appears. The procedure should be repeated to set up the parameters of the navigational system e.g. BAUD rate, PARITY etc, as shown in the example of Fig. 25.16.

RAD 1 ⊓ or RAD 1 ⊓ should be selected and by using SELECT DATA and the joystick the cursor should be positioned alongside the NAV.SYS. menu. Pressing MODIFY DATA will annotate NAV.SYS. ON and the menu should appear as shown in Fig. 25.17.

```
┌─────────────────────────────┐
│       NAV.SYS   MENU        │
├─────────────────────────────┤
│  OWN  LAT/LONG   >      OFF  │
│  JSTK LAT/LONG         OFF   │
│  WAYPOINTS             OFF   │
│  AUTO FIX MAP          OFF   │
└─────────────────────────────┘
```

Fig. 25.17 Setting up the parameters for Nav. Sys. (courtesy Kelvin Hughes)

Using SELECT DATA control, the joystick and MODIFY DATA, the parameters can be set up as required. The parameters that are available to the operator for displaying data within the radar screen are:

- *Own LAT/LONG*   The ship's position, in latitude and longitude, will be displayed at the bottom of the screen. This will be the most recent geographical position supplied by the position fixing system connected to the display.

  The LAT. and LONG. are displayed in degrees and decimal minutes, i.e. LAT 35 18.39N is 35 degrees and 18.39 minutes, not 18 minutes and 39 seconds.

- *JSTK LAT/LONG*   The position of the joystick marker, in latitude and longitude, based on the ownship's position as supplied by the position fixing system. With this facility ON, the joystick RANGE and BEARING field, at the lower right corner, will display the LAT/LONG of the joystick.

- *WAYPOINTS*   If the positioning system has the facility for storing way points, these will be displayed on the screen in their true geographical position, based on the latest information from the position fixing system. They will be displayed as :

$$\boxed{\text{Wp}}$$

  Depending on the system fitted the way points may not be displayed immediately; some positioning systems only output way point data every 10 seconds.

  To avoid continual updating of way point positions, which could prove a distraction to the operator, the position of each way point is only updated every 5 minutes.

- *AUTO FIX MAP*   True maps, which are saved while a position fixing system is connected, will have their geographical location stored with them. During map retrieval this facility will automatically position the map as previously saved as follows:

  If a map with a stored geographical position is retrieved, and the map position fixing function in the NAV. SYS. menu is turned on, it will automatically be positioned at the same geographical position (i.e. the same place relative to the land/coastline) as it was when it was saved.

To turn the map positioning function on, the menu cursor should be moved to AUTO FIX MAP and the MODIFY DATA control pressed. Repeating the operation will turn the automatic map position fixing function off.

Setting up the display for PRINTER

With the display in STANDBY mode the main MENU should be selected and the following operations carried out:

Using SELECT DATA and joystick controls, CHANNEL should be selected and MODIFY DATA control pressed to give CHANNEL B.

Using SELECT DATA and joystick controls the cursor should be moved down to DEVICE, the MODIFY DATA control pressed and PRINTER selected. This selection will produce another two fields at the bottom of the menu showing PRINT OUT and EVERY, see Fig. 25.18.

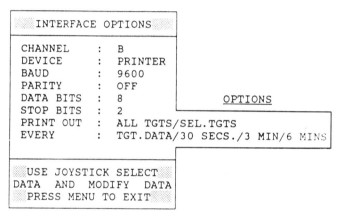

Fig. 25.18 Setting up the display for Printer (courtesy Kelvin Hughes).

As the BAUD, PARITY, DATA BITS and STOP BITS are fixed within the processor memory, the SELECT DATA and joystick controls may be used to move the cursor to the PRINT OUT selection. Pressing MODIFY DATA will allow the selection of ALL TARGETS or SELECTED TARGETS.

Moving the cursor to the EVERY position, again by the use of SELECT DATA and joystick controls,and using the MODIFY DATA control, allows the print out time to be set.

Print Out

- *All targets* This selection will result in the time, day and date, ownship data (including LAT. and LONG. if fitted) and all targets, tracked by the ARPA computer, within the radar picture area being printed out.

All targets selected

11:15	THURSDAY		15 AUGUST

OWNSHIP DATA

COURSE	000 DEG	SPEED	9.9 KTS
DRIFT	OFF		
LATITUDE	044 56.55N	LONGITUDE	045 06.12E

TARGET 1

BEARING	125 DEG	RANGE	4.23 NM
COURSE	151 DEG	SPEED	23.45 KTS
TCPA	−6.5 MIN	CPA	2.4 NM

TARGET 2

BEARING	165 DEG	RANGE	3.23 NM
COURSE	185 DEG	SPEED	15.10 KTS
TCPA	−7.4 MIN	CPA	0.99 NM

TARGET 3

BEARING	15 DEG	RANGE	7.63 NM
COURSE	225 DEG	SPEED	6.72 KTS
TCPA	29.7 MIN	CPA	0.4 NM

- *Selected Targets* This selection will give a print out of time, day and date, ownship's data (including LAT. and LONG. if fitted) and selected targets, tracked by the ARPA computer, within the radar picture area.

Target 2 selected

11:15	THURSDAY		15 AUGUST

OWNSHIP DATA

COURSE	000 DEG	SPEED	9.9 KTS
DRIFT	OFF		
LATITUDE	044 56.55N	LONGITUDE	045 06.12E

TARGET 2

BEARING	165 DEG	RANGE	3.23 NM
COURSE	185 DEG	SPEED	15.10 KTS
TCPA	−7.4 MIN	CPA	0.99 NM

To achieve this response, the SELECT control should be used, together with the joystick cursor on or close by the required target. The target will start flashing and pressing the TARGET DATA control will give a print out of the data on ownship and the selected target.

- *Every* Selection of this facility will enable the ARPA computer to transmit data to the printer at designated times or instantly when the TARGET DATA control is pressed. The designated times vary between every thirty seconds, three or six minutes.

- *Doppler log* A doppler (dual axis) log can be connected to the display via a Doppler log interface board and via Channel B of the RS422/423 serial data link on the Radar expansion board (see Section 24.9).

The display may be set by selecting the INTERFACE OPTIONS menu on the display, selecting CHANNEL B and selecting DEVICE D LOG (or LOG & PRT if ownship and ARPA target data print out is required).

Once selected in the interface options menu, the display will take log and drift information from the doppler log while the LOG INPUT data line is set to D LOG. Manual speed and manual drift will still be available. On the ARPA display, if targets are designed as fixed, AUTO DRIFT is generated and will override D LOG drift.

25.8   ARPA acquisition and tracking accuracy

The source of the target information fed to the ARPA computer is the same video signal that is fed to the PPI display. Any target giving a strong, clear signal to the PPI display will also give the ARPA computer an echo that can be acquired and tracked.

The requirement for automatic acquisition within the guard zone is for three out of four visible 'hits' on the target with successive antenna revolutions. Successful tracking, on the other hand, requires five out of ten 'hits'. Any target that is not displayed for seven successive antenna revolutions will be dropped by the tracker and denoted as lost (L).

It follows that any adverse conditions that affect the state of the received signal by the PPI display will also affect the ARPA system. Clutter or spurious reflections can degrade the accuracy or reliability of the ARPA tracking. Also, unexpected swinging of vectors may arise due to the fast response of the computer if an echo appears unstable due to target glint or local abnormal reflections of the radar beam (glint is caused by the apparent movement of the centre of the radar echo as the ship rolls, pitches and yaws, and could lead to random bearing errors). These effects are not due to malfunction of the ARPA system and should be recognised as such by the operator.

Errors in the displayed data can be due to many sources, some due to incorrect data inputs and some due to incorrect interpretation of the displayed data. Some key sources of error are listed below as an indication to the user:

- *Ownship log error*   This will result in a vector error for 'true' speed and course for every other ship. Also all stationary targets being tracked will indicate an apparent speed. The amount of error obviously depends on the amount of deviation of the actual log value to that indicated, but it could give rise to misassessment of a situation with the inherent danger that implies.

- *Ownship gyro error*   This will result in errors in the predicted course of other ships. However this is unlikely to affect an ARPA collision situation since all course data is affected, including that of the navigating ship. A misassessment could occur however when dealing with collision avoidance.

- *Tracking errors*   Raw radar data has to be converted to digitised form for processing and this could lead to quantisation errors in range and bearing. The tracker uses mathematical filters which smooth out the signal variations with time to give an indication of a steady track. The filters should also be able to respond quickly to manoeuvres. Observation of the effect of a manoeuvre on a known stationary target may be a useful method of gaining an impression of the accuracy of a system.

- *Target swop*   This is a phenomenon caused by the transfer of computer tracking from one target to another and may happen when targets are very close or merging. The tracker circuitry is designed to minimise the likelihood of the effect occurring, but the operator should always be alert to the possibility.

- *Errors in interpretation*   It should always be remembered that the data displayed on the screen may be the result of imperfect inputs and complete reliance on the information should be avoided. Errors are quoted in the IMO performance standards (Appendix 1) and due allowance should always be made for these.

  Time should be allowed to elapse, after the completion of a manoeuvre, to allow the data to settle. The system should provide an indication of target's motion trend in a period of not more than one minute, and display within three minutes the target's predicted motion, in accordance with specified tolerances. The operator should be mindful of these timing requirements before using the ARPA data as the basis for making any critical decisions.

Appendix 1
IMO PERFORMANCE STANDARDS FOR AUTOMATIC RADAR PLOTTING AIDS (ARPA)

1 INTRODUCTION

1.1 Automatic radar plotting aids (ARPA) should, in order to improve the standard of collision avoidance at sea:
   .1 reduce the workload of observers by enabling them to automatically obtain information so that they can perform as well with multiple targets as they can by manually plotting a single target;
   .2 provide continuous, accurate and rapid situation evaluation.

1.2 In addition to the general requirements for Electronic Navigational Aids, the ARPA should comply with the following minimum performance standards.

2 DEFINITIONS

2.1 Definitions of terms used in these performance standards are given in Annex 1.

3 PERFORMANCE STANDARDS

3.1 Detection

3.1.1 Where a separate facility is provided for detection of targets, other than by the radar observer, it should have a performance not inferior to that which could be obtained by the use of the radar display.

3.2 Acquisition

3.2.1 Target acquisition may be manual or automatic. However, there should always be a facility to provide for manual acquisition and cancellation: ARPA with automatic acquisition should have a facility to suppress acquisition in certain areas. On any range scale where acquisition is suppressed over a certain area, the area of acquisition should be indicated on the display.

3.2.2 Automatic or manual acquisition should have a performance not inferior to that which could be obtained by the user of the radar display.

3.3 Tracking

3.3.1 The ARPA should be able to automatically track, process, simultaneously display and continuously update the information on at least:

Reproduced by kind permission of the International Maritime Organisation from its publication 'Performance Standards for Navigational Equipment', Sales No. IMO-978E.

  .1 20 targets, if automatic acquisition is provided, whether automatically or manually acquired;

  .2 10 targets, if only manual acquisition is provided.

3.3.2 If automatic acquisition is provided, description of the criteria of selection of targets for tracking should be provided to the user. If the ARPA does not track all targets visible on the display, targets which are being tracked should be clearly indicated on the display. The reliability of tracking should not be less than that obtainable using manual recordings of successive target positions obtained from the radar display.

3.3.3 Provided the target is not subject to target swop, the ARPA should continue to track an acquired target which is clearly distinguishable on the display for 5 out of 10 consecutive scans.

3.3.4 The possibility of tracking errors, including target swop, should be minimised by ARPA design. A qualitative description of the effects of error sources on the automatic tracking and corresponding errors should be provided to the user, including the effects of low signal-to-noise and low signal-to-clutter ratios caused by sea returns, rain, snow, low clouds and non-synchronous emissions.

3.3.5 The ARPA should be able to display on request at least four equally time-spaced past positions of any targets being tracked over a period of at least eight minutes.

3.4 Display

3.4.1 The display may be a separate or integral part of the ship's radar. However, the ARPA display should include all the data required to be provided by a radar display in accordance with the performance standards for navigational radar equipment.

3.4.2 The design should be such that any malfunction of ARPA parts producing data additional to information to be produced by the radar as required by the performance standards for navigational equipment should not affect the integrity of the basic radar presentation.

3.4.3 The display on which the ARPA information is presented should have an effective diameter of at least 340 mm.

3.4.4 The ARPA facilities should be available on at least the following range scales:

  .1 12 or 16 miles;

  .2 3 or 4 miles.

3.4.5 There should be a positive indication of the range scale in use.

3.4.6 The ARPA should be capable of operating with a relative motion display with "north-up" and either "head-up" or "course-up" azimuth stabilisation. In addition, the ARPA may also provide for a true motion display. If true motion is provided, the operator should be able to select for his display either true or relative motion. There should be a positive indication of the display mode and orientation in use.

3.4.7 The course and speed information generated by the ARPA for acquired targets should be displayed in a vector or graphic form which clearly indicates the target's predicted motion. In this regard:

  .1 ARPA presenting predicted information in vector form only should have the option of both true and relative vectors;

  .2 an ARPA which is capable of presenting target course and speed information in graphic form should also, on request, provide the target's true and/or relative vector;

  .3 vectors displayed should either be time-adjustable or have a fixed time-scale;

  .4 a positive indication of the time-scale of the vector in use should be given.

3.4.8 The ARPA information should not obscure radar information in such a manner as to degrade the process of detecting targets. The display of ARPA data should be under the control of the radar observer. It should be possible to cancel the display of unwanted ARPA data.

3.4.9   Means should be provided to adjust independently the brilliance of the ARPA data and radar data, including complete elimination of the ARPA data.

3.4.10   The method of presentation should ensure that the ARPA data are clearly visible in general to more than one observer in the conditions of light normally experienced on the bridge of a ship by day and by night. Screening may be provided to shade the display from sunlight but not to the extent that it will impair the observer's ability to maintain a proper lookout. Facilities to adjust the brightness should be provided.

3.4.11   Provisions should be made to obtain quickly the range and bearing of any object which appears on the ARPA display.

3.4.12   When a target appears on the radar display and, in the case of automatic acquisition, enters within the acquisition area chosen by the observer or, in the case of manual acquisition, has been acquired by the observer, the ARPA should present in a period of not more than one minute an indication of the target's motion trend and display within three minutes the target's predicted motion in accordance with paragraphs 3.4.7, 3.6, 3.8.2 and 3.8.3.

3.4.13   After changing range scales on which the ARPA facilities are available or resetting the display, full plotting information should be displayed within a period of time not exceeding four scans.

3.5   Operational warnings

3.5.1   The ARPA should have the capability to warn the observer with a visual and/or audible signal of any distinguishable target which closes to a range or transits a zone chosen by the observer. The target causing the warning should be clearly indicated on the display.

3.5.2   The ARPA should have the capability to warn the observer with a visual and/or audible signal of any tracked target which is predicted to close to within a minimum range and time chosen by the observer. The target causing the warning should be clearly indicated on the display.

3.5.3   The ARPA should clearly indicate if a tracked target is lost, other than out of range, and the target's last tracked position should be clearly indicated on the display.

3.5.4   It should be possible to activate or de-activate the operational warnings.

3.6   Data requirements

3.6.1   At the request of the observer the following information should be immediately available from the ARPA in alphanumeric form in regard to any tracked target:

  .1   present range to the target;
  .2   present bearing of the target
  .3   predicted target range at the closest point of approach (CPA);
  .4   predicted time to CPA (TCPA);
  .5   calculated true course of target;
  .6   calculated true speed of target.

3.7   Trial manoeuvre

3.7.1   The ARPA should be capable of simulating the effect on all tracked targets of an own ship manoeuvre without interrupting the updating of target information. The simulation should be initiated by the depression either of a spring-loaded switch, or of a function key, with a positive identification on the display.

3.8   Accuracy

3.8.1   The ARPA should provide accuracies not less than those given in paragraphs 3.8.2 and 3.8.3 for four defined scenarios. With defined sensor errors the values given relate to the best possible manual plotting performance under environmental conditions of plus and minus ten degrees of roll.

3.8.2   An ARPA should present within one minute of steady state tracking the relative motion trend of a target with the following accuracy values (95 per cent probability values).

Scenario	Data		
	Relative course (degrees)	Relative speed (knots)	CPA (nautical miles)
1	11	2.8	1.6
2	7	0.6	
3	14	2.2	1.8
4	15	1.5	2.0

3.8.3   An ARPA should present within three minutes of steady state tracking the motion of a target with the following accuracy values (95 per cent probability values).

Scenario	Data					
	Rel. course (deg's)	Rel. speed (kts)	CPA (naut. miles)	TCPA (mins)	True course (deg's)	True speed (kts)
1	3.0	0.8	0.5	1.0	7.4	1.2
2	2.3	0.3			2.8	0.8
3	4.4	0.9	0.7	1.0	3.3	1.0
4	4.6	0.8	0.7	1.0	2.6	1.2

3.8.4   When a tracked target, or ownship, has completed a manoeuvre, the system should present in a period of not more than one minute an indication of the target's motion trend, and display within three minutes the target's predicted motion, in accordance with paragraphs 3.4.7, 3.6, 3.8.2 and 3.8.3.

3.8.5   The ARPA should be designed in such a manner that under the most favourable conditions of ownship motion the error contribution from the ARPA should remain insignificant compared to the errors associated with the input sensors, for the defined scenarios.

3.9   Connections with other equipment

3.9.1   The ARPA should not degrade the performance of any equipment providing sensor inputs. The connection of the ARPA to any other equipment should not degrade the performance of that equipment.

3.10   Performance tests and warnings

3.10.1   The ARPA should provide suitable warnings of ARPA malfunction to enable the observer to monitor the proper operation of the system. Additionally, test programmes should be available so that the overall performance of ARPA can be assessed periodically against a known solution.

3.11   Equipment used with ARPA

3.11.1 Log and speed indicators providing inputs to ARPA equipment should be capable of providing the ship's speed through the water.

ANNEX 1
DEFINITIONS OF TERMS TO BE USED ONLY IN
CONNECTION WITH ARPA PERFORMANCE STANDARDS

Relative course	The direction of motion of a target related to ownship as deduced from a number of measurements of its range and bearing on the radar, expressed as an angular distance from north.
Relative speed	The speed of a target related to ownship, as deduced from a number of measurements of its range and bearing on the radar.
True course	The apparent heading of a target obtained by the vectorial combination of the target's relative motion and ship's own motion, expressed as an angular distance from north. (N.B. for the purpose of these definitions there is no need to distinguish between sea and ground stabilisation).
True speed	The speed of a target obtained by the vectorial combination of its relative motion and ownship's motion (see note on ship's motion above).
Bearing	The direction of one terrestrial point from another, expressed as an angular distance from north.
Relative motion display	The position of ownship on such a display remains fixed.
True motion display	The position of ownship on such a display moves in accordance with its own motion
Azimuth stabilisation	Ownship's compass information is fed to the display so that echoes of targets on the display will not be caused to smear by changes of ownship's heading.
/north-up	The line connecting the centre with the top of the display is north.
/head-up	The line connecting the centre with the top of the display is own ship's heading.
/course-up	An intended course can be set to the line connecting the centre with the top of the display.
Heading	The direction in which the bows of a ship are pointing, expessed as an angular distance from north.
Target's predicted motion	The indication on the display of a linear extrapolation into the future of a target's motion, based on measurements of the target's range and bearing on the radar in the recent past.
Target's motion trend	An early indication of the target's predicted motion.
Radar plotting	The whole process of target detection, tracking, calculation of parameters and display of information.
Detection	The recognition of the presence of a target.

Acquisition   The selection of those targets requiring a tracking procedure and the initiation of their tracking.

Tracking   The process of observing the sequential changes in the position of a target, to establish its motion.

Display   The plan position presentation of ARPA data with radar data.

Manual   Relating to an activity which a radar observer performs, possibly with assistance from a machine.

Automatic   Relating to an activity which is performed wholly by a machine.

Appendix 2
ARPA VIDEO SYMBOLS AND CONTROL NAMES AND RECOMMENDED CODE OF PRACTICE

ARPA VIDEO SYMBOLS

E.1 IMO Resolution A 422 (XI) requires that certain indications and warnings be given on an ARPA for anti-collision purposes.
ARPA video symbols 1 to 12, illustrated in ANNEX 1, shall be used to conform with these IMO mandatory requirements.

E.2 Other symbols may be used for other anti-collision or navigational functions provided they do not conflict with the symbols 1 to 12 in ANNEX 1. The use of these other symbols shall be limited to ensure that they do not obscure the anti-collision requirements of the ARPA.

E.3 For the three warning alarm symbols (Symbols 7, 8 and 9) the following priorities shall be used:

3.1 An unacknowledged warning alarm is always a higher priority than an acknowledged warning alarm;

3.2 CPA/TCPA warning has a higher priority than a target entering guard zone alarm;

3.3 A Guard zone warning has a higher priority than a Lost target warning.

ARPA CONTROL NAMES

E.4   The names indicated shall be used to describe ARPA controls.

E.5   If the ARPA has any of the 23 radar display controls of IMO Resolution A.278 (VIII), then those radar display names shall be used on the ARPA.

E.6   Abbreviations of names may be used.

IMO/IEC REFERENCES	ARPA SYMBOL NUMBER	DETAIL	DESCRIPTION OF SYMBOL
IMO A422 PARA 3.2.1			A cross is to be used as the cursor for manual acquisition.
IEC 872 PARA 6.2.1	1	Manual Acquisition (IMO 3.2.1).	

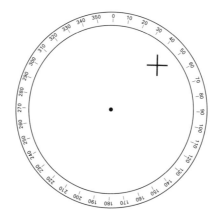

NOTES
1. The cross shall be at least 10mm in height and width, to avoid confusion with other navigational and chart symbols, and for ECDIS harmonisation.
2. The cursor is also used for other radar purposes.

CONTROL NAME
MANUAL ACQUISITION

IMO/IEC REFERENCES	ARPA SYMBOL NUMBER	DETAIL	DESCRIPTION OF SYMBOL
IMO A422 PARA 3.2.1		AREA OF AUTO-ACQUISITION "On any range scale where acquisition is suppressed over a certain area, the area of acquisition shall be indicated on the display".	If facilities are provided for suppression of acquisition, continuous lines are to be used to define the limits out-side of which auto-acquisition is suppressed.
IEC 872 PARA 6.2.1	2		

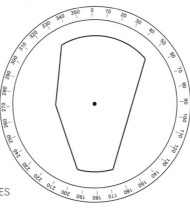

NOTE
IMO PARA 3.2.1 places no restriction on the number and shapes of auto-acquisition/ suppressed zones.

CONTROL NAME
AUTO-ACQUISITION LIMIT LINES

IMO/IEC REFERENCES	ARPA SYMBOL NUMBER	DETAIL	DESCRIPTION OF SYMBOL
IMO A422 PARA 3.2.2 IEC 872 PARA 6.3.2	3	TARGET BEING TRACKED. "If the ARPA does not track all targets visible on the display, targets which are being tracked shall be clearly indicated on the display".	A broken square around the echo to indicate the initial stage of tracking steady state tracking.

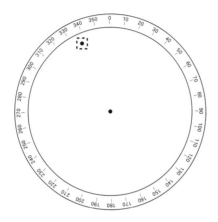

CONTROL NAME
ACQUIRE

IMO/IEC REFERENCES	ARPA SYMBOL NUMBER	DETAIL	DESCRIPTION OF SYMBOL
IMO A422 PARA 3.4.7 IEC 872 PARA 6.4.7	4A	COURSE AND SPEED VECTOR. TARGET BEING TRACKED WHEN TRACKING IS IN STEADY STATE. "The course and speed information generated by the ARPA for acquired targets shall be displayed in a vector or graphic form".	A vector to indicate the target's predicted true or relative motion, which may have a fixed time scale or time adjustable scale. The vector origin is to be defined by a small bright dot or the centre of a circle. The circle shall be at least 2mm in diameter.

NOTE
This symbol may be combined with SYMBOL 3 to show an indication of the target's motion trend during the period when an indication of that is required (see IMO A422 PARAS 3.4.12, 3.8.2, and 3.8.4 and IEC 872 PARAS 6.4.12, 6.8.2 and 6.8.4).

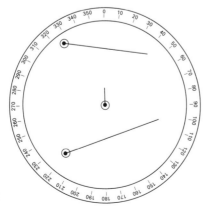

CONTROL NAMES
VECTOR
VECTOR TIME
TRUE VECTORS
RELATIVE VECTORS

IMO/IEC REFERENCES	ARPA SYMBOL NUMBER	DETAIL	DESCRIPTION OF SYMBOL
IMO A422 PARA 3.4.7 IEC 872 PARA 6.4.7	4B	COURSE AND SPEED VECTOR. TARGET BEING TRACKED WHEN TRACKING IS IN STEADY STATE. "The course and speed information generated by the ARPA for acquired targets shall be displayed in a vector or graphic form".	As for SYMBOL 4A. In addition, it is permissible to give a positive indication on the vector at equal intervals corresponding to fractions of the time scale selected. NOTE As for SYMBOL 4A.

CONTROL NAMES
AS FOR SYMBOL 4A

IMO/IEC REFERENCES	ARPA SYMBOL NUMBER	DETAIL	DESCRIPTION OF SYMBOL
IMO A422 PARA 3.4.7 IEC 872 PARA 6.4.7	5	COURSE AND SPEED GRAPHIC. TARGET BEING TRACKED WHEN TRACKING IS IN STEADY STATE. "The course and speed information generated by the ARPA for acquired targets shall be displayed in a vector or graphic form".	The graphic can take the form of a shape such as a hexagon (see example) or ellipse. The vector origin is to be defined by a small bright dot or the centre of a circle. The circle shall be at least 2mm in diameter. NOTES 1. The form of the graphic shall avoid shapes that are being used for other ARPA symbols. 2. The meaning of the graphic shall be fully explained in the manufacturers handbook, and must specifically include how the graphic represents target speed.

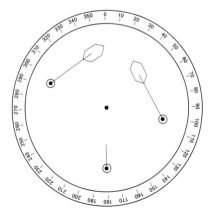

CONTROL NAMES
AS FOR 4A

IMO/IEC REFERENCES	ARPA SYMBOL NUMBER	DETAIL	DESCRIPTION OF SYMBOL
IMO A422 PARA 3.3.5 IEC 872 PARA 6.3.5	6	PAST POSITION OF TARGET. "The ARPA shall be capable of displaying on request at least 4 equally time spaced past positions of any targets being tracked over a period of at least 8 minutes".	At least four equally time spaced past positions to be shown on request as dots or small circles.

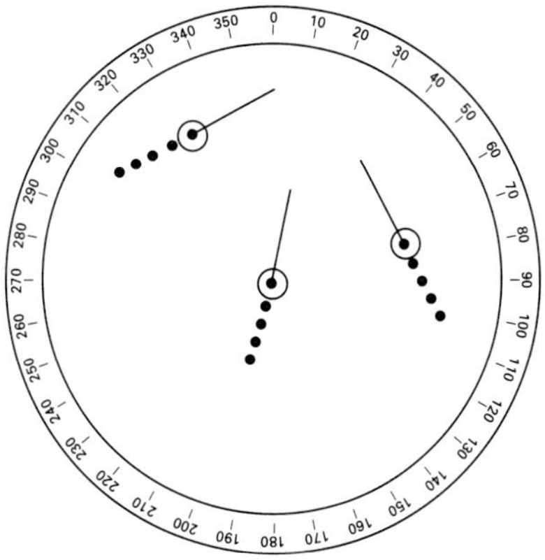

CONTROL NAME
PAST POSITIONS

IMO/IEC REFERENCES	ARPA SYMBOL NUMBER	DETAIL	DESCRIPTION OF SYMBOL
IMO A422 PARA 3.5.1 IEC 872 PARA 6.5.1	7	TARGET ENTERING GUARD RING OR ZONE WARNING. "The ARPA shall have the capability to warn the observer with a visual and/or audible signal of any distinguishable target which closes to a range or transits a zone chosen by the observer. The target causing the warning shall be clearly indicated on the display.	A flashing triangle, apex down, shall be used to mark the target. A guard ring shall be displayed as a continuous line. A guard zone shall consist of continuous lines bounding the area chosen by the operator.

NOTES
1. Flashing is a frequency of about $\frac{1}{2}$Hz to 1Hz.
2. After acknowledgement it is permissible to cease flashing.
3. The area chosen by the operator shall be narrow enough to avoid any confusion with SYMBOL 2.

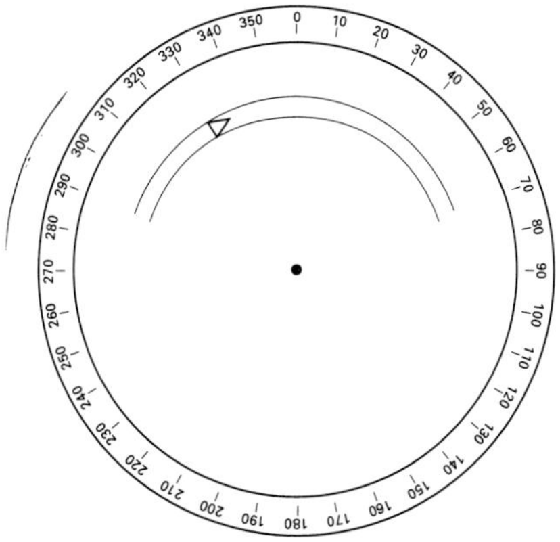

CONTROL NAMES
GUARD RING
GUARD ZONE

IMO/IEC REFERENCES	ARPA SYMBOL NUMBER	DETAIL	DESCRIPTION OF SYMBOL
IMO A422 PARA 3.5.2 IEC 872 PARA 6.5.2	8	CPA/TCPA WARNING. "The ARPA shall have the capability to warn the observer with a visual and/or audible signal of any target which is predicted to close within a minimum range and time chosen by the observer. The target causing the warning shall be clearly indicated on the display".	A flashing triangle, apex up, shall be used to mark the target. In addition the target vector may be flashed. NOTES 1. Flashing is a frequency of about $\frac{1}{2}$Hz to 4Hz. 2. After acknowledgement it is permissible to cease flashing.

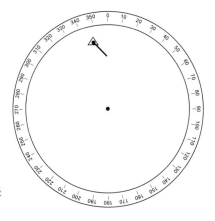

CONTROL NAMES
CPA
TCPA

IMO/IEC REFERENCES	ARPA SYMBOL NUMBER	DETAIL	DESCRIPTION OF SYMBOL
IMO A422 PARA 3.5.3 IEC 872 PARA 6.5.3	9	LOST TARGET WARNING. "The ARPA shall clearly indicate if a tracked target is lost, other than out of range, and the target's last tracked position shall be clearly indicated on the display.	A diamond shall flash. The diamond shall be formed from two equal triangles (one apex up, the other apex down). NOTES 1. The form of the diamond, consists of two equal triangles which are used as warning symbols. 2. Flashing is a frequency of about $\frac{1}{2}$Hz to 1Hz. 3. After acknowledgement, it is permissible to cease flashing.

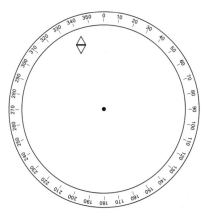

CONTROL NAME
LOST TARGET

IMO/IEC REFERENCES	ARPA SYMBOL NUMBER	DETAIL	DESCRIPTION OF SYMBOL
IMO A422 PARA 3.7.1	10	TRIAL MANOEUVRE. "The simulation shall be initiated by the depression, either of a spring loaded switch or of a function key with a positive identification on the display".	The letter "T", at the bottom of the display shall flash.
IEC 872 PARA 6.7.1			

NOTES
1. The letter "T" shall be at least 15mm high, and the letter width at least 2mm.
2. Flashing is a frequency of about $\frac{1}{2}$Hz to 1Hz.

CONTROL NAMES
TRIAL MANOEUVRE
(TRIAL) COURSE
(TRIAL) SPEED
(TRIAL) DELAY

IMO/IEC REFERENCES	ARPA SYMBOL NUMBER	DETAIL	DESCRIPTION OF SYMBOL
IMO A422 PARA 3.10.1	11	TEST "Test programmes shall be available so that the overall performance of the ARPA can be assessed periodically against a known solution".	A letter "X" at the bottom of the display and on the test target shall flash. During a trial manoeuvre the letters "XT" shall appear at the bottom of the display.
IEC 872 PARA 6.10.1			

NOTES
1. The letter "X" shall be at least 15mm high, and the letter width at least 2mm.
2. If an automatic test programme is incorporated the indication of an ARPA system failure shall be given.
3. Flashing is a frequency of about $\frac{1}{2}$Hz to 1Hz.

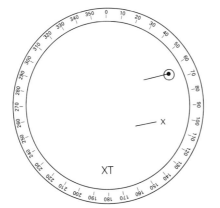

CONTROL NAME
TEST

IMO/IEC REFERENCES	ARPA SYMBOL NUMBER	DETAIL	DESCRIPTION OF SYMBOL
IMO A422 PARA 3.6		DATA requirements.	A square is to be used as a symbol to mark the data reading target.
	12		
IEC 872 PARA 6.6			

NOTE
If data is required for more than one target, at the same time, each mark shall be separately identified, e.g. with a number adjacent to the symbol.

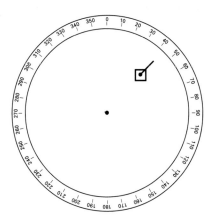

CONTROL NAME
DATA READING

Appendix 3
Brief details of the microprocessor and support chips referred to in the text

8086 A 16 bit processor. Some of its signal lines may have their functions redesignated according to the mode of operation selected. Control signals in one mode may be suitable for a single processor system while in a second mode the control signals may be assigned for multiprocessor use. Data and address busses are multiplexed on the same lines and the upper four address bits are multiplexed with status signals. An external clock generator (8284) is necessary while bus control may be achieved by a bus controller (8288) device. The processor is contained in a 40 pin package and operates with a single +5 V power supply.

Signal functions

AD0–AD15	Multiplexed address/data I/O tristate.
A16–A19	Address/status outputs tristate.
S3, S4	Segment identifier outputs.
S5	Interrupt enable status output.
S6, S7	Status outputs.
RD	Read control output tristate (active low).
INTR	Maskable interrupt input.
NMI	Non-maskable interrupt input.
RESET	Reset input.
READY	Wait state request input.
TEST	Wait for test input (active low).
CLK	Single phase clock input.
BHE	High order byte strobe output (active low).
MN/MX	Minimum/maximum mode select (MX low).

When MN/MX is set high, for minimum system configuration, the following signals appear on pins 24–31:

pin number:

24 INTA	Interrupt acknowledge input (active low).
25 ALE	Address latch enable output.
26 DEN	Data bus enable output tristate (active low).
27 DT/R	Data transmit/receive output tristate (R low).
28 IO/M	IO/Memory strobe output tristate (IO low).
29 WR	Write control output tristate (active low).
30 HLDA	Hold acknowledge output.
31 HOLD	Hold request input.

When MN/MX is set low, for maximum system configuration, the signals on pins 24 to 31 are as follows:

pin number:

24 QS1	Instruction queue status output.
25 QS0	Instruction queue status output.
26 S0	
27 S1	Machine cycle status output tristate.
28 S2	
29 LOCK	Bus hold control output tristate (active low).
30 RQ/GT1	Bus priority control, bidirectional.
31 RQ/GT0	Bus priority control, bidirectional.

8087   A 16 bit coprocessor which is designed to be connected in parallel with the 8086 (or 8088) device acting as the CPU to produce a high speed numerical processor which is much faster than the 8086 (or 8088) device alone. The 8087 may be considered as an extension to the CPU, providing register, data types, control and instruction capabilities at the hardware level. From the software level the CPU and the 8087 are seen as a single unified processor.

Signal functions

A0–A15	Multiplexed address/data I/O.
A16–A19	Address/status I/O.
S3, S4, S5, S6	Status information I/O.
S7	Status information input.
RQ/GT0, RQ/GT1	Request/grant I/O (active low).
QS0, QS1	CPU instruction queue status inputs.
INT	Interrupt output.
BUSY	Busy output.
READY	Ready acknowledgement input from memory device.
RESET	Reset input.
CLK	Single phase clock input.

8088   An 8 bit processor which is a modified version of the 8086. An 8 bit data bus is used instead of the 16 bit bus of the 8086. The processor is contained in a standard 40 pin package and operates with a single +5 V power supply.

Signal functions:

AD0–AD7	Multiplexed address/data I/O tristate.
A8–A19	Address outputs tristate.
S3, S4	Segment identifier outputs.
S5	Interrupt enable status outputs.
S6, S7	Status outputs
RD	Read control output tristate (active low)
INTR	Maskable interrupt request input.
NMI	Non-maskable interrupt request input.
RESET	Reset input.
READY	Wait state request input.
TEST	Wait for test condition input (active low).
CLK	Single phase CPU clock input.
BHE	High order byte strobe output (active low).

MN/MX   Minimum/maximum mode select input (MX low).
Configuration for pins 24–31 for MN/MX high or low is the same as for the 8086 device.

8251   Universal synchronous asynchronous receiver transmitter (USART). The device accepts data from the CPU in parallel format and converts the data to a continuous serial stream for transmission. Simultaneously it can receive serial data and convert it to parallel form for the CPU. The USART signals the CPU whenever it is ready to receive data from or transmit data to the CPU. The CPU can read the status of the USART at any time. 28 pin dil package with +5 V power supply.

8253–5   Programmable interval timer (PIT). Provides three independent fully programmable timer/counters with each counter consisting of a 16 bit counter register. Counter selection is via the A0 and A1 address lines. Six modes of operation are available for each counter. A delay may be set up under software control by initialising a counter with a set quantity. On command the device will count out the delay and interrupt the CPU on completion. Other counter/timer functions that are non-delay are possible and include Rate generator, Event counter and Real time clock. Package is 24 pin dil with a power supply of +5 V.

8255   Programmable peripheral interface (PPI). Provides 24 programmable input-output lines which may be individually programmed in two groups of 12 and used in three major modes of operation to interface with an 8 bit microprocessor data bus:

MODE 0   Each group of 12 I/O pins may be programmed in sets of four to be input or output.
MODE 1   Each group may be programmed to have eight lines of input or output. Three of the remaining four pins are used for handshaking and interrupt control signals.
Mode 2   is a bidirectional bus mode which uses 8 lines for a bidirectional bus and 5 lines, borrowing one from the other group, for handshaking.
   A 40 pin package with a +5 V power supply.

8259   Interrupt controller. Allows up to eight interrupts to be serviced in the order of their priority. The priority of an interrupt signal from a device is established by the interrupt request input of the 8259 device to which it is connected. IR0 has the highest priority while IR7 has the lowest in normal operation.

8284   Clock generator and driver. Using a crystal or TTL signal for a frequency source this device generates a system clock for the 8086 and 8088 microprocessors. An 18 pin package with a +5 V power supply.

8288   Bus controller. Provides command and control timing generation for the 8086 or 8088 microprocessor. A 20 pin package operating with a +5 V power supply.

Z80   An 8 bit procesor. Available in a standard 40 pin dil package and operates from a +5 V power supply.

Signal functions
D0–D7   Data bus tristate.
A0–A15   Address bus tristate.

RD   Read strobe (active low).
WR   Write strobe (active low).
M1   Machine cycle one (active low).
MREQ   Memory access indicator (active low).
IORQ   I/O operation indicator (active low).
RFSH   Dynamic memory refresh indicator (active low).
HALT   MPU in halt state (active low).
WAIT   Wait state request (active low).
INT   Interrupt request (active low).
NMI   Non-maskable interrupt request (active low).
RESET   Reset MPU input (active low).
BUSRQ   Request for control of the data, address and control
busses (active low).
BUSAK   Bus acknowledge (active low).

Z80 DART (Dual asynchronous receiver/transmitter). This device provides two independent full-duplex channels that can operate asynchronously to give serial to parallel and parallel to serial conversion. Additionally the device provides modem control for both channels. In the event that modem controls are not needed, the lines can be used for general purpose input-output. Also the device has a programmable interrupt vector and standard Z80 peripheral daisy-chain interrupt structure which allows automatic interrupt vectoring without external logic.

Signal functions
B/A   Channel A or B select input (high selects Channel B).
C/D   Control or data select input (high selects control).
CE   Chip enable input (active low).
CLK   System clock input.
CTSA, CTSB   Clear to send inputs (active low).
D0–D7   System data bus bidirectional tristate.
DCDA, DCDB   Data carrier detect inputs (active low).
DTRA, DTRB   Data terminal ready outputs (active low).
IEI   Interrupt enable in input.
IEO   Interrupt enable out output.
INT   Interrupt request output (active low).
M1   Machine cycle one input (active low).
IORQ   Input/output request input (active low).
RxCA, RxCB   Receiver clocks inputs.
RD   Read cycle status input (active low).
RxDA, RxDB   Receive data inputs.
RESET   Reset input (active low).
RIA, RIB   Ring indicator inputs (active low).
RTSA, RTSB   Request to send outputs (active low).
TxCA, TxCB   Transmitter clocks inputs (TxD changes on the falling
                                edge of TxC)
TxDA, TxDB   Transmit data outputs.
W/RDYA, W/RDYB   Wait/Ready outputs (open drain when programmed for
Wait function, driven high and low when programmed for Ready function).

Appendix 4
Glossary of terms used in Part 2 (ARPA)

Active   A signal may be described as active high or active low to indicate which of the two logic levels (logic 1 or logic 0) causes the digital circuit to be enabled.

Address   A coded instruction which specifies the location in memory of data which is stored or is about to be stored.

AEN   Address enable.

Alphanumeric   A system where the required information is in a combination of alphabetic characters and numbers.

Analog   A system where the signal can be considered to vary continuously with time. A digital system on the other hand may be considered to consist of a finite number of discrete levels. The number of levels may be two as in the case of a binary system.

ARPA   Automatic radar plotting aid.

BCR   Bow crossing range.

BCT   Bow crossing time.

Bit   Binary digit. The basic data unit in a system; may have the value 0 or 1.

Buffer   An electronic circuit connected between other circuit elements to prevent interaction between those elements. The buffer may also provide extra drive capability. A buffer may be used also as a temporary storage device to hold data, which may be required at a later time, while the processor is engaged on other tasks.

Bus   A collection of conductors used to transfer binary information in parallel around the system. For microprocessor applications there would be an address bus, used by the CPU to identify storage locations, and a data bus used for the transmission of data around the system.

Byte   A collection of eight bits. In a microprocessor system using 8 bit data busses and a 16 bit address bus, then data may be contained in one byte while the address needs two bytes to define it.

CCK   Counter clock. Used in those counters with a register to differentiate between the clock input to the register.

CCLR   Counter clear. Used in those counters with a register to indicate that the counter, not the register, is being cleared.

CD   Centred display.

CE   see Chip select.

Chip select　An input to an integrated circuit which, when active, allows the integrated circuit to be operative. If the input is not active then the integrated circuit is inactive. This control signal is sometimes called a Chip enable (CE) input.

CK, CLK, Clock　A regular train of pulses used to provide timing control in a system.

CLR　Clear. To remove data and return status of device to an initial condition, usually '0'.

CMOS　Complementary metal oxide semiconductor. A form of integrated circuit using field effect transistors.

Command　A signal, or group of signals, used to begin or end an operation.

Computer　In the case of a digital computer the basic system consists of a central processing unit (CPU), memory, input and output units and a control unit. The computer is able to perform such tasks as: manipulate data, perform arithmetic and logical operations on data and to store data.

Counter　A circuit used to count the number of pulses received. The counter may be arranged to start from a predesignated value and incrementally count upwards (an up-counter), or to start from a predesignated value and count downwards (a down-counter).

CPA　Closest point of approach. The predicted range of a target that represents a collision risk.

CPU　Central processing unit. The part of a microprocessor that controls operations, interprets instruction codes and executes instructions.

CS　See Chip select.

DART　Dual asynchronous receiver/transmitter. For more detail see Appendix 3.

Data　The information to be transmitted or stored. Usually in binary form.

Digital　Information in discrete or quantised form, ie not continuous as in the case of an analog signal.

Dil　Dual-in-line. The most common form of packaging for microprocessors and associated devices. Connections are made via a row of pins each side of the device.

Display　A means of presenting information required by a user in visual form. Includes the use of CRT (cathode ray tube), l.e.d. (light emitting diode), liquid crystal, gas discharge and filament devices.

DRAM　Dynamic RAM. A memory in which data is stored as a charge on a capacitor. Since charge can leak away the memory element must be continually refreshed by writing data to maintain the current value.

Driver　An electronic circuit that provides the input for another circuit or device.

DSC　Digital scanning conversion.

D-type Flip-flop　An electronic circuit which on receipt of a clock pulse will give an output logic level the same as that present at the input terminal prior to the arrival of the clock pulse. It is widely used as a data latching buffer element.

EBL   Electronic bearing line. An EBL control can set a bearing line on the screen which can radiate from the radar origin, or be offset as required.

Enable   A control signal which allows a circuit or device to receive or transmit information.

Flip-flop   An electronic circuit having two stable states that can be used to store one bit. The circuit uses two gates, the output from each being cross-coupled as an input to the other. The output from one gate is usually referred to as the Q output while the output from the other gate, being the complement of the first output, is called $\bar{Q}$.

Gate   This is a circuit with two or more inputs and an output which allows a logic level 1 to exist at the output, or not as the case may be, when certain defined criteria are met.

Hexadecimal   A number system with a base of 16 using 1,2,3,4......9,A,B,C,D,E,F.

IEC   International electrotechnical commission.

IMO   International maritime organisation.

Input/output (IO) ports   These are circuits which allow external circuits to be connected to the computer internal bus system.

Integrated circuit (ic)   A small chip of silicon processed to form several elements directly interconnected to perform a given unique function.

Interface   A common boundary between systems to allow them to interact.

Interrupt   A break in the execution of a program that allows control to temporarily pass to another software routine.

Interrupt masking   A technique which allows the computer to specify if an interrupt will be accepted.

INTA   Interrupt acknowledge. A control signal sent by the CPU to a peripheral device that has requested an interrupt.

Keyboard   A unit which forms part of an input device. This may have a full QWERTY type key layout or be a specialised arrangement to suit the needs of the system.

Latch   A temporary storage element, usually a flip-flop.

LED   Light emitting diode. A semiconductor device which emits light when current flows in a certain direction through the device.

Logic   Electronic circuits which control the flow of information through the system according to certain rules. These circuits are known as gates since the 'gates' are opened and closed by the sequence of events at the inputs.

LSI   Large scale integration that allows more than 100 gates on a single silicon chip.

Memory   In a digital system, it is that part of the system where information is stored.

Microprocessor   A processor constructed of one or more chips using LSI.

Monostable   An electronic circuit which has only **one** stable state. The circuit is normally in the stable state and is triggered into the unstable state where it remains for a period of time determined by a CR time constant value of external components. After this period of time the circuit returns to the stable state.

Octal latch   An integrated circuit package that offers eight separate flip-flop (or latch) circuits.

PCB   Printed circuit board. A board made of insulating material covered with copper where areas of copper have been etched away to leave conducting tracks and pads for the connection of passive components and active devices.

Port   Terminals (input and output) which allow access to or from a system.

PPI   Programmable peripheral interface. The 8255 is an example of a PPI and details of this device can be found in Appendix 3.

PPI   Plan position indicator. A type of display where the trace rotates and presents an all-round picture centred on ownship position.

Printer   The output peripheral of a computer system which allows a hard copy to be obtained.

Processor   A device capable of carrying out operations on data.

Program   A sequence of instructions logically ordered to perform a particular task.

PROM   Programmable read only memory. A memory programmed to be read but not written into. This type of memory is programmed by the supplier.

Pulse   A signal used to energise a circuit digitally. There is a transition in signal level between discrete values and each level is maintained for a period of time.

RAM   Random access memory. A memory that can be read without altering its state or can be written into with a new value.

RD, Read   The process of determining the data in a memory location without altering its contents.

Readout   A presentation of output information from a computer. It can be displayed on a screen, stored on tape or disc, or be a hard copy when it is usually referred to as a printout.

Register   A group of memory cells used to store groups of binary data in a microprocessor.

Reset   This could be an input to a flip-flop to bring the Q output to the logic 0 state, or that facility which allows a microprocessor to be returned to a predetermined state. Where the point of return is situated in memory depends on the system.

ROM   Read only memory. A memory element containing information that cannot be altered under computer operation. The data can only be read by the computer.

RW, Read write   A control signal that can determine whether a memory element is to be read or overwritten. If the control line is common then one function occurs when the control line is high and the other when the control line is low.

Shift Register   A register in which the stored data can be shifted, one bit at a time, to the left or right.

Signal   An electrical variation, either continuously variable or variable between discrete levels, which can be interpreted as information.

Software   A program which can be loaded into a computer system and resides in RAM. Such programs can be changed at will.

Storage A term used to describe any device capable of storing data. Memory elements are storage devices.

Test A routine for establishing that a device or system is responding as it was designed to do.

TCPA Time to closest point of approach. The predicted time to achieve CPA with a target that represents a collision risk.

TTL Transistor-transistor logic. A form of integrated circuit that uses bipolar junction transistors.

VRM Variable range marker. A VRM control provides a dashed ring, the range of which can be varied, with respect to radar origin.

WR, Write The process of transferring data into a memory or other device.

Index